NEGOTIATING FOR YOUR LIFE

NEGOTIATING FOR YOUR LIFE

NEW SUCCESS STRATEGIES
FOR WOMEN

NICOLE SCHAPIRO

The National Association
for Female Executives
Professional Library

HENRY HOLT AND COMPANY
New York

Henry Holt and Company, Inc.
Publishers since 1866
115 West 18th Street
New York, New York 10011

Henry Holt® is a registered
trademark of Henry Holt and Company, Inc.

Library of Congress Cataloging-in-Publication Data

Schapiro, Nicole.
Negotiating for your life: new success strategies
for women / by Nicole Schapiro.—1st ed.
p.   cm. — (The National Association for
Female Executives professional library)
Includes index.
1. Women—Psychology.   2. Success.   3. Negotiation.
4. Conflict management.   I. Title.   II. Series.
HQ1206.S345   1993   92-35767
305.42—dc20   CIP

ISBN 0-8050-1383-0

First Edition—1993

Designed by Ann Gold
Produced by New Chapter Press

Printed in the United States of America
All first editions are printed on acid-free paper.⊗

10   9   8   7   6   5   4   3   2   1

to my mother, who taught me that everything in life is negotiable without compromising your own or others' ethics

and to my children, Robert, Erik, and Jessica, who kept me in practice and who taught me the art of understanding and knowing the other side's needs to come to mutual satisfaction as well as the difference between arguing and negotiation

CONTENTS

Preface   xi

Acknowledgments   xv

Introduction by Wendy Reid Crisp, National Director,   xvii
National Association for Female Executives

PART I
UNDERSTANDING NEGOTIATION

1   What Is Negotiation, Anyway?   3

2   Is It Negotiable?   16

3   Discovering Your Negotiating Style   30

4   Negotiating Personalities   50

5   Special Considerations   68

PART II
STRATEGIES FOR PREPARATION

6   Setting Goals   87

7   Learning About Your Negotiating Partners   104

8   Anticipating Scenarios   126

9   The Tactics of Time, Place, Agenda   145

10   Readying Yourself   162

PART III
NEGOTIATION IN ACTION

11 Getting into the Game   181

12 Working Toward Agreement   207

13 Tactics for Special Circumstances   224

    Epilogue   243

    Index   245

PREFACE

Has your world ever turned upside down in an instant? Mine did. All it took was a piece of shocking news to throw me off course—and send me heading in a direction radically different from the one in which I'd been traveling for years.

Let me tell you what happened. My California home was the final product of years of vision, hard work, and good negotiations; it represented security I never had as a child growing up in Hungary. My house was located on a hilltop above Berkeley; it had a majestic view of San Francisco and its bay. Dwelling in the midst of ever-changing surroundings of mature pines, fog, sun, and occasional visits from deer gave me a real sense of freedom. The house was filled with an eclectic collection: mementos of my roots in Hungary, arts and crafts from other cultures, gifts from clients, a photo spread of my children reminding me of my other identity as a mother. In the house, too, was my business office with twenty-five years of records, research, and books essential to my work.

Then came October 20, 1991. It was a Sunday, and I was away. On that day, the Oakland Hills firestorm destroyed more than three thousand houses—my home among them. Everything was obliterated. In the days and months that followed, I went through that recovery course familiar to all people who have experienced a devastating loss: denial, rage, depression, and grief. Eventually I moved toward acceptance and beyond it into recovery.

To initiate the healing, I had to witness the physical evidence of my loss. For several days after the fire, residents were not permitted to visit their home sites. We waited as the embers of charred houses and trees cooled—a renewed lesson in patience. Finally,

with my three children and several close friends, I began the ascent
on foot. The firestorm's fury had melted the narrow roads leading
up the hillside and covered them with debris. We carried back-
packs and shovels; we wore combat boots, heavy gloves, and clear
plastic masks to protect our faces from hazardous particles blowing
about. Slowly, we edged our way up treacherous embankments—
past blackened remnants of the once lovely neighborhood, the
mutilated monuments of other people's lives: crumbling chim-
neys, burned-out metal hulks of cars, cracked concrete stairs that
led nowhere. The dead, lunarlike landscape looked worse than
Europe after World War II.

As we drew closer to my property, my head filled with a babble
of inner talk. Hope: some homes, after all, had miraculously survived. . . . The cheerleader: You'll be okay, Nicole! You can do it,
you're a survivor. . . . The pragmatist: Just push on, don't feel, and
you'll get there. . . . And then the victim: Why me—haven't I paid
my dues already? Do I need another test?

When I saw a neighbor's brick chimney standing naked
against the sky, I knew the bleak reality that would greet me. Now
I, the longtime, skilled negotiator, would have to negotiate again—
within myself, the toughest negotiating place of all. Negotiate between denying and accepting. Between the surface and the core.
Between the illusion of control and the reality of how little control
we actually have. Between giving up and going on.

My three-level house was a great mound of rubble. Its huge
steel girders and its vertical supports, driven deep into the hillside
to withstand earthquakes, had been twisted like discarded hair-
pins. Jagged pieces of walls and flooring jutted up like smashed
bones in a vandalized cemetery. Combing through the wreckage,
we found some objects we could identify, although they had
melted into almost unrecognizable forms. None was salvageable.
All else had vaporized in the blast-furnace heat. Every material
thing I had striven so hard to keep inviolable in my home was
now gone.

I searched for understanding. "What is the meaning of life?" I
absurdly asked myself aloud, exhausted and despairing. My son
Eric, sifting through junk and ashes where my office once had
been, was silent. Either he hadn't heard me or he had just dismissed my banal question. Then suddenly this strong young man

crumpled and began to sob. He had found something very fragile. Gently, I took it. It was a single piece of paper, burned at its edges, reduced to the size of a small file card. There was printing on it, and I read the words: "The meaning of life? . . . is life!" It was the only remnant of the burned manuscript of this book.

This was the message I needed to take away with me from that dark, burnt mountain. While giving the place and its vista one final, departing look, I glanced down. There at my foot a tiny plant—some future weed or tree—had emerged. It was rising up from the ashes, a thin green shoot already unfurling two brave and tender leaves.

Thirty-five years ago, when I first arrived in America, I walked along Broadway in New York City and saw my first billboard. Dazzlingly lit, it may have used more electricity than was available in all of Hungary. From then on, I made a habit of picking up or making "mental billboards"—provocative sayings I filed away in my head, to call up at a moment's notice, usually to help me deal with a difficult situation.

I recalled now a favorite one, its two words succinctly conveying an attitudinal switch we can make whenever the game of life deals us a worthless card or a really lousy hand: "Shift happens." We always have choices—alternatives—for how we want to look at the world, how we want to respond to people and situations, how we want to think and feel.

As we pursue our life goals, detours and roadblocks sometimes occur. Though we don't welcome them, we can learn from them. We cannot control our destinies, but we can choose to shape our response to misfortune. These are survival tactics.

Much of the negotiating we do is a creative process to satisfy our needs to establish and maintain a sense of control over our lives. We often get into conflicts with others over what we perceive as scarce resources—whether they relate to food, money, jobs, opportunities, power, or love. Through our ability to communicate, we can negotiate solutions to the eternal differences that make us partners instead of opponents.

Also, we often get into conflicts within ourselves because our many selves feel different ways and want different things. In negotiating life it is crucial to acknowledge and honor our inner needs. In seeking the best pathways toward our destinations or goals, we must heed these internal guides—including the ethical "billboards" we live by—as well as the external signposts along the way that show us direction and mark our progress en route.

We communicate and negotiate successfully with others if we can understand and accept valid alternatives to our own beliefs, actions, values, and words. While working on differences in perspective or style, we may wish to shift our own position, making adjustments that move toward compromise, the heart of the negotiation process.

We always have a choice in our own attitudes. So when negotiating any inner problem or outer conflict into a satisfactory solution, always remember: Choose choice. Leaving options for possible shifts and for later changes in your life will allow you the freedom to become who you really are. Realize, too, that you can always renegotiate aspects of your life whenever you see a chance for improvement ... or the need for survival. You're never truly stuck.

I invite you now to travel with me on a journey toward discovery of yourself and of your life's negotiating partners.

Nicole Schapiro
Mill Valley, California
April 1993

ACKNOWLEDGMENTS

A book is the result of the collaborative efforts of hundreds of people who in one way or another help in its creation. This book is no exception. That it is being published at all restores one's faith in miracles because the 1991 Oakland fire that destroyed my home and office destroyed the work in progress and the book had to be re-created. Responsible in large measure for this miracle are all those friends who were there for me at the time as well as all the new friends who came forward to help me find the physical and mental energy and the creative spirit to begin again.

First I must thank Barbara Marinacci, who devoted so much time to making sense of my notes, seminar materials, and interview tapes, and did it all with such skill and always with a sense of humor in the face of very difficult circumstances. She is definitely a co-parent of this book.

Thanks also go to those people whom I interviewed and who shared their experiences with me so generously. They include Sarita Ledett, Susann Namm, Rochelle Deneen, Terry Linda Hodge, Elena Asturias, Susan Jones, Rosa Perez, Gail Harris, Bobbie Rich, Barbara Beck, Juanita Owens, Liz Rigali, Judy Miller, Beverly Zoller, Marlene Leverette, Nancy Monson, Celeste Matarazzo, Susan Lesker, Carlota Del Portillo, Jackie Spear, Jessica Schapiro, Erik Schapiro, Louise Bender, Andrea Falesby, Jane Snook, Joan Kemp, Joan Brozovich, Robert Schapiro, Alice De Forest, Dave Ackerman, Len Silvey, Gregg Chow, Steven Kopstein, Allen Sauer, and Arnold Schapiro.

I am grateful to Anthony J. Alessandra, Ph.D., and Phillip S.

Waxler, authors of *People Smart*, and to members of the National Speakers' Association for sharing their thoughts and information.

I also want to acknowledge the wonderful people who participated in my seminars, conferences, and consultations, as well as in various negotiating sessions, both personal and business, where the material for the book was tested and retested. After each session I walked alway richer, having always learned something new, and those seeds of knowledge are part of the book.

Special thanks go to the following who believed in and cared about me, and whose love and encouragement was a major support throughout this whole period: Juanita Owens, Evelyn Fisher, Judith Briles, Joyce Turley, Simma Lieberman, Maureen Mulvaney, Rebecca Morgan, Roz Newton, Patricia Tripp, Bee Epstein, Judy Kafka, Vicki Schneider, Dana Gribben, Sylvia V. Mills, and Paula Statman.

I've already acknowledged the help of my professional family, The National Speakers' Association, in my research for the book, but I must further thank the members for their financial and emotional support and for going out of their way to assist me in putting my life back together again after the fire. I am grateful, too, to the people at NAFE for their continued enthusiasm for the book, to Wendy Crisp, my editor at New Chapter Press, for her invaluable guidance, vision, and patience, and finally, to my publishers, Henry Holt, for their lasting faith in me and my book.

INTRODUCTION

The intricacies of negotiation were impressed on me many years ago. A friend's father—the type of man who always has the right answers and who never willingly enters a situation in which he has no control—decided to buy a horse. This venture required scouting the local ranches, questioning other people in town about the relative honesty of various ranchers and their hired men, and talking to the veterinarian about specific clues to a horse's health, well-being, and promise of longevity. At long last, after what seemed like an eternity of preparation to my eager-to-be-Dale-Evans friend, the three of us drove out to the country to examine a prospective purchase.

The horse was beautiful—deep shiny mahogany coat, strong legs, long black eyelashes, good teeth. After quickly determining the price was right, my friend's father announced he would buy the horse. "A fine looking animal," he said to the rancher's hand.

"Oh, I don't know," said the hand. "She don't look too good to me."

"Nonsense!" laughed the father. "She's perfect."

"Well," said the hand, "Nobody working here thinks she looks good. That's why she's for sale."

The father chuckled at his good fortune. The next day a truck brought the beautiful mare to my friend's house.

And there we discovered that the hand was right. Not only did she not "look too good," she didn't "look" at all. The mare was, in fact, totally blind. "Nancy's dad buys a horse" was an excellent lesson in the art of negotiation from the careful preparation stage to the pitfall of not listening to, or understanding, the other side—

what Nicole Schapiro calls our "negotiating partner." Unfortunately, such vivid parables are rarely available in life to teach us the way to go about achieving our goals and satisfying our needs. We have often learned, usually ineffectively, negotiating techniques through our family interactions—techniques that seldom succeed in the "outside" world.

When I first heard Nicole Schapiro speak—at a National Association for Female Executives conference in San Francisco—it was only a few weeks after the earthquake that had toppled bridges and freeways and left a part of the city in ruins. In her presentation on negotiating, Nicole talked about the disaster and about how our negotiation skills are as relevant to coping with unforeseen events in our private lives as they are to implementing the long-range plans of our business lives. In teaching these skills—the lessons that are shared in this book—Nicole instructs us to anticipate with confidence opportunities for negotiation and to see potential confrontations as arenas for growth and accomplishment.

After studying *Negotiating for Your Life*, learning and practicing its techniques and strategies, we will all be better able to get that promotion, salary increase, family leave, business loan, production contract, property purchase—or that big sale, good advance, or improved living situation. There is nothing—well, almost nothing, as Nicole asserts—that can't be negotiated, and the rules of successful negotiation apply as equally to the brief, casual interaction that determines who will pay for lunch as they do to the lengthy, complex discussions regarding a transnational corporate merger.

And rule number one? Watch out for any deal that don't look too good.

> Wendy Reid Crisp
> National Director
> National Association for Female Executives

PART I

UNDERSTANDING NEGOTIATION

"Negotiation is the highest form of communication used by the lowest number of people."
—President John F. Kennedy

1
WHAT IS NEGOTIATION, ANYWAY?

"You have to believe in the impossible."
                                   —Howard Hesol

Thirty feet or so away from me the young soldier set a rifle against his right shoulder and began locating me in its sight. What did he see? A fifteen-year-old Hungarian girl dressed in peasant's clothing. Hoping the disguise would get me safely across the border into Austria, my mother had hastily assembled the outfit. She'd wept when I left, afraid she would never see me again. This was the second time we had to part; the first time we were separated, during World War II, it had taken her eight years to find me.

This time, it was 1956. Hungary's brief, glorious uprising against the Soviet-imposed Communist rule had been brutally snuffed out. As a teenage freedom-fighter, I'd teamed up with some young insurgents and hurled Molotov cocktails at tanks. My aim was good; I helped destroy three of them. Now I was running for my life.

The group I'd been traveling with—there were about twenty of us—had been caught the night before, about fifty miles from the Austrian border, and freedom. Shoved into a barn, we bedded down on straw. When dawn came, we were roughly lined up and told to march; to each of us was assigned a soldier-guard. Having left our assigned zones against the rules and then attempting to escape, we were considered traitors.

As we trudged along the path, I glanced at my soldier-guard. He could not have been any older than I. His smooth face showed no sign yet of a beard. He was short and thin, and the green jacket he wore was several sizes too large for him. Its sleeves drooped over his hands. His boots, loose around his feet, flopped as he walked. Whenever his big cap fell over his eyes, he'd push it back. He did not look like a soldier; he looked like a boy forced into the army, with no more control over his fate than I now had.

We had been ordered not to talk, but I took a risk. If I was to die anyway, what was the risk? "Isn't this crazy?" I whispered, turning my head slightly toward him. "Here you and I are, the same age, and you are supposed to kill me." He said nothing, but I knew he was listening. "All I did was get caught. On my way to America."

"America?" I heard him whisper back, hoarsely. For a brief moment we partnered in a common vision. And that was all he said. All he dared to say.

We walked past fields where only stubble remained from the summer's crops. In a few minutes, we came to an old building, and we prisoners were lined up against a picket fence, three feet apart. Meanwhile, the guards we'd walked with stood opposite us, readying their rifles.

If ever I'd have to bargain for my life, this was it. But how could I do it, at such a distance from my adversary? I could only repeat in my head, with total concentration, the words I'd already said to that boy, and then briefly move my hands to indicate the utter madness of his killing me. I looked at him with the focus of sunlight through a prism, beaming one last message. Our eyes connected and in my silence I screamed, "Let me live!"

There was the command, "Fire!" But I didn't hear the shots blasting at us. All I know is that I awoke later to find myself alive and unhurt. On both sides of me sprawled the bodies of my companions. I probably fainted just as the rifles started shooting, and nobody checked to make sure I, too, was dead. Did the soldier boy miss me on purpose? Had he opted to share vicariously a life of freedom?

Realizing that the soldiers would soon return with grave diggers, I got up quickly and ran as far as I could toward the northwest, the direction we were headed when we'd been captured.

Five days later I crossed into Austria on the first leg of my journey to America.

Ever since that day of intended execution over thirty-five years ago, I have often wondered: Did the young soldier deliberately aim his bullets to the side or above my head? Or had the cap just fallen over his eyes, making him miss his human target? I will never know what really happened. But I like to believe he became a willing partner in my life: one of many good negotiating partners I've had along the way.

Never in my busy life—a life that has included a career as a professional negotiator and negotiation trainer—have I conducted such intensely intuitive, personal negotiating as I did in those brief instants. But after all, I was negotiating for my life. What would have become of me if I hadn't?

Fortunately, not many of us ever find ourselves looking into the barrel of a rifle. But all of us at some point have felt as if we were on the firing line with a life-or-death issue confronting us, or hanging in the balance. In those times of conflict, when we are in a critical and vulnerable position and have almost lost hope, we reach *inside* to negotiate within ourselves and we reach *outside* to negotiate as skillfully as we can with others.

Every day, in far less stressful encounters in our work, in our relationships with the people in our lives, and in our practical, daily world, we do the same kinds of negotiating: within ourselves and with others. We negotiate resolutions to conflicts, decisions on issues, peacemaking compromises, and the setting and readjusting of plans and goals.

Our lives continue onward each day because of the process of negotiation.

Most of the time, we are unaware that the process we are undergoing is negotiation. At the same time, we wish we could make better decisions, reach more satisfying agreements, be strong and fair in meeting the challenges of everyday life. By realizing what negotiation is, by identifying how and when you negotiate, and by learning—and practicing!—negotiating skills, we will improve the quality of our life. We will be successfully negotiating for our life.

That's what this book is all about.

What Does Negotiation Mean?

The verb *to negotiate* comes from the Latin *negotiare:* to transact business with someone. It is also defined as "settling by bargaining," and "discussing with a view to finding agreement."

We're all in the business of living. What do you hope the business of living will bring you? You want to prosper, of course. Not just economically—to be financially secure enough to surround yourself with material comforts. You also want to prosper emotionally—to have a sense of fulfillment by reaching the goals you've set for yourself in both your work and your personal relationships. How do you successfully transact the business of living? By negotiation.

When I ask women to tell me about memorable moments of negotiating they've done in their lives, they often respond incredulously. "What, *me* negotiate? You've got to be kidding!" What are their mental images of negotiation? Diplomats seated at a long conference table, scowling at each other over piles of documents? International tycoons in pin-striped suits hammering out global deals in fancy hotel suites? Shouting matches between labor and management? Old-style politicians trading favors in smoke-filled back rooms?

While you're thinking about how you might define *negotiation,* here are what some other women have said.

"When two people have different goals, negotiation is the communication process you both enter to get to an agreement that is something both of you can live with. It may not be the ideal situation for either one, but it makes an 'agreement zone' that's comfortable for each." That's human resources manager Barbara Beck talking.

Psychologist Joan Brozovich approached it this way: "Negotiation happens when two people or parties both want something that may cost the other something. The art of negotiation is to see this point of conflict as a creative moment. For both can actually end up getting more than what they originally went after."

With top saleswoman Bobby Rich, the pies of life may not be so equitably divided: "It's a process by which the parties involved come to a place where each one manages to get at least a piece of what she wanted."

And here's Canadian educator and trainer Susan Dowler: "It's like a seesaw going up and down, back and forth, finally leveling—where you both have your feet on the ground and everybody wins." Her image is vivid, apt; it establishes the important criterion of balance.

Producer Susan Lasker viewed the negotiation process as getting a clear vision of what she wants, gaining insight into the other party's goal, and finally arriving at a compromise that makes everyone feel like a winner.

College administrator Juanita Lee Owens went straight to the point: "Negotiating is what we do to achieve something we want." She's not a materialistic person. The objects of the "want" Juanita mentioned usually have to do with changes that will benefit the community. As we will learn, the word *want* can serve us well in a wide variety of negotiating circumstances.

Rosa Perez, counselor and educator, mined a similar vein, with humor and honesty. "Negotiation in its crassest form is 'How to get what I want without making you feel bad?' To make you feel that you gained something in the process of my getting what I want." She paused and laughed. "But I've fine-tuned it in my own life."

Negotiation changes its form and purpose according to the situation. Architect Jennifer Hill worked on a kibbutz during the 1950s, when she was a college student. She noted significant differences between the sort of negotiating that took place in the daily lives of Americans and what she experienced in the Israeli farming community. "People teamed together for the common goal. Their basic survival depended on this. So there was less arguing over individual rights. Since success has to be for the whole community, individual needs are set aside, and negotiating is for the common good."

At first, Gail Harris confessed, "I didn't think much about negotiating. That term just didn't come to mind. But yes, I guess you could say, 'We are doing some negotiating to get to an agreement.'" Now, Gail's terrific at selling. She is persistent. Looking at the activity from a sales-oriented view, she said, "Negotiation's a strategic interchange—a trade-off that is time-limited, an event, rather than a long-term process or building relationship. You decide to do business together and then you negotiate the terms."

Here are some of the meanings I assign to negotiation when I'm conducting workshops and seminars.

Negotiation is:

- Getting what you want
- A learning process in which each party reacts to the other's concession pattern
- Maneuvering for advantage
- Conferring or interacting between individuals with a specific goal in mind
- Ideas exchanged in an effort to influence thought or behavior
- Exchanging and interchanging different interests and value systems
- A field of knowledge and endeavor that focuses on gaining the favor of people from whom we want things
- An exchange in which participants work side by side in attacking problems, not each other
- The seeking and exchanging of information to effect a "winwin" solution
- A process of communication that avoids having to choose between the satisfactions of getting what you deserve and want, and being "decent"
- The working out of wise solutions to shared problems with different interests
- Arranging a joint opinion or course of action

What is *your* definition of negotiating?

Isn't Negotiating Just Bargaining?

No. We negotiate on many levels, beginning with the relatively simple bartering or bargaining that goes on when someone wants to sell something and another person wants to buy it. Certainly, negotiations involving prices, costs, services, labor, and other financial considerations are kin to the marketplace bartering that have characterized economic dealings since the beginning of time.

But at its higher levels, negotiation applies more to problem solving and conflict resolution than to monetary transactions.

Good negotiation is a partnership.

Negotiating often has connotations of being serious, formal, rigid, tough. It's done well by the meanest guy with the most forceful ego and the most troops at his command. But the style of negotiation we will be exploring, while it may be serious and formal, is not rigid or tough. It is cooperative. Negotiation, as we will discuss it, is the give-and-take, back-and-forth process of resolving problems, large and small, that arise every day while we try to obtain something or accomplish something. Cooperative negotiating achieves a balance—there's that seesaw again—between two differing or opposing points of view. I call this cooperative process *partnership negotiation*.

Partnership negotiation is an opportunity for information exchange in which two people, or two "sides," strive to present their positions honestly, and to listen carefully to understand the other side's situation as a crucial preparatory step in reconciling the differences between them. Partnership negotiation is a mutual education process.

Partnership negotiation eliminates a style called "ego exchange"—negotiating only as an opportunity for people to put on a display of their individual power and pretense.

Is Manipulation a Form of Negotiating?

Manipulation is *not* a form of partnership negotiation. Often, in fact, the word implies underhanded dealings, and occurs when a person wants to get someone to do something contrary to an already expressed intention. It may be used by someone who feels inferior to a person in a stronger "power" position and does not want to alert him or her to ulterior motives. Equally, people in power positions employ manipulation in persuading others to perform what they wish to have done which may be disagreeable, demeaning, or unethical from the doer's point of view. If positive inducements such as promises of rewards won't work, then negative ones such as threats may be used. This kind of manipulation is routine for people in influential positions.

Manipulation can become a lifelong habit. A disposition for using it as the primary way of achieving goals usually shows up in early childhood, and may remain as an adult characteristic. Most of us as adults in fact retain behavior tendencies that are vestiges from successful childhood manipulations.

Some people plan their manipulations carefully in advance, gradually introducing key elements and moving toward yes. This process is often confused with negotiation. How can you tell the difference? *Manipulation*—the word actually means "to operate with the hands"—has a subject (the manipulator) and an object (the person who is being manipulated). There is usually an unfair power differential. The needs of the subject are being met by the object. And in no way is there equal power; manipulation in no way resembles a partnership.

What About Conflict?

But, you are asking, doesn't most negotiation have an element of conflict? The answer is yes. Conflict is a part of everyday life. It comes with the condition of being human, of being connected to other people. We also have inner conflict; we must deal with the many "different people" inside of us, each clamoring for recognition and control.

When confronting conflict, we may feel uptight, frustrated, angry, helpless, insulted, upset, devalued, deprived. I'm sure you're familiar with the negative feelings that crop up when things aren't going the way we'd like them to or when there's a difficult situation to solve in the workplace and we're not sure we can bring it off successfully.

For example, you want or need to have something; so does someone else, and it's in limited supply: a job, a concert ticket, a chocolate pie. Who gets it? Can it be divided up? How?

Or maybe you want to do something, and someone else has an entirely opposing idea about what should be done. Perhaps you and I are in business together. You like exploring new ways of doing things, and I am only comfortable with the old ways. If our business is to succeed, we must resolve our differences or call it quits.

Maybe you have a close relationship with someone and think you're not being treated fairly. If you say so, however, you risk a fight; you fear you'll lose out altogether.

What can you do in these problem situations? You've got to

negotiate. Remember, negotiation does not engender conflict; negotiation *resolves* conflict. Some people say, "I'm not good at negotiating. I try to avoid conflict." And I tell them, "Good!" Skilled partnership negotiation is the best way to avoid conflict and resolve differences.

Why Negotiate?

For many people less fortunate than we, life involves a daily quest for the means of sheer survival: water and food, shelter, protection from harm. To obtain the bare essentials to sustain existence, negotiating goes on incessantly with other humans, with nature, with deities, with the universe itself. It's often an I'll-do-this-if-you'll-do-that, quid pro quo exchange.

Somewhere high in priorities, beyond such bottom-line basics, there's also the yearning to be loved by others. The infant's emotional need never quite leaves us; it evolves slowly from utter dependency on others to the nurturing we do within intimate relationships, parenting, and mentoring. Abraham Maslow's famous pyramid-shaped hierarchy of needs alerts us to the fundamental human concerns that must be sequentially satisfied as we begin our lifelong journey toward "self-actualization," or fulfilling our potential. On each step of the way, we're likely to encounter conflicts with aspects of the outer world—with people, with the environment, with chance happenings. We also run into interior squabbles, when one part of us wants to do something that another part resists.

Translating a prioritized, survival-oriented collection of needs into our own life circumstances can be highly useful. In spite of all our differences, each of us negotiates for sustenance, then advancement—physical, social, economic, emotional, mental—in individual ways. Often our needs and our wants conflict. Our ability to negotiate—a skill that combines aptitude, knowledge, and experience—largely determines how well we do.

What Do You Need to Negotiate?

Let's consider the past. When did you last negotiate? Whom did you negotiate with? Were you pleased with the outcome?

And the future. What would you like to change in your life right now?

- Advancement on the job
- A better salary
- A new job or position or career
- More satisfying personal relationships
- A more manageable (less exhausting!) home life
- Improvements in your community or neighborhood
- Special opportunities for friends or family members
- A change in where you live
- Changes in your workload (at home, at your job)
- Adjustments in the way you spend your time
- More profitable or manageable financial agreements

What are the obstacles, the difficulties, the opposing points of view that you will have to negotiate about to achieve these changes? Here are some common sources of conflict with others:

- Unclear jurisdiction (whose possession or territory is it?)
- Disputed interest (what's in it for us, for the other person?)
- Poor communication (we can't understand each other)
- Defective relationship (there's an inequity, an imbalance in power)
- Different objectives (we don't want the same thing)
- Conflicted assumptions (we view life differently)
- Personality discord (we are not the same "type" of person)
- Opposing methods (we don't do things the same way)
- Unshared values (we don't have standards or rules in common)

There is one other major source of conflict: within ourselves. We must not forget the importance of self-negotiating. From start to finish in handling a problem, we've got to be attentive to our own motives and expectations. We have to be aware of our feelings of fear, rage, and shyness that may be handicapping our ability to negotiate.

The process of skillful negotiation that we will explore includes learning more about the "people" inside of us. I find that when I regard my identity not as a monolith but as mosaic made up of bits and pieces of many colors, sizes, textures, and shapes, that metaphor allows me to see the multiple elements in my character. And it helps me negotiate with them in an effective internal partnership.

Self-negotiation may also involve "reframing" the way we look at the world, and abandoning the negative behaviors that distort our perspective and keep us from solving problems and achieving our goals.

In your own way, you may be facing a firing squad of your own right now. Confront it. And learn to negotiate now—for your life!

▬ EXERCISE 1 ▬

AGREE TO NEGOTIATE CHANGE

We can negotiate new circumstances for ourselves in most aspects of our lives, personal and professional. But the first step is not developing the strategy, or even learning the negotiating techniques; the first step toward negotiating change in our lives is to make a commitment to that change. Many people—and I'm one of them—find that making a contract with themselves seals and strengthens their commitment. Below is a sample of a self-contract:

The problem or circumstance I need to negotiate is:

To prepare for negotiating those circumstances, I need to:

Research _____
Assess _____
Call _____
Write _____
Learn _____
Discuss _____
Confront _____

Today, I will:

By (date), I will have accomplished:

▬ EXERCISE 2 ▬

How do you rate yourself on the skills listed below?
Give yourself: 5 for Excellent, 3 for Good, 1 for Fair.

	EXCELLENT	**GOOD**	**FAIR**
Have quick understanding of issues			
Display good problem-solving skills			
Able to depersonalize situations			
Able to think under pressure			
Can maintain positive self-esteem			
Exercise patience			
Am a good listener			
Take calculated risks			
Keep an open mind			
Enjoy competition			
Have ability to prepare			
Am clear on purpose			
Attack problems and issues, not people			
Develop strategies			
Create options for alternative plans			
Keep tally of concessions			
Make assessments of people			
Keep focused			
Separate facts from assumptions			
Offer what is deliverable			
Am appropriately creative			
Pay attention to nonverbal signs			
Make proper use of silence			
Able to put self in opponents' shoes			

	EXCELLENT	GOOD	FAIR
Maintain long-term vision during negotiation			
Leave room to move. Avoid cornering self and others			
Get a clear agreement before leaving			
Keep a sense of humor/perspective			
Be an observer rather than a judge			
Understand timing			
Follow up			
Am a team player			
Have a sense of wanting to win			
	TOTALS		

2
IS IT NEGOTIABLE?

"To predict the future, you have to create it."
—Thomas J. Peters

Like everyone else, I negotiated long before I knew that what I did had a name. After escaping from Hungary in 1956, I ended up—after some unplanned detours around border guards—at the American embassy in Vienna. A young clerk there told me that no way could I go to the United States. Not only was the quota for immigrants from Hungary already filled, but there was also a long waiting list. "But maybe some time in the past officials let more people in than the quota allows," I said. "If you can find that this ever happened, I believe you and I will find a way to get me there." Unconsciously, I made this young man my partner. He had told me, "I'm only a clerk." But now I empowered him to look beyond his self-limited role.

Later, joyously, he gave me the big news: there had indeed been a quota-breaking precedent. "We did it!" he exclaimed, demonstrating how negotiation is always a *we* situation. Our partnership wasn't over yet. How could I now persuade the U.S. government to admit me among the lucky ones? My mother had always said to me, "If you want something, go to the very top—the decision maker." So who was the "boss" of America? I asked. President Eisenhower, I was told. "Then I'll write to him," I decided. "You just don't understand!" my new friend said. "Your letter will go to the immigration department, and some bureaucrat will throw it out." "Maybe so," I said, "but I want to write to him anyway. Will you please help me?"

Sixteen years old and naive, I instinctively talked out, on paper, the dream I had had since the age of nine. I started out by saying, "Dear President Eisenhower: You and I want the same thing. We both want everybody to know that America is a great place to live. . . ." My embassy friend then translated my letter into English. "This is the craziest thing!" he insisted. "He'll never see it." Still, I believed Eisenhower would read my letter.

By some miracle this happened. The president was holding my letter in his hand when I went to meet him in his White House office. "It shocked me when you said, 'You and I,'" he told me. "'Who is this person?' I wondered. So I was simply compelled to read on." He said that soon after reading my letter, he asked for the quota to be expanded to let in Hungarian refugees who had escaped from Soviet rule. And my name was put on the list.

That's how I got to America—through negotiating something that appeared to be nonnegotiable.

Through the years you've doubtless made important life-altering decisions, too. Or you seriously considered doing so, even if you ultimately kept your status quo. You knew, or at least sensed, that a good many circumstances around us can be altered—if we choose them to be. Not that these choices will be easy for us to make or implement.

Whenever you negotiate for something important in your life, think beyond the limitations that our culture, our upbringing, our self-doubts usually put on us, restricting our thinking and actions. Too often we negotiate as if we've swallowed a pill that limits our dimensions: only two by two, or four by six. That way, we forget that almost everything in life is negotiable—provided we are willing to pay the price.

Let's take a look at two women's negotiation situations:

After three months of making the payments on my business's bank loan, I realized that I had made a mistake and overestimated how large a payment I could make and still keep the business running. At first I panicked, and tried to think of ways I could earn the extra money to make the payments.

. .

As more and more people were laid off, their responsibilities fell on my lap. Finally, I was working at the office thirteen and fourteen hours a day, with no increase in pay and a real decline in my health and in my relationship with my family. I thought about quitting, but the economy was bad, and I needed the job. My anger at my employer's taking advantage of me caused a lot of additional stress. I felt trapped.

Anger, resentment, stress, fear, and fatigue. Feelings of being trapped, of desperation.

How many times have you felt this way? How many times have you heard yourself tell someone, "There's nothing I can do about it—this is just the way it is." Or, "I can't believe this is happening to me."

Everything is negotiable (well, almost). Before we analyze these stories and learn how these two women negotiated successful resolutions to their problems, let's get real for a minute and take an inventory of those very few things that are *not* negotiable.

Here's an assignment right now. Think about all the circumstances in your present life that you can do nothing about. Nothing at all. Except change your own attitude. Attitude adjustment requires the consistent habit of looking at the "3 A's":

1. *Awareness.* What am I aware of about me and the people I deal with?
2. *Attitude.* How is my attitude about what I am aware of?
3. *Action.* I have control and can do something about the above two things.

Be honest as you ponder these seemingly nonnegotiable facets in our lives:

• *Age.* We can't change it, but we can do a number of things to minimize its influence on our lives. We can practice preventive health measures to stay well, we can follow good exercise and diet regimens, we can have regular medical checkups. We can take various measures (some risky, perhaps) to make ourselves look younger. And, most important, we can change our *attitude* about aging. Attitude adjustment is accomplished by negotiating with ourselves. You will be learning the techniques of self-negotiation later—it is a skill as specific and as necessary as the ability to negotiate with others.

• *Gender.* For some people, for whom birth-gender is an unbearable psychological burden, medical science offers radical solutions. Here, however, we are addressing ourselves—women who sometimes wish they were men so they would be paid more for the same job, listened to with more respect, be less conspicuous on the job, or have more opportunities. Yet most of us like who we are.

• *Parentage and family.* We can't change our status as the offspring of biological parents and, in some cases, the adopted children of another set of parents. We can't change the children to whom we have given birth. And we can't change the family members who come with those packages. But we can alter aspects of our interactions with these people. We can work on changing some of our attitudes. We can consider moving, leaving difficult situations, changing our name. We can seek counseling or therapy to resolve our own conflicts about relationships. In other words, we can negotiate within ourselves and with others to either resolve relationship conflicts or minimize the negative results of unresolved conflicts, or we can change our exposure to them.

• *Physical handicaps.* We cannot negotiate for better eyesight or stronger legs or clearer speech, but we can negotiate for the circumstances that we require to perform effectively and successfully in our work and at home. We can educate people as to how we want to be treated or what and how we feel when they act a certain way.

• *Illness.* Disease would seem to be a part of life that, surely, is not negotiable. How do you negotiate with cancer? With AIDS? And yet, courageous people who have battled these and other debilitating afflictions have learned that illness can be negotiated. We can determine the nature and course of treatment, we can choose how much of our life to give over to management of the illness, we can make attitudinal changes that significantly affect the state of our health. Each of these choices is a negotiation.

So, you see, in some way *everything is negotiable.* Still, there are some obstacles we must overcome before we can begin to negotiate for what we want in our life.

To evaluate if any of these obstacles is preventing you from confidently entering into negotiations, answer the same questions I would ask if you were to meet with me as a negotiation consultant:

1. A risk is an action, the result of which is unknown and involves potential loss. What was the last risk you took? Did it pay off? If so, how? Would you characterize yourself as a risk-taker?

2. Do you make many decisions in your daily life? Do you make them fast, or ponder about them for a long time?

3. How did your family make decisions when you were growing up?

4. List three or four decisions you were required to make this week.

5. Is your decision about these issues the final one? If it is not the final one, is it the prevailing one (the one with the most authority)?

6. Who in your work and/or family or community life makes decisions that affect you?

7. How much control or authority do you have over your own life?

8. Do you easily get frustrated when others can't make up their minds quickly or make decisions different from yours?

First, we must confront our willingness (or unwillingness) to take risks. Living equals risk management. We must understand our risk awareness. How often have we accepted situations as they are—grumbling about it, making ourselves and the people around us miserable, yet not speaking up and out? How frequently do we try to change a situation for the better? To do so means challenging the status quo, the "powers that be." It means taking risks—and risking loss: loss of someone's love or friendship, loss of a job or an income, loss of respect or security or power.

Sometimes we hope others will take the risks for us: circulate the petition, bring in the lawyers, call the police, confront management, meet with the neighbors. We admire their daring, but wonder at their vulnerability, their potential loss. We think: Isn't there a safe way to protest, to seek improvements in the situation? The answer is no. One of my favorite "billboards"—those quotations that help me keep my eyes on the goal and my perspective clear—is from my Hungarian grandfather:

"If you have tried to do something and failed, you are vastly better off than if you have tried nothing."

Negotiation is a process in which we can make a difference. The cost is risk. Accepting the possibility of loss is key to the ability to take risks. There is a difference, however, with the *negotiated* risk. The negotiated risk is not a winner-take-all, "scorched earth" approach. The negotiated risk rests on the idea of partnership, and in a partnership the goal is to have the gains on both sides outweigh the losses.

The second step in preparing for negotiation is to become aware of how many events—large and small—in your life are negotiable. Most decisions that we make every day contain possibilities for negotiation, with ourselves and with others. Here are a few examples taken from the worksheet of one of my seminar participants:

DECISIONS MADE IN THE LAST WEEK

- Car repair: I'll have the parts replaced, but skip the body work.
- Community work: I said no to a request to serve on a committee at church.
- Children: No to going into the city for a rock concert; yes to spending the night at Tim's; yes to using the car to get to a new job; no to use of the telephone after 9 P.M.
- Husband: I'll take the "good" printer from his system and trade him for the "good" terminal on my system.
- Job: It's okay for Peter to turn his final report in a week late. We won't use any temporary help until after the first of the month; we will increase the size of the test mailings.
- Personal: Decided to swim before work instead of after work, and to visit Gram after work at least three times a week.

Does that sound anything like your life? Do you see in the above list the endless possibilities for negotiation—or, in some cases, the results of some good negotiating? You may not have realized how often you actually negotiate!

To evaluate how effective a negotiator you are, look at your answers to question 4. Is there a pattern in how the decisions were made? Did you act on information or emotion or a balanced combination of both? Did you make the decisions quickly, or did you take extra time to weigh the considerations? What kind of conflict exists in any of the situations? How did you respond to the conflict? Did all the decisions have to be made, or could some of them have been postponed? Did you make some of the decisions as a compromise measure or to avert another problem? Are you satisfied with the results of your decisions?

Are you an effective negotiator? The proof is easy: Are you getting the results you want and expect?

Effective and Ineffective Negotiators

Some of us never evolve beyond a young child's negotiating techniques. We may go through life sulking, crying, or wildly "acting out" to get what we want . . . and wonder why our behavior doesn't produce notable success. Or we might imitate some elder's early modeling—a parent or a sibling, say—but not recognize that this person's tactics have never yielded desirable results or won respect.

These unsuccessful negotiators I call *unconscious incompetents*. They may never learn how to negotiate because they don't know that they don't know.

Of course, some people are natural negotiators. Perhaps the skill was inborn, or maybe learned through hit-or-miss experience. However they acquired the talent, they depend completely on instinct and chance. They have never analyzed why they have been successful; they can't explain their procedures or tactics. Consequently, they are not able to replicate their triumphs nor can they effectively train others. I call them *unconscious competents*. They don't learn from their experiences, good or bad, because they don't reflect upon them. Unconscious competents run a serious risk of failing—and not knowing why. They don't plan, nor can they share strategies with other team members. They make no adjustment plans in case something goes wrong.

Other people have greater insight. When they finally recognize that their action has brought disappointing or detrimental results, they start to wonder why. This brings them to a realization that they need to learn some things about negotiating—to know what works and why. These people I call *conscious incompetents*. They know that they don't know, and they're alerted to the need to learn—maybe from workshop training, books, and seminars, or from mentors and observing others.

Last of all is the blue-ribbon class, the *conscious competents*. These people are always aware of what they are doing when they negotiate. That doesn't mean they are consistently successful. They, too, have their percentage of failures. After each negotiation, to learn from the pluses and minuses within the process, consciously competent negotiators think about the following:

1. What worked well?
2. Why did it work?
3. What didn't work?
4. Why didn't it work?
5. To achieve what I want in the future, I must . . .
6. In order to get, I should remember . . .

Both successful and unsuccessful negotiations provide feedback for the consciously competent negotiator. Many negotiations mix positives and negatives, and there's always something to learn.

Examining the Results of Our Negotiations

To illustrate the above evaluative points, we can reflect on the answers to those questions given by our workshop attendee mentioned earlier, who had summarized various decisions she had made in the previous week.

• Car repair: Satisfied. I asked for estimates for replacing the damaged parts and doing the body work and a separate estimate just for the damaged parts. When given the costs, I asked about installing used parts instead of buying new ones, and the safety factor in used parts. I got good answers, and believe I made a safe, economical decision. What might have changed? My decision would have been different if the car was newer and body work would have increased its market value.

• Community work: Not satisfied. I've said no a lot lately and I felt guilty, especially since these people really helped me out when I was without a car (see above!). So, I found someone who would love to be involved on the committee.

• Children: Satisfied, with reservations. Not sure about the decision to let my son use the car—even if it is for a new job—so soon after he ran it into a ditch (see above again! It was that kind of week!).

• Husband: The best deal of the week. We're both happy.

• Job: Not satisfied. I didn't feel I had a choice but to give Peter the deadline extension; he hadn't finished the report. What could I do? Fire him? I don't think cutting temporary help right now was the right way to save money this month, especially when we're increasing the test mailing. Had to make the decisions very quickly, reacting all the time to crises. Didn't really negotiate anything.

• Personal: Some self-negotiating here, trading off evening and morning hours to accommodate my need to visit my grandmother. Good compromising. As a reward, I will give myself an hour alone at least once a week.

We can see the patterns emerging. Where this woman confidently recognizes the opportunities to negotiate, she does so deliberately and fairly. She is beginning to understand what worked, what didn't, and why. She can make decisions without unduly procrastinating or agonizing over them, and then can stand back and objectively survey the results of her decision making, including her own dissatisfactions with some of them. As she moves along through life, day by day, week by week, she will continuously provide feedback to herself about how well she handles problems that come up. And she will increase her negotiating skills as she learns from experience. She seems well on her way to becoming a fully conscious, competent negotiator.

Who's the Authority in Your Life?

Review your answers to questions 5, 6, and 7 (on page 20) regarding obstacles to decision making and negotiating. You will have fairly identified who has the real authority in your life. Are you satisfied, or do you need to renegotiate who is in charge of your life?

Are you making most of the major decisions that affect you? Or are those decisions made by a spouse, a parent, a child, an employer, a co-worker, a friend? Often the people whom we allow to influence or make decisions for us have been dead for years: a parent whom we could never please, a religious figure, a teacher. In the next chapter, I discuss these childhood influences that continue to affect many of the negotiations we engage in daily, sometimes contrary to our best interests.

Claiming authority over your own life is a critical step in preparing to negotiate for your life—and it is a nonnegotiable requirement. You cannot trade off the right to make decisions about your life for money, love, security, prestige, affection, or fame. Not until you reclaim yourself or understand what you are about will you go forward.

Let me be clear. Do not confuse "authority" with "control." The desire to have total control over our lives is unrealistic since we depend on others also. We cannot control the behavior of other people—in our own families or in the world—and we cannot control the course of nature. Within that reality, it is foolish to think that we, who function every moment of our lives in connection with other people and the natural world around us, can be in total control.

However, we *can* have authority over our lives. We choose to be the *final decision maker* on important issues that concern our minds, our bodies, and our work. To put it as simply as possible:

Control: Planning and moving events and people in ways that achieve our goals and satisfy our needs.
Authority: Making the final decisions on issues that directly concern us.

Lastly, check your answer to question 8. This is the final, important step in negotiation preparation: respecting the timing of others. Remember, we are talking about *partnership negotiation*. We are learning how to negotiate in a way that involves give-and-take on the part of both—or all—"sides." As we have seen, almost everything in the world is negotiable. We just don't see it that way because sometimes we only want to see it our way. And sometimes that's the way the other person sees it, too—his or her way. The result is that we both act as tyrants.

If you are impatient with the negotiating partner, you are not only jeopardizing the chance of a fair outcome, you are not respecting that person's own proper authority. Patience is the life blood of negotiating. But too much patience is foolish.

To put these qualities in short order:

TO PREPARE TO NEGOTIATE FOR YOUR LIFE

1. Be willing to take the negotiated risk.
2. Recognize negotiating opportunities in daily life.
3. Assume authority for your own life.
4. Respect the negotiating rhythms of others.
5. Accept the fact that most everything is negotiable, and be conscious of the price.

Everything Is Negotiable (Well, Almost)

Now that we have reviewed some of the elements of our lives that are negotiable, and the steps we must go through in order to prepare to negotiate, let's take another look at the two negotiating challenges that opened this chapter.

Both women felt they were in a bind, trapped, and, as is often the case, economically vulnerable. Although it is rarely true that we are as restricted in our decisions, sometimes we are told that an issue is *not negotiable*. That may be a tipoff that you will have to begin significantly altering, or severing, your connection. In most situations in life, however, some lines of communication are kept open, and both parties are willing—or become willing—to discuss possible solutions.

Financial arrangements are, by their very nature, continually negotiable. Institutions respect this reality and are eager to "work out" solutions that are to their benefit by helping the customer. Here's how the first example turned out:

I was panicked. I thought I was going to lose my business, everything. And then I thought, "Wait a minute. Banks are in the business of loaning money. It's to the bank's advantage that the business grow and eventually prosper. It's to my advantage to keep my energies focused on that goal." I did a cash-flow projection that showed how I would invest the difference— between what I could pay and what I was supposed to be paying—in promotion and marketing, and how this investment would pay off. Then I went back to the bank, presented the plan, and renegotiated the terms of the payment to our mutual advantage.

Even when you think you're occupying a position of little or no formal power, you may have more bargaining power—more room for asserting yourself—than you believe. The kinds of power available to you are:

- positional power
- expert power
- perceived power
- personality (charisma) power
- power of connection

Usually people who consider themselves powerful depend upon others to sustain them. Are you taken for granted? What would happen if you were to suddenly disappear? If your absence would cause some consternation and distress, you know there is perceived value to your role, however you or others may have minimized it. On the other hand, we are all ultimately replaceable; we negotiate often to "up" our measurable value.

Here's what happened to the overworked office manager:

One day, my boss said to me, "Nancy, I don't know what we'd do without you." I decided to believe him. I went home and made a short, to-the-point list of my responsibilities on the job, and made a second list of what I needed to do those responsibilities well (either significantly more money and an understanding that an assistant would be hired at a certain specified point in time, or significantly reduced responsibilities for the same pay and more convenient hours). My boss quickly agreed to Plan A. I felt valued and empowered. My commitment to the company was strengthened, my work was effective, and the stress completely disappeared. Well, almost!

Negotiation frequently works like the bargaining example above. Each side wants to get something out of the matter, whether it is the change in ownership of material objects or the settling of a dispute in a fair manner. People with power in a situation rarely yield on the points unless inequities or deserved benefits are brought to their attention.

Few people want to be in an uncomfortable circumstance for long, where issues have not been resolved. Frequently, however, until a matter is brought to mutual awareness, many people find they are unable to discuss the problems.

Learning the Jargon

Whatever the negotiating circumstances, there are terms and phrases that people use to define certain strategies, tactics, and behaviors. The following is a list of a few of the most common terms.

ASPIRATION LEVEL: How well you expect to do in the negotiations; your expectations.

CLOSED-ENDED QUESTION: One that can only be answered with a yes or a no.

COUNTERMEASURE: Action taken as a consequence of the other side's negotiation tactics.

COUNTEROFFER: A change, modification, or concession from an original offer; made in an attempt to reach a zone of agreement.

DEAL-BREAKER: Point that a side will not concede; requirement that is nonnegotiable.

FALLBACK POSITION: A backup offer; part of negotiating strategy; an alternative solution that avoids loss or failure.

NEED: What is required to establish a feeling of mutual satisfaction in a negotiation; includes intangibles such as self-esteem, trust, values, and reputation. Rarely negotiable.

NEGOTIATION: The process of communication that focuses on influencing yourself and others to accomplish mutual goals.

OPEN-ENDED QUESTION: Elicits complex answers with many variables; cannot be answered with yes or no.

OPENING POSITION: The first offer in a negotiation.

STRATEGY: An overall plan to reach recognized objectives.

TACTIC: A specific maneuver and technique incorporated into a strategy.

"YES" ZONE: The area where minor points are negotiated.

▬ EXERCISE ▬

Reread the above terms and personalize them. For each term, think of a specific situation in your business or personal life to which such a term could be—or, from the past, could have been—applied. For example, here is part of the exercise as completed by one of my workshop participants:

ASPIRATION LEVEL: When I presented my master's dissertation to the committee, I expected it to be praised and accepted.

CLOSED-ENDED QUESTION: Do you intend to increase the promotion budget for our department?

COUNTERMEASURE: When told I would not be given a three-month maternity leave, I began to investigate the possibilities of job-sharing with Eileen.

3
DISCOVERING YOUR NEGOTIATING STYLE

"No one can make you feel inferior without your consent."

—Eleanor Roosevelt

The first step toward becoming a conscious competent negotiator is to reconstruct your early lessons—positive or negative—in negotiating.

What's your first memory of negotiating? I don't mean when you persuaded your high school boyfriend to take you to a movie you wanted to see instead of his choice, or when you got your boss to give you a day off from your first summer job. I'm talking about something that went on, perhaps as a small incident, way back in your early childhood.

That something may embody or symbolize the very way you were initiated into the negotiation process. It usually involved people who—for better or for worse—influenced you. This event set a tone for future negotiating, which later in life you may have had to unlearn or modify when you discovered more effective ways to get what you want.

I always ask women to talk about how they got what they wanted when they were children. I also ask them how their parents or other family members negotiated. Each person has a unique background that affects her current negotiating style.

JANICE. I was a good girl. Good girls are supposed to get what they want. I'd ask for what I wanted and then be very good. Good meant always acting happy. If I was angry or sad, I would have to go to my room and be alone with those feelings. I was supposed to stuff them.

Years later, at work, I was still doing a lot of stuffing. And it would all suddenly come leaking out—usually, of course, at some inappropriate time.

Now, dealing with all those years of good-girl stuffing is part of my self-negotiation. I've got to be aware of it when I'm working closely with people in our small company or negotiating with customers.

CAROLYN. I was sitting in my high chair. We were living in Maryland or Washington, D.C., then. It was summertime—hot and steamy. Somebody went out and bought a bunch of bars from the ice cream man. When I got one, I saw it was coconut-covered. I loved chocolate but hated coconut. So I just began screaming and shouting. My mother had to take off all the coconut coating before I'd eat it. That was how I learned to get my way.

Were you a "good girl" or a "bad girl"? Or somewhere balanced in between? Early in life we start playing by certain scripts—given to us by other people to start with—our parents primarily—until we begin to invent our own. Often we play the same roles over and over in all life situations—unless something happens to change our course.

The way we negotiate life is built into that early script. We have to examine carefully what that script is if we want to become deliberate negotiators—conscious competents—and not people who are simply reacting to what very often are inappropriate, childish, and emotional historical dialogues. In this chapter, we hear from a number of women about their own individual scripts: the ones that began in their childhood.

But first, let's look at how the negotiating behaviors of the two women's stories just mentioned played out in adult life.

JANICE. I had a major customer give me an order for half a million dollars in parts and a delivery deadline. When Manufacturing told me the delivery would be delayed, I called the customer, flew to his location, met with his production people, and worked out the problem, even taking a commission decrease to lower his costs. When the parts were delivered—at the new time promised—the customer refused the order. When my boss called me and told me, I really blew up—at him and, later, at several key people at the customer location. I was furious. And I lost the account.

CAROLYN. When I was in college, I was elected to a women's service organization—an honors group. At the second meeting, I suggested a fund-raising project, and someone else said it wouldn't work, it wasn't a good idea. I shouted at her and at the rest of the group, and they were intimidated. We did the project, it raised money, and I used my "firepower" as my friend called it to run that group. For years, people walked on eggs around me. I never negotiated anything. I always won.

To understand our own basic negotiating style, we must look not only at how we negotiate now and how we have negotiated in the past, including during our childhood and adolescence, but also at the examples of negotiating tactics (or utter lack of them) in our upbringing. These examples are most particularly between our parents, or, if we had a single parent, between her (or him) and other adults, and with the children.

Did You Want to Be Like Mom?

How do I get what I want? [Laughs] Manipulation. You just keep persisting and try to turn the situation around. That's how my Mom has always done it. She makes people around her feel guilty so they may end up doing what she wants. My sisters and I are the same way. We're no different from the past generations. They did it all before we did.

It's generally agreed that daughters usually look first to their mothers as models for their behavior. Thus, to understand your own attitude toward negotiating, you might look first at your mother.

Did she know what she really wanted—specifically, and in life itself? Did she expect others to give it to her, or did she often take the initiative to secure things for herself? Was she basically satisfied and happy? Or sad and depressed? Or angry, punishing everyone around her for her disgruntlement? To what extent were others (such as your father) blamable for unhappiness? Did the home atmosphere in good part reflect your mother's attitude and her sunny or dark moods? Maybe you thought you'd succeed if you acted as your mother did when she was determined to get her way. That was the case of one very successful woman who told me:

> My mother? She's one of those who goes by the rule, "You've got to know when to hold 'em and when to fold 'em." She only went after what she wanted on the really important stuff. I've learned a million things from her, and that's one of them. Fight the battles you can win, walk away from ones you can't win, and make a decision about the ones that could go this way or that.

This woman's mother's "hold/fold" message is an important lesson in negotiation: You've got to know when to enter negotiation and when not to. Some battles you may never win no matter what you do. But you may want to enter them anyway, just for the experience and education you'll get from them. Understand your motives—and the odds—in advance.

Some daughters pattern their negotiating styles as mirror opposites of what their mothers did:

> My mother is a dynamite woman. She can self-negotiate, but she won't negotiate with other people. She makes demands, and either you meet her demands or she doesn't want to deal with you. She is not a compromising individual. Either it's her way or no way.
>
> And how did her way affect me? I decided I was going to be nice. Everything that I saw in her I didn't want to be! So from the beginning, I was a people pleaser. I didn't want to hurt any feelings or step on any toes as she always did. Since I didn't want to be the bad guy, I allowed myself to get stepped on. I really felt that if you give something, you'll get something. So if I was friendly and did all kinds of nice things for other

people, I'd eventually get what I wanted from them. But of course I never did. Instead, I got hurt.

What do you make of this woman's tale of the effect of her mother's rigidity on her childhood, which made her reluctant to assert herself in her own behalf? As a girl she felt disappointed and embarrassed that her mother was so different from the "ideal" mother, and from the other women around her. This uneasiness caused her to design an identity for herself that conformed to the conventional "nice" one expected of women.

The "good girl" reaction is a common one among even seemingly tough professional women. As one woman recalled:

We had an interesting family dynamic. Nothing was ever good enough for my mother. She didn't fight fair. She got what she wanted—she "negotiated"—by telling my father that he never did anything right, that he never did anything for her, that he owed this to her. She used guilt through and through.

My father was a very kind and caring man, and conflict really hurt him. I remember having a lot of discussions with him and also observing what the conflict with my mother and sister did to him.

So I was always the good girl. And I still have to fight back in my life. To be able to say, "No, you may not do that to me or anybody else." Also, to fight a lot the temptation to avoid conflict—the idea that conflict isn't healthy. Watching my father when he was put in those situations has made it hard for me. And you're right: I'm never going to become my mother!

In the workplace, I don't mind participating in a conflict situation as long as it's not around me. I'll fight for others, but I'm not comfortable fighting for myself. I can't remember a time when I went in and said, "I should get a higher salary."

This woman doesn't come off as a pushover, either on the job or in her personal life. But she always has to pay attention to that abiding inner self who is reluctant to be assertive or demanding—especially, perhaps, with men. In spite of their occupying the power positions around her, she may sometimes feel she must be extraordinarily protective and considerate, as she did so long ago with her own father. And she doesn't want to resemble her mother.

One woman's childhood perception of her parents' negotiations seems idyllic:

> How did I get this way? I have two of the most wonderful parents on Planet Earth. My mother is extremely sweet-natured, and my father is very, very calm. So I never saw them argue. Argument was not a way to negotiate in our family. The way my father negotiated was that he'd find something he wanted and then would just talk about it and gradually wear my mother down so she'd give in. Probably because of having had polio very early in life, she acquiesced a lot. That was okay with her unless she had a very strong opinion about something.
>
> If my mother herself really wanted something, she would just say to my father straight out, "You know, Paul, this is what I want and these are the reasons I want it, so you should listen to me." She didn't ask often for things, so he'd usually give in. Early in their marriage, I think, they made a pact about how they'd always negotiate with each other. They waited for seven years to have children, so they had a long time to talk about how they'd negotiate with them when they came along. So they had done their homework. By then they knew who they were and who the other person was, and had their own values lined up so they could always give a united front. My parents were good negotiators, certainly in talking things out with each other and with us.
>
> We could never go to one parent and get something that the other parent didn't know about. The important things they'd discuss and consider maybe for weeks and weeks. If a new reason for something came up, they'd just throw it in the pot and think about that, too. Then they'd finally sit down and come to a decision based on what would be the best outcome for the family.

Your birth-order placement (being first or last born or in the middle) may also structure a particular early negotiating role and style within the family, and subsequently affect your later career and private life. (The oldest tends to be the most assertive and self-confident, the middle child the most flexible and accommodating, the youngest the most likely to let others take charge and do it while she does "her own thing.") Here is one example of the negotiating edge given the middle child:

My first negotiation? Obviously it had to be with my brother and sister. I was the middle child and somehow was always put in the mediator position. My mother did that very early on. It would always be, "Maureen, settle the argument between Wayne and Susie and get them to play nice." So it was my task to negotiate a deal between them. Like if they were playing Monopoly, I'd say, "Now, Susie, I'm sure Wayne didn't mean to do that! If he gives you that little hotel on the corner, will you give him such-and-such and stop being angry with him? And Wayne, if Susie does so-and-so, we can settle this." And that was how it went. I did this kind of thing with candy, too.

Another thing I negotiated had to do with neighborhood games. I was good at sports. But though my brother was about two years older than I, he was not well coordinated and had no natural athletic ability. Still, he wanted to play. The kids always wanted me to play football with them. But my brother was there too, and nobody wanted him in the game. Usually I would get picked first by the captain, so then I'd say, "You know, the only way I'm going to play on your team is if you'll let Wayne play with me." And almost always they'd go for the deal.

As we might expect, this woman has a built-in propensity for negotiations that lead to peacemaking, not just between herself and others but also in settling other people's disputes. At the same time, because she tries to keep the peace herself, she tends to back off from conflicts and also do more than her share of work. Her "worst negotiations" happen when she takes on responsibilities that really are other people's and realizes belatedly that they have failed to do anything at all. Only then, when she gets angry, refuses to perform further, and demands action from the others, does she get results.

Here's an example of a middle-child negotiator who did not have successful role models:

My immediate family was really dysfunctional. All our "negotiations" were hostile and argumentative. My mother was like her own mother: unbalanced and out of sorts. As for my father, he wanted things the way he wanted them, and that was that. It's interesting how my parents picked each other: they fought all the time. And their children—I was the middle one—were the bane of their existence.

It is difficult to overcome negative habits of thinking and behaving instilled in us through poor modeling witnessed daily, even hourly, as we were growing up. On the other hand, some adverse experience at an early age can prepare you for the world outside, where you must eventually deal with a wide variety of people who will not have the same calm, considerate, and well-planned approach to negotiating as some parents demonstrate for their fortunate offspring. Moreover, you may not always have the luxury of large blocks of time for slow, deliberate discussions leading up to decision making.

Be confident, then, that if you have survived a less-than-perfect childhood and are already gaining a good understanding of the deeply pervasive influences of your past on both your self-negotiating and your interactions with others, you can certainly become a conscious, competent negotiator.

Now, What About YOU?

Having considered a wide spectrum of other women's remembered interactions with mothers and fathers, let's consider what your own parents were like when they were in a "negotiating" situation.

Was one parent dominant? Did he or she usually get things to go his or her way? If so, how did they do it? If this is how it was, you could have learned various things from them and shaped your own negotiating tactics accordingly.

Have you identified by now your first remembrance of negotiating? Later, you might write about it to summarize what it portended for the rest of your childhood negotiating, and in your adult life, too. Maybe you can even write a scene with characters, dialogue, and descriptions. You might surprise yourself at how

much you recall when you focus on it, and then amplify its implications.

If a precise event doesn't come to mind, make a composite—
a summary—of dozens of negotiating situations that show your
early style either in trying to get something you wanted or else in
avoiding something you *didn't* want. (We tend to forget that negotiating is also about *evading* the negatives, the undesirables.)

Does Gender Make a Difference?

I don't know how men negotiate. All I know is that they make
a hell of a lot more money than I do, so maybe what I need to
do is take a look at it.

The first thing we usually notice about person is gender. Along
with general age group, of course; we note whether the person is
an infant, an adolescent, or a senior citizen. Ethnicity or race is
nowhere as significant. Height, eye or hair color, body type, and
facial structure are details considered later, too.

We relate also to other people through our own gender, mod-
ifying aspects of our behavior in accord with the other person's.
Our response to another person's gender, whether the same or opposite, is especially revealing when we deal with adults.

Most people relate differently to girls than to boys. They are
more rough-and-tumble, more bantering and offhand with boys,
and feel they should be gentler, more sensitive and complimentary
with girls. We talk to each gender differently too, since each expects to hear language and subjects appropriate to one's own kind.

In other words, people usually generalize about the members
of a particular gender. And, although we should always remember
there are important exceptions to the rules, as groups, men and
women *do* negotiate differently.

How do we differ? Psychologist Joan Brozovich (whose clien-
tele is 80 percent women) readily traces contemporary women's
challenges with negotiation to both biological and societal sources:

It's women's biological nature to be connected with others.
Our caring begins in the womb. It's instinctual, but reinforced
by culture. We are scanners of the environment: How is every-

one doing here? Basically we're okay if everyone else is okay. It's unusual for a woman to consider: How am I doing, what do I need? . . . to change the mirror to the inside and read the self rather than others.

In our culture women play secondary roles. Most of us don't feel we deserve to get what we want. So we use indirect ways of getting it. We might give off an air of sadness to get attention. Someone just might ask us what's wrong, and then we get to tell that person what we'd like to have. Since women are assigned a second-class status, we've had to be indirect to get what we want, to be secretive in our dealings, and hope our message gets through.

Think for a minute about how you were raised as a girl. If you had brothers or male cousins, or if you had close friends who were boys, were they given any different instructions, rules, or encouragements? Were different things expected of them? If so, what were they?

I wasn't taught to negotiate at all, other than the way women negotiate with men when they want something. You use your sexuality. I did that, and when I was younger it worked very well. I was reared to understand how powerful sex is for a Southern woman in a genteel socioeconomic group. That's all they've got and they are well groomed to use it. "Don't do that!" my mother would scold me when I picked up something whenever a man was around. "Let him carry it. Don't wear yourself out. It makes him feel better that you don't do it, that he's doing it for you. Once he sees you doing that, he'll keep letting you do it. He'll begin looking at you like an equal. And that won't work."

I remember friends, and women in the neighborhood, talking about how to get what they wanted from husbands. Never ask them for it when they're hungry. Always ask after they've eaten. When you've fed them, given them a nice glass of wine, massaged them, and are making out. Then ask at the very beginning of sex. But never after sex! By then it's too late.

How did you learn, and how were you *taught*, gender differences in negotiating when you were a child? Did your mother and other female relatives just model the appropriate behaviors for your edification, or did they also deliver mini-lectures on the subject? Was manipulation a typical, approved tactic in feminine negotiations, particularly with males? Did it carry over naturally into adult life, as in these examples? And how much power did sexuality, implicit or explicit, have in manipulating?

Are you fully aware of your own personal roots in creating your gender identity when you're negotiating? Perhaps you did it in accordance with the models you saw in your family and community. Or maybe you did it partly as a reaction to them, knowing instinctively what you did *not* want to be or do. You might then have discovered other styles for female negotiating that seemed more enlightened and suitable for you.

• Who were your role models in stories you read as a girl and young woman? In history accounts? In biographies and autobiographies? Why did you admire them?

• Who were the heroines who impressed you in stories? In movies and TV programs? Did you try to be like them? Are you like them at all now?

• Were you more impressed with what boys and men did in stories, in history, and in the entertainment media?

• Which gender do you prefer to work with or for? Negotiate with? Women or men? And why?

Do Men and Women Negotiate Differently from Each Other?

First, ask yourself that question. In what significant ways do you think men and women, or boys and girls (because these start in childhood), differ from each other when trying to get something they want? Think about it for a minute or two. Then record your initial impressions on a piece of paper divided into two columns, Male and Female, with contrasting behaviors or attitudes relating to negotiation on the same line.

Now let's see what some other people think.

The rules and expectations that hold for one sex somehow

don't fit with the other's rules. Listen to this story, told by a woman speaker at a conference for women in business:

Two women decided to do something different. They'd go on a hunting trip, just like "the boys" always did. So they went out and got outfits: plaid wool shirts, boots, hunters' jackets, food. They also bought two rifles, took lessons in shooting, borrowed a truck and drove off to the woods. Walking along among the trees, they looked for deer. What they saw was a huge black bear. It gnashed its teeth and roared, then lunged toward them. They turned and ran as fast as they could. But the bear came crashing after them, getting closer and closer. Finally, one of the women stopped, pulled off her boots, looked in her bag, and pulled out a pair of Nikes. "What are you doing?" her friend asked. "People can never outrun bears." Her companion laced up her sneakers and took off. "I don't have to outrun the bear," she said. "All I have to do is outrun *you!*"

Ever heard that story? It's an old story; you probably have. But I'll wager you heard it told about two *men* going hunting together. And everybody laughed. Isn't that just like men—being competitive with each other, even to death! And they can joke about it, too.

But told about *women?* When the female speaker at a professional women's conference used that tale in its slightly altered form to illustrate a point she wanted to make, her audience tittered uneasily. I didn't laugh. I was shocked that simply altering the gender of the two hunters totally changed the tone of the story. There was nothing funny about it. It was mean-spirited and wicked. The disturbing factor, of course, was this: Women rarely compete in the ruthless way that men are socialized to do. Far likelier, when being pursued women would figure out they could outsmart the bear together.

Some people see gender differences as the contrast between a power struggle (male) and a need to find a consensus (female). A conscious, competent female negotiator had this to say about working with males, who are her principal job associates:

Men approach negotiation from a different standpoint. It's a game that has to be won. Since I realize it's a power struggle, I can't be too upfront. I come at it a bit by the back door. I get them to negotiate on a goal—an inanimate object—and change the focal point. Most of my negotiating anyway goes on around projects or about policies being developed. I get people to depersonalize the issue. And I talk about it in global terms, like benefits to the company; and then how their own needs can be fulfilled within the context.

Men are very much into recognition, so you have to give away the kudos they need to get their support for what you need: a favorable decision. You can talk all you want about the good feelings and all the other side benefits, and nothing will happen. But then boil it down, whether in terms of dollars or real labor, into the universal language of corporations: money.

Even when they are dealing with totally impersonal matters that require a wide focus, men want to "win" their points. Women, by contrast, seem more emotionally invested, so they may find it difficult to "get the big picture" when negotiating. They aren't as much interested in "winning" as they are in reaching accord or consensus, often leading them into a submission not always intended by their negotiating partner.

Here's how a man differentiates between the two genders' negotiating styles:

When I'm problem solving with women, I first handle it by depersonalizing. I try to find out what they really need to get out of the negotiation or something they want to accomplish. I ask questions that lead that way. If I want to initiate a new process or product, I ask them to talk about what they've heard, how people feel, and so on. They I say, "OK, let's take all the information you've explained here and find out who the recipient is of this new process or product."

I go through this routine because I've seen that women often must release on emotions before they can focus. They do this more than men. Men will personalize some issue because of ego. Women do it because they want to meet some need and don't know how to go about it. Men are more self-directed, women more other-directed.

Clearly, conscious competent negotiators of both sexes always consider the gender of their negotiating partners an important factor, particularly whenever they are dealing with prototypes and generalities rather than individuals whose personal negotiating styles are already known to them. The experience of one female police officer is revealing:

> The men at my workplace certainly negotiate differently from how the women do. But then they're mostly policemen and police administrators. They are demanding. They make their requests or handle negotiations or meetings forcefully. When they are making their point, they raise their voices and pound their fists. When I see a woman do it, or when I do it, it's a much gentler and quieter approach. I'll also ask them for feedback before I actually come out and ask for what I want. And then I get them to think it was really their idea, so they'll take the first steps. It works!

If a woman tries negotiating in a forceful "macho" style, she can harm her position, no matter how rationally and eloquently she presents it. This happens because she either offends the opposite side (who expects something kinder and gentler from a female), or distracts them from the points she is making because they are busily pondering the reasons for her unfeminine demeanor. Girls learn early on that it is not "politic" to talk like a boy. They are supposed to be more subtle and decorous.

There's also a prevailing opinion that in some ways women as a group may not negotiate as effectively as men because they have insufficient exposure to male-oriented athletic activities, whether playing competitively in teams or taking part in individual outdoor pursuits like golf or fishing, which require perseverance and patience.

This comment comes from a female bank executive who is also an accomplished athlete:

I've seen far more men negotiate than women, but I've noticed that women come to the bottom line much faster. They just don't have the confidence to stretch out that experience. That ability may come from playing sports. Women who take time negotiating usually know that it takes a while to take the ball down the court and get it into the basket, or make just the right shot in a tennis match. Part of the negotiating is getting there.

Though many men and women do not negotiate differently from each other in significant ways, we should recognize this reality: they are usually *perceived* as negotiating according to their gender's style, whatever that may be. In other words, people have different *expectations* of how their sex or the opposite sex negotiates. We tend to notice the conformities rather than the exceptions, according to our own notions of them as positives or negatives.

Anomalies—people who seem to cross these established gender barriers when they negotiate—may be considered wimps (men) or ballbreakers (women) by traditionalists. Most men will therefore strive to negotiate "like men," and most women "like women"—that is, unless they see some definite advantages in doing otherwise.

Thus we may be locked, consciously or unconsciously, into a particular gender's negotiating style just to avoid disapproval or ridicule. We slip into our role-playing especially when partnering with someone of the opposite sex, whether negotiating on the same "team" or on opposite sides. Sometimes the gender-linked separate stances are so taken for granted that they can sabotage each other, as in the following story:

We were quite interested in buying a piece of property being sold by a couple who I knew were going through a rather messy divorce. When a bank assessed it at a much lower figure than the asking price, my husband and I decided to make a lower offer than we'd intended to pay. We were turned down. "You know," I told Jack, "I'm going to call the woman. You can't talk with her husband since you've never been able to stand each other. She wants to sell the property and I want to buy it. I want to see if, woman to woman, we can decide what each of us needs and what we can give up—to make this work for us both."

So that night when I went up to bed, Jack said, "It won't work." I asked, "What do you mean?" And he said, "I just called her and told her what we would pay . . . and that was it."

Well, that *was* it! I just about killed him. He simply couldn't understand why I was so angry at him. "So what's the big deal whether you call her or I call her?"

Jack's very direct. That's one of the things I love about him. He's clear straight through! You never have to wonder about what he's thinking. But he just doesn't understand subtleties at all.

When we heard soon afterward that the property had gone into escrow, we were both devastated. We'd both wanted it more than anything. "We absolutely blew it," I told him. "We were willing to pay what they said they wanted, but we let an outside opinion change our minds." I then phoned the woman and asked if there was any way she could get out of the escrow if we paid their asking price. "No," she said, "when your husband called and told me your offer was final and inflexible, I took what he said at face value."

Well, I was so upset over losing this property that I got really furious with him all over again. But he'd listened in on our conversation: what she was essentially saying was that his approach had really screwed us up. So all of a sudden he put more credibility into the fact that there's much more to negotiating than what you say. It's the way you say it, the environment you say it in, the medium you choose, the timing. And relationships. None of these, of course, meant anything to him until that moment.

Around that time I read an article that described my husband's and my differences in just that situation. It said that when men communicate, just as they do everything else, it's competition. In their conversations they're always trying one-upmanship. But when women communicate, it's a sharing of ideas within a relationship that you have or are creating.

In this couple's case, the husband automatically assumed the spokesman role as "head of household." Only when he realized how his way of doing things had sabotaged his wife's negotiation plan could he value the difference in their separate, distinctive approaches.

Women in general *do* seem to place a high value on interpersonal communication that moves toward community and away from competitiveness. Associated with their negotiating style as well are honest emotionality, compassion or empathy, and cooperation. In contrast, men in negotiating situations are competitors who seek to win (whether as individuals or on a team). They veer away from showing personal feelings, and clam up when this "defect" is pointed out to them by women. Cooperation with others is not regarded as a goal but as the temporary means of achieving the goal—which is winning, of course.

Let's not forget about one more special attribute of women. Men, who pride themselves on their skeptical rationality, dismiss it as a figment of the female gender's gullible emotionalism. Many women ridicule the whole idea of such a thing, and relinquish any ownership. I suggest, however, that you pay attention to our claim. Because "women's intuition" can be a powerful directive when you are negotiating.

What About Intuition?

A significant mental factor that differentiates males from females during negotiation is the female's built-in radar system that searches below the surface of a situation to pick up and process hidden messages about other people's intentions, character, emotions, distractions, and motivations.

Most women I've talked with grew up believing that any intuition they felt they had was of no value, and therefore should be discounted. In our left-brain-oriented, analytical culture, many of us are detached from this element within our psyches, particularly if family members ridiculed it as we were growing up. Women whose own mothers honored their own intuitions are more likely to be consciously and skillfully intuitive themselves.

Women who negotiate well have learned to pay close conscious attention to this intuitive sense. They don't readily dismiss it as momentary madness; all too often they've realized, in retrospect, that their intuition had tried to alert them to underlying factors in a situation—negative or positive, dire warnings or special opportunities. Their conscious mind simply was unaware of, and therefore they did not heed, the messages.

That's why we often hear women say with regret things like: "I knew we shouldn't trust that man, but my husband just laughed when I told him what I was feeling." Or, "I wanted to tell her not to go, but she'd have thought I was crazy." Not always, of course, is our intuition correct. It isn't intended to be. It's a kind of Red Alert system. And it gives us beneficial messages as well as warnings.

Since intuition is universal among womankind, it must be inherent and biological in design and purpose. It is not "extra-sensory" at all, because it pulls in subtle information from the environment, which bypasses the conscious mind. This shortcut accesses in milliseconds some nether region of our brain. If pressed for "facts" that document fears and suspicions of others or, conversely, crosscurrents indicating a favorable subterranean but possibly accessible trait, women can usually come up with a surprising quantity of precise external data that were rapidly configured and synthesized into a forceful response.

Since we no longer perpetually wander across the African savannas, and most of us no longer spend all of our life, or perhaps any of it, as mothers or domestic caregivers, expectably our intuition now functions to process wholly different environmental signals. Our sensory equipment is constantly on the alert for clues alerting us to someone's need for rescue or for nurturance. Sometimes that endangered or needy person must be ourselves, as others' primary providers. As one woman said:

> I have to continually remind myself to listen to my intuition and not sell out in relationships. I need to do what I am best at: using my intuition and my determination.

Make sure, however, you always discriminate between intuitive feelings and messages from your emotional projections—fears, expectations, anger, longings—that may look and sound like intuition but are not. They are your own displaced, not yet consciously identified feelings put out to roost elsewhere—and they could lead you astray.

We'll discuss various ramifications of women's intuitiveness later on, as we learn more about the negotiation process.

▬ EXERCISE 1 ▬

STRETCH YOUR MEMORY

1. Think of something you wanted as a very young child—a bicycle, a new dress, a pony, a doll, a piece of candy. How did you ask for it? What were the reactions of your adult family members? Did you get what you wanted? How many and what kind of tactics did you use?
2. Who was or were the authority figure(s) with whom you were negotiating? What influence did the outcome of your behavior have on future negotiations with that person? Could that person be considered a significant influence over your present negotiation style?

▬ EXERCISE 2 ▬

From your experience, do men and women negotiate with different styles? What single words come to mind as you analyze these styles? Focus on a particular male-female negotiating situation from your experience. What differences can you observe? What similarities?

▬ EXERCISE 3 ▬

HOW DID YOUR FAMILY HANDLE CONFLICT?

Blamed	Confronted fairly
Got involved	Listened to each other
Were silent	Withdrew
Denied	

1. Do you reflect any of these traits in your negotiating style?
2. In which situations are your negative traits dominant?
3. In which situations are your positive traits dominant?
4. What type of conflicts cause you the most stress?

5. What type of conflict personalities do you find most threatening? Most communicative?

6. What skills do you use to handle conflict?

> Negotiate   Stop, think, come back
> Get even   Attack
> Withdraw   Others:

7. Which conflict-resolution skills or traits would you like to emphasize? Which would you like to eliminate?

▬ EXERCISE 4 ▬

WHAT ARE YOUR BEST NEGOTIATING TOOLS?

1. Do you value intuition? Think of past experiences when you ignored your intuition and ones when you acted upon it. Do you trust those "feelings" when you are negotiating in business?

2. Intuition is only one of many personality qualities or behaviors— let's call them tools—that each of us already has to greater or lesser degrees. We can consciously adjust them to suit situational needs in interactions with people, including negotiating.

To evaluate your "tool chest," do an inventory of personality characteristics, arranged in a continuum or spectrum from a state of deficiency to the balanced optimum condition to a state of excess. (You can regard extremes as having too little or too much of a good thing!)

I have found that the qualities in the continuum are excellent ones to have during the negotiation process. Look over this list and assess honestly how closely you attain or stray from the center.

TOO LITTLE (−)	BALANCED (+)	EXCESSIVE (+ +)
indecisive	decisive	controlling
impatient	patient	indulgent
submissive	cooperative	domineering
unimaginative	innovative	overimaginative
fact restricted	intuitive	fanciful

4
NEGOTIATING
PERSONALITIES

"The goal of negotiation is to build bridges, not walls."
—Nicole Schapiro

Listen whenever someone new is talking to you. Often, you can discover a person's negotiating style immediately.

Suppose I call someone for the first time. I'm preparing to exclaim when the person answers, "Isn't it a beautiful day?" But what I get is "Smith here." I switch my style and attitude immediately. "Schapiro here," I respond, because I have to pace that person—pick up his or her energy. "Who the hell is Schapiro?" Smith barks. I know I've got what I call a "Steamroller." (Like the three other types of negotiators, I have names for each style. I'll introduce you to them soon.)

Personalities—
and Matching Negotiating Styles

As important as knowing your own basic negotiating style is knowing the negotiating style that characterizes the person sitting across from you—at the bargaining table, at the breakfast table, or on the other end of the telephone line. To be a successful negotiator, you need to find out as much as you can about the opposite side: who they are, and where they are coming from. Whether you're negotiating with one person or a group, the more you understand the other side's positions, perspectives, and possible behavior, the better your chances will be to resolve the issue.

The information you learn about personalities—directly and

indirectly—should tell you enough for you to infer their probable negotiating mode (and mood!). You should learn whether they are naturally confrontational and competitive, or whether they are cooperative and approach negotiating with a partnering point of view. This information will help you design your strategy: how you will meet, match, cooperate, or compete.

While seeking information, keep in mind that each side brings to the negotiations its unique set of background issues and attitudes based on experience or personal history. The key to successful negotiating is to understand these issues, accept them, and plan for them.

The primary types of personal issues are:

- Personality type
- Motivation
- Gender
- Perceived amount of control or power
- Actual power of position
- Age and generation
- Ethnicity, nationality, race
- First and second languages
- U.S. regional styles
- Perceived social and economic realities (class)
- Level of fear and risk
- Experience level of the negotiator
- Self-esteem
- Amount of time or financial pressure

The most important variable is personality type. It is the overriding issue in negotiating; frequently, the other variables include tendencies toward one type or another. We'll look at those other factors in the next chapter. For now, let's focus on personalities.

The Origin of Personality Types

People have innate temperaments. Consider how four very different types of people might behave when they're trying to get somewhere. Picture them driving cars along the highway. What kind of cars would each drive? How fast would they drive? Would they

stick to all the rules, or sometimes break or stretch them? Would
each go in the fast lane, occupy the middle lane at moderate speed,
or poke along sensibly, even rigidly, in the slow lane? Do they
weave in and out of all lanes, working always to get their place
ahead of, and faster than, all the other drivers? (And how about the
ones that zip along the shoulder of the road and then push in front
of the line?)

Would these drivers pay close attention to the road ahead, or
be busy chatting to a companion, turning their head to focus on a
friend, not a stop sign or the truck next to them? Would they be
glancing in the mirror—applying lipstick and mascara, combing
their hair, shaving, or be reading the morning paper at a stoplight?

Each of these drivers fits a particular model, a personality type:

1. Aggressive: eager to win at any price, get ahead, get it over
   with.
2. Analytical: exercising caution at all times—"better safe than
   sorry."
3. Expressive: sociable and emotive with others.
4. Amiable: anxious to please everyone.

You see the same kinds of widely varying behavior when
people negotiate. Some people want to show they are in control
of whatever is going on, in terms of time, power, knowledge, and
space. Some want to feel safe and not look like a fool. Some want
to be noticed, to be acknowledged for their very presence and
their participation, though knowing others may not agree with
them. And some want to be included but don't want to take a position that might offend anyone. For several decades, researchers
and management specialists have worked with variations on a
model that broadly identifies these four basic personalities in the
workplace. These distinctive types, which are generalized compos-
ites of individual characteristics, provide a useful handle when
looking at the participants in a negotiation.

Many people in different situations fit the overall profile of one
of these personality types—not wholly and consistently, but
enough so that certain traits determine how they design a negotiating strategy and then carry it out. These traits also determine how

a person interacts with the opposite side, particularly when encountering obstacles.

There are different names for the four types (which some negotiation commentators expand to a half-dozen or more). I've added my own name for each, and I use my names throughout the book, since sometimes what I say about these types breaks from other negotiators' classifications.

USUALLY KNOWN AS	I CALL
Aggressor (sensor, driver, bottom-liner, bulldozer, dominant, director)	Steamroller
Analytical (analyzer, thinker, conscious thinker)	Datacrat
Expressive (socializer, intuitor)	Butterfly
Amiable (feeler, pleaser, soother)	Mr./Ms. Nice Guy

These self-explanatory names convey images of the people we meet in a negotiating situation. What we'll do now is suggest the different external aspects of their individual appearance and behavior that provide clues to their identity. (Please remember that, like a caricaturist, sometimes we need to distort or magnify so as to provide that useful handle.) Also, you may discover some things about your own personality type that will help you be a more conscious and competent negotiator.

■ THE STEAMROLLER

The most extraordinary negotiating session I've ever had with a Steamroller occurred in Denver, where I had flown to meet with the entrepreneur who had founded a successful cookie company. I had just seated myself in a chair next to her desk when she bounced up and said, "Well, I gotta go!" I was astonished. "Go?"

She looked down at her appointment calendar. "You were down today for sixty seconds," she said, "and—" she glanced at her watch—"you've had sixty-three." This is how she operates; she *really* schedules sixty-second appointments.

She was the perfect example of a Steamroller. A one-minute conversation with an unknown entity seems ideal to a Steamroller.

"Whoa!" I quickly warned myself. Fortunately, I've had a lot of experience with Steamrollers, so I could make the right shift happen. "Where are we going?" I asked her, instantly.

"*We?*" she wondered, taken aback.

"I'll go with you," I said firmly, standing up, ready to take off.

"But I'm driving seventy-two miles out of the city for an appointment," she protested, heading out the door.

"Good, let's go!" I replied, matching her pace as she strode through the parking lot.

"Then how are you going to get back?" she asked while inserting a key in the car door.

"I'll figure that out when I get there," I told her. She flipped up the lock on the passenger side, and we were on our way.

When you deal with a Steamroller, you have to keep the goal in mind and act quickly. You've got to manage that shift smoothly, with no gear-grinding. I wanted to talk with this woman. That's why I'd come to Denver. There was no room for blame. (Who made such a stupid one-minute appointment?) Steamrollers respect quick solutions, and creative ones—along with "guts." We could talk in the car, all the way to her meeting, I figured. And we did. I'm resourceful, I knew from a history of successes. I'd find some way to get back home from our destination point.

If you can adapt your own attitude and style to get along with a Steamroller, you can handle any kind of negotiating situation life throws at you. Be flexible, take risks, think on your feet, and don't get hung up thinking about what a bully this person is. It helped that I could "read" her style instantly and gear my strategy to it. I didn't beat myself up for making the assumption that this would be a "nice Cookie Lady."

What to Know About Them

They are easy to spot. Steamrollers move around fast. They dress with quality without being ostentatious or trendy. They always speak in a forthright, authoritative tone of voice. Their handshake is a real cruncher. Often they have a corporate, military, or team-sports background. They embody the standard image of the American negotiator. They have a know-it-all, "full of themselves" attitude. Their whole demeanor says, "Hey, I'm the boss"—whether they are or not.

How do Steamrollers get what they want in business? Well, they just assume that they're going to get it—not a bad vision for the rest of us. And don't think that the Steamroller's domain is occupied exclusively by males. As you saw, women can also belong to this group. They assume that they must fight in order to win anything. As managers they say, "My way, or the highway," making others feel that not many things with them are negotiable.

Steamrollers will call you, or come in and say, more or less, "What can you do for me?" *What* is their key word (as in "What's in it for me?)—their Open Sesame—so say it a lot when you're negotiating with them. *What* forces you to a bottom-line approach like theirs. Expect many of their questions to start with the word.

Steamrollers may pace back and forth like a caged tiger. They tap or slap impatiently on desks and tables and walls. They rarely sit down for long. When they do, they invariably place themselves at the head of a table, even if they really have no business being there.

When you meet a Steamroller, look for nonverbal clues. The most telling items come from them in the first thirty seconds. (See also the section on Body Language in Chapter 11.) They establish and maintain intense eye contact, which may result in a staring contest. Take a break from time to time by looking away, but always come quickly back, locking eyes often enough so they'll know they aren't intimidating you. They may keep their eyes focused on you, with the intent of getting a quicker resolution. Also, it might be a lesson they learned early: "Look at me when I talk to you."

If their gaze is unnerving, look steadily at their "third eye" in the forehead between the eyes. They won't know you're doing this. They are seeing how strong (or weak) you are. This is the style they've developed for winning every contest in their lives. They love the psychological equivalent of arm-wrestling.

Steamrollers speak rapidly. They often don't finish their own sentences and may not let you finish yours. Watch this when you're negotiating. If it becomes incessant, it's a sure sign that information you're spouting is too detailed to interest them, and you should shift to summarizing and bottom-lining.

Their Fears and Concerns

Steamrollers' greatest fear is that their time will be wasted. They want all transactions to go quickly and efficiently.

Wordlessly they convey the command, "Recognize and respect my power." They use this power as a weapon or added advantage in negotiating. But they are perpetually afraid of losing it. Their fear of losing the power of their position is tied up with their concern that if they don't have power, they'll have to wait for a slow decision maker. They can never make decisions as fast as they want to make them, and hate it if they must wait for other people to make up their minds about something. To them everyone else is a snail on Valium.

Steamrollers want information right now—but without details—and they need quick responses, quick solutions from you.

■ THE DATACRAT

Brenda, a friend who's a real estate broker, frequently sounds off to me about the clients who never seem to get enough information to make a decision. Or at least the *fast* decision that would be to her liking. "They want two hundred years of the history of a town where they want to buy some property." She heaves a sigh.

"And that's just a small part of their expectations," she goes on. "They badger me for the exact dimensions of an irregular lot, and house size down to the cubic inch, including the attic and basement space as separate figures. They need to know the exact population figures going back to 1900, the number of children in the local elementary school, and how many retail stores are within the town limits. They expect lists of all elected local officials in the past quarter-century, and their party affiliations."

While Brenda paused in her recitation to take a deep breath, I asked her, "So how do you handle them?" "Well," she said, "I *feel* like saying, 'Buy it or not, I don't care!' But of course I *do* care, because I want to stay in business. So I scurry around and try to supply them with all the information they're asking for. And believe me, I've really earned my commission once I get their signatures on the title deeds!"

Brenda's a Steamroller who's chosen a career that often requires her to negotiate with Datacrats. Sooner or later, that improbable combination is bound to happen.

What to Know About Them

Datacrats dress conservatively and neatly. Men may have an array of mechanical pencils neatly lined up in their shirt pockets or on a desk tray. They walk slowly. And they talk slowly, because they must always carefully consider what you've said. If they do extend their hand to shake yours, it is limp. Or they'll do a half-handshake, with a stiff arm that keeps you at arm's length.

They may avoid looking directly at you. Their eyes usually look down—at their desk, at the rug, at their shoes. (This minimal eye contact is due to the fact that they can only properly think about one thing at a time, and are easily distracted by people's presence, which makes them nervous.)

How do you discover them when you cold-call? A person who's a Datacrat may answer the phone, with or without an initial greeting, in great detail that provides you with first name, middle name, last name, position, department, and corporation. Or they'll just give a noncommittal "Yes" if they don't want to identify themselves until they know who you are.

Their voices will be toneless, impersonal, and perhaps slightly hesitant, as if they didn't want to answer the phone at all. Which is true. Because they dislike surprises, they always treat a phone call as a surprise—unless they're expecting a particular call and can prepare themselves for it. Let them know exactly when you will call them to discuss anything.

Listen to the speed of their voice and match it. Slow down your self-introduction when you know you're talking to a Datacrat. If you're a fast talker, they will feel threatened and will withdraw, which is not to your advantage. Trust is their short suit; they seemingly speak and think slowly, and always think before they talk—which takes time. Furthermore, they won't *want* to negotiate with you because they think speed demons are trying to put something over on them.

Avoid seeing Datacrats in person whenever you can, because they act as if they don't particularly like you. Because they are usually uncomfortable when dealing face-to-face with people, negotiate through E-mail, fax, messengers, computer modems. You can even get their signature that way on a deal without ever meeting them. What kind of professions are likely to have a high percentage of Datacrats? Engineers, computer analysts, lawyers, accountants, some professors, librarians, technicians, and researchers.

Their Fears and Concerns

Since people often behave out of fear when negotiating, we must look at the symptoms. With Datacrats, what's the cause of resistance that takes the form of procrastination and decision blocking? Their biggest fear is making a mistake. When deciding anything they need time to think about every minuscule pro and con. They assemble every conceivable fragment of information before they give a decision, move on a position, or make up their minds. They sometimes go off on wild goose chases—or get others to do so—in search of abstruse data.

They won't feel safe if anyone is pushing them. When they are pressured to decide, they balk. They dig in their heels and won't talk, or start procrastinating aloud ("Now, we haven't seen the full report"), withdraw altogether and sit in silence, or fail to return your phone calls.

Respect their personal space, especially if you're a natural hugger. They're definitely not! Don't stand closer to them than eighteen inches, either; it will make them nervous. Yet you might check your intuition about them. Sometimes Datacrats, because they are shy and detached from others, will warm up when trust is built. But let them lead the way. Be very cautious in initially giving them affection or assurance—it's best done in a note. You don't want them to feel cornered or overwhelmed, though you do want them to feel respected and appreciated, in spite of their socially awkward and at times austere manner.

Datacrats have a low trust of others—their intentions, modus operandi, abilities, intelligence, or reasoning ability. They don't trust quick answers. Expect them to scrutinize you constantly and critically, particularly when they first deal with you.

Their self-expectancy is "Be perfect." Part of their elusive, distanced quality is that they are hiding the fact that they, like the rest of us, are not perfect. But they *seek* to be perfect and want to be surrounded by perfection.

▪ THE BUTTERFLY

Marilyn got dressed up in a favorite outfit, a shocking-pink jumpsuit with a purple print silk scarf, and drove to the closest Mercedes-Benz dealer. She was thinking of buying a car for herself for Christmas. Shopping for it was going to be fun.

It was a Saturday afternoon, and the showroom was jammed with people who were just looking around. That was just how she liked her surroundings: full of people who would certainly notice her. She strutted around like a peacock, opening car doors, climbing in and sitting in the luxurious leather seats, getting a feel for the steering wheel and gears. After ten minutes of this, she tried to catch a salesman's eye. They all seemed busy with other customers, who were kicking tires and asking interminable questions.

Everyone kept ignoring her, as though she weren't there at all. She climbed into another car, left the door open, turned the radio on to a rock station.

People just stared at her. "Doesn't anybody want my money?" she suddenly exclaimed loudly. Silence. Infuriated, she quickly headed for the door. A heavy-torsoed salesman close to the exit opened the glass door for her. "Were you really interested in buying a car?" he now asked—dubiously. Marilyn gazed at him in clear distaste. "Maybe I'll have a better time at the BMW dealer's," she said. The salesman shrugged. "We sell cars," he commented dourly. "And I plan to buy one," she said. "But not *here!*"

Marilyn drove away fast. And in less than an hour, she'd bought herself a new BMW. A red one. And had fun doing it, because the salesman and then the manager served her with good customer service and gave her lots of attention. She was a hard bargainer, and got a thousand bucks off the list price while persuading them to add a bunch of no-cost options like a CD player. They saw she'd be a moving advertisement for the dealership, as well as an unsalaried PR deputy.

Marilyn looks and acts like a pea brain, but she's not. She is a successful businesswoman and competently runs her own cosmetics-manufacturing firm. Sure, she flits around, but she always knows where she is and why she does what she does. She negotiates in her own way, and when her need is reasonable—as in expecting good customer service—she takes it personally and may become vindictive. ("I'll buy, but not from *them*.")

Trouble is, a lot of people don't take Butterflies like Marilyn seriously. And that can be a mistake. For them. Never underestimate a Butterfly.

What to Know About Them

Butterflies walk into the room hoping that all eyes are upon them. The women wear stylish clothes in bright, even flamboyant colors. They always aim to look like fashion plates. They put a lot of color around them in their homes and offices. They love flashy business and note cards, rich leather attaché cases, and gold pens. If you arrange to meet them somewhere, they'll probably drive up in a Porsche, BMW, or Mercedes. Or some hot little sports car, which most likely is red.

The male form of Butterfly is somewhat more subdued and less "flitty" than the female, but has its own personable warmth and display. (Non-Anglo men, particularly of Mediterranean, Latin, and African ancestries, often have the Butterfly's social characteristics.)

Their high-energy movement is graceful; they know that people will be—or should be—watching them. They move as if to music . . . even when there isn't any. Their voices can be melodic and dramatic, and strong enough so that people across a crowded room might hear them, or at least notice that they've arrived. They underscore at least one word in every sentence they utter.

Butterflies are social creatures. They are natural huggers. They stand as close to you as they can get without stepping on your toes. One-to-one, they establish intense eye contact. But it's fleeting in a group situation, for they're always looking around at who's looking at them.

They enter your office and exclaim "Darling, what a fabulous place!" and then rave over the view, the decor, the artwork on display. They are creative, quick thinkers. But their enthusiasm and energy are somewhat indiscriminate. They often insert interruptive jokes in serious talk.

They might ask snoopy or totally inappropriate questions. "Where did you get that? It's just marvelous!" All the while, they may be running their fingers over the herringbone weave in your jacket . . . or through your hair. They are touchy-feely folks. They can be wonderfully fun to have around, for people who appreciate their brazen flair.

What if you don't see them in person for the first time, but talk with them over the phone? If the person you've targeted for negotiation says a cheery and hearty "Good morning!" (but no sweetness in the tone), you're almost certainly talking to a Butterfly. You should have no trouble talking right then and there. They love phones and can't have too many of them. If they could all ring at the same time, the Butterfly would be delighted.

Butterflies want instant attention and service from those around them. They, in turn, are willing to return it abundantly. A Butterfly has an eternally expressive style. Whatever they think or feel is on display. They love people. If they can't be surrounded by people, they need reminders; photographs, scrolls, postcards, thank-you notes adorn the walls of their offices and homes. They are builders of "I love me" walls.

Butterflies aim to act and look theatrical. They often create drama in their lives. You'll hear two words from them about how things are going: fun or boring. That judgment applies to negotiation, too. Butterflies enjoy negotiating if the process doesn't take too long or involve too many details. So if Butterflies are having fun with you, you'll close the deal. They will move off of their position if they feel accepted and liked—and it's a smart deal. What does "fun" mean to a Butterfly who is negotiating? No papers, no lawyers, no details, no high tech.

Some people find Butterflies irresistible. Others—Datacrats particularly—are appalled by them. A Steamroller will tolerate a Butterfly, especially if the deal is a good one and it goes through fast.

Their Fears and Concerns

The greatest fear Butterflies have is that no one will remember them. They require inclusion. They would rather have attention of any kind, even negative attention, than no attention at all.

■ MR./MS. NICE GUY

The law firm had expanded so rapidly that it needed new quarters. The office manager asked the law clerks to visit the larger office that had been leased on the floor above them. It was being set up now for the staff, she said. Each employee was expected to choose a partitioned area that would be most convenient for him or her. The favored sites must be known at once; otherwise, people might be stuck somewhere not to their liking, randomly assigned by someone unfamiliar with their needs and functions.

Kevin had listened to the talk, which encouraged the clerks to come to a group consensus that would be practical and fair to everyone. And now he stood there in the new office, watching the other clerks staking their claims on the floor plan, arguing hotly with each other about windows and furnishings, flipping coins to settle possession without coming to blows. Kevin kept smiling throughout the noisy negotiation process going on around him. But he looked increasingly uncomfortable.

Finally the rest of the crew quieted down. Each had his or her final place. "But Kevin!" they exclaimed. "You haven't picked your spot yet." He blushed as he smiled. "Oh, any place is all right with me," he said. "Wherever there's an extra place. It doesn't really matter."

"But Kevin, it *does* matter!" his associates pointed out. "You should be concerned about your own convenience. Make a decision, for heaven's sake!" But Kevin could not oblige. He could not stop being amiable, even though he saw his associates frustrated. By remaining passive, Kevin refused to negotiate at all.

Of course Kevin ended up with a dark, hole-in-the-wall area

located clear across the office from the reference books and electronic equipment he most needed to do his work efficiently. Twenty times a day he hiked across the floor, passing the other clerks situated close to what they needed.

Kevin had missed his chance. Again.

If "all the world loves a lover," everyone should appreciate a Mr. or Ms. Nice Guy. Is this why many men and women grow up to be congenial, affable, pleasant, amiable—all those wonderful words that characterize the nicest people you've ever known?

Nice Guys aim to arrange life around them so that everything will flow smoothly, without employing friction or pressure or heat. They expect everyone, themselves included, to be happy. When people around them act angry or mean or upset, Nice Guys try to soothe. They bring hot tea or cold sodas. And if they don't succeed at changing someone else's ugly mood—actually, their valiant efforts might irritate out-of-sorts persons further—they can become unhappy themselves. Any perceptible down mood usually passes quickly over most Nice Guys, however.

What to Know About Them

Actually, there are so many Mr. and Ms. Nice Guys that you're bound to wonder why murders and wars happen at all. Taken collectively, they're a poster for peace on earth. So how is it that our society can have so many problems when all these Nice Guys are out there?

A large percentage of our time may be taken up contriving and carrying out strategies for negotiating with Nice Guys. When we deal with them, we may be almost unaware of the process—it often doesn't seem like negotiation at all. But negotiating successfully with Nice Guys can require as much patience, stamina, and skill as dealing with any other personality type.

Nice Guys smile. They usually manage to smile even when somebody is saying something disagreeable to them or to someone else. They smile when they talk on the phone, when they work at the computer, when they ride in the elevator, when they fix up the office coffeemaker. (Even Nice Guys in supervisory or executive positions may take care of domestic duties, democratically emptying a wastebasket or straightening up magazines in the reception room.) Their office may contain candy bowls and cookie jars, bouquets of flowers, philodendron plants with clean and glossy leaves, pictures of dogs and cats done in cross-stitchery, and desk plaques with upbeat messages.

When you meet them, they don't come right out and offer their hand, but if you extend yours for a handshake they'll easily respond. If you shake hard or soft, they follow the pattern. They'll gaze at you but then look away, as if they might seem too bold or curious if they maintained strong eye contact. (As with any style mode, be sure to take into account cultural and geographic values and norms. Women in some cultures are not supposed to keep eye contact with men or superiors.)

There's a sense of caution, even unsureness about Nice Guys; perhaps they are carefully taking your measure so that they won't offend you by saying or doing the wrong thing. Since they want you to feel comfortable and happy, and worry that you may not, they may inquire solicitously about your needs and desires. When they are uneasy, they may giggle or clear their throats a lot. If you glance at them, having noticed the sounds they emit, they might shrink back, knowing that they've brought unwelcome attention to themselves. They are self-effacing.

Because they are such agreeable people, Nice Guys inevitably wonder why some people don't like them. Worse, they wonder why people they considered friends abandoned them, why spouses leave them, why their children don't phone them every week. They won't, can't, or dare not make decisions. Or they decide and then fret over the consequences, causing others to share in their misery. They may decide only because they are forced to do *something*, and resent the pressure. Risk-taking is almost impossible for Nice Guys.

Since they try to have such a great smile on their faces all the time, you might never know when they're angry, sad, or tormented. Maybe they won't know either. But you can ask them sometime. And help them realize that you will like them and involve them even when they are not "happy."

Understanding the Nice Guy Type

How can we identify the Nice Guys? Nice Guys do not stand out like the other types. They are not pushy, or fusspots, or showoffs. They do not interrupt our train of thought, step on our toes, or grab our cookies. So we are apt not to notice them, except for when we need them or are giving them an occasional glance toward the sidelines. We take their benevolence and patience and calmness quite for granted. Only when they fail to perform as we fully expect them to are we apt to notice that they're not there, gone.

Nice Guys are persons with characteristics as complex and contradictory and deep as everyone else; they've simply been schooled, from the start of their lives, to present a placid, two-dimensional surface. They were probably born with temperaments that did not express themselves in tantrums, defiance, independence, domination, theatricality. Or society quickly taught that there is no payoff, only punishment, in being outspoken, demanding, or even clear with their own feelings.

Uncomfortable ever being the center of negative attention, they failed to get into the limelight either, the way a Steamroller or Butterfly would. Little Nice Guys clean their rooms and wash the dishes and polish their shoes. They do their homework every night and never forget to bring home their lunchbox from school. They get appreciative parental and teacher approval. Whenever things go wrong, they feel responsible for fixing it all.

Dependably good girls and boys, the Nice Guys in time grow up to be larger adult editions of their childhood selves—or at least the selves, the personas they present to the people around them every day.

How do I know this much about them? Because we—you and I—are really "they" to some degree. Especially since we are women. Most girls are raised to be Ms. Nice Guys—amiable drones who someday will serve the needs of everyone around them, especially husbands and children and aging parents, and (possibly) employers and neighbors. Our prevailing fear is that we may sometime offend someone and then be excluded from the privilege of being a helper. We avoid doing anything that would annoy anybody, not realizing that our very niceness and inaction can be irritating.

What's Your Own Style?

Just as the people you negotiate with will likely fit a particular personality type with a matching negotiating style, you too are inclined toward being a Steamroller, Datacrat, Butterfly, or Ms. Nice Guy. During negotiating, your style can often influence your partners' attitude and behavior. Certainly, too, you can consciously modify it to work in accord with their style.

▬ EXERCISE ▬

1. As a quick review of personality types, choose A or B as a tactic.

   BUTTERFLIES:
   A. Takes care of business first
   B. Socializes first

   STEAMROLLERS:
   A. Gives as much information as possible
   B. Gives bottom-line information and moves on

   DATACRATS:
   A. Sets a clear date, time, and quiet place
   B. Catches them anywhere, anytime to negotiate

   NICE GUYS:
   A. First gives a lot of *what* and *how* information
   B. Gives *why* information first

2. To remember the benefits of negotiating with certain personalities, choose between these answers for each type. The results of your negotiations will be:

   BUTTERFLIES:
   A. Fun and creative
   B. Priced competitively

   STEAMROLLERS:
   A. Quick and competitive
   B. A safe bet

DATACRATS:
A. Rapid results
B. Perfect calculations

NICE GUYS:
A. A long-term business relationship
B. High-powered connections

5
SPECIAL
CONSIDERATIONS

"O brave new world/ That has such people in't!"
—William Shakespeare, *The Tempest*

Now that you've been introduced to the four basic personality types and their negotiating styles, it's appropriate to see how negotiation can also be affected by other factors that reflect personal circumstances and cultural backgrounds.

Gender Considerations

As we learned in Chapter 3, no matter what someone's age or cultural background, that the person is male or female can be a main indicator of how your partner will negotiate. Some women have very definite opinions about male-female differences:

Men see women as vulnerable. Oftentimes women can be much more honest about their feelings than men, but men see that as a weakness, not as a strength. I think men are very naive in that sense. Basically I'm not a liar; I like to speak the truth.

Women are less risk-taking than men. Men are more out in the world, more used to negotiating there. Many women act helpless and let men do it all. Often we're not in a strong position when negotiating with men. We may actually be fearful of honest, equal negotiation because we've been secret in our dealings, having to be indirect to get what we want. And women also don't want to make trouble for someone. Calling attention to oneself is being selfish.

Women are more interrogative, men more affirmative. In establishing a connection, women ask questions, which makes them look weak. Men are raised to be competitive, to take stands, whether they know anything about the situation or not. Their stance, posturing, voice say something definite. "The facts are ..." vs. women's "I think that...." So people may choose the first one, the sure one, to go with, though he may not really have the facts. Women try to endear themselves, so show a softer side.

It would be reasonable to anticipate that a man you've not yet met, whom you know little or nothing about, will negotiate in the traditional and standard male manner, tending toward "winner take all," and to predict that an unknown woman will negotiate in a distinctly female way, cooperative and sharing. Maybe 75 percent of the time you will be correct.

Don't let stereotypes and appearances mislead you as to negotiating styles. For instance, a man with subdued demeanor who's wearing a casual sportshirt with a flower design might lead you to expect a Mr. Nice Guy. If a woman is dressed in a tailored suit, with crisp deportment, you might anticipate she will be a Steamroller. Yet when the actual process begins, the man may become rushed and aggressive, whereas the woman may act more interested in establishing rapport.

Of course, there's also a good chance their negotiating style will conform to their appearance. Your strategy should prepare you for either eventuality.

Be attentive to the fact that most men were raised as Steamrollers, if not by their parents, then in the school playground by their peers and coaches. They learned in stories, movies, and TV that behaving otherwise would indicate weakness, leaving them vulnerable to attack by other males and to disrespect by females.

Some men refuse even to negotiate at all, with employees or with their wives and children. Their every word is a command. Whenever you must negotiate with such a man, you may have a problem in getting through to him on your terms—or any terms other than his.

I'm sure you've had the experience of being relegated to the "women's circle" at some professional meeting that combined socializing with serious business talk. You were perceived as some male delegate's wife, not as a professional with the host company. Or, possibly worse, if you're attractive, you've been treated as an airhead; or, if you're not, then you've been treated as a nonentity.

> It really infuriates me how at a meeting when we're trying to solve some big problem I will offer a solution and nobody pays a bit of attention to it. Then ten minutes later some guy comes up with exactly the same proposal, and the whole group seizes it as if he's created some miracle! I don't think they even *hear* me when I talk. It's just background buzzing or something.
>
> By now I've developed a technique for handling this whenever it happens to me. I'll say something like, "Mr. Jones, I'm pleased to hear that Sam now agrees with me. So if you like the idea, that makes three of us now."

In their generic tendency to discount females' value, men may also assume that because you're a woman, no matter who you are and what you do otherwise, you're the likeliest candidate to do whatever go-fer work needs doing, such as making the coffee in the morning or fetching it.

A wonderful example of this happened to me years ago when I was assigned the role of lead negotiator for our bank in talks with a client corporation. A small group of us filed into the corporation's conference room and took our seats. I was at one end, my pen and pad already in place for making running notes of the meeting for my own use. We were introduced to the men on the other side of the table. I was the only woman present. Their chief obviously thought that I was a secretary for the bank's executives, for he turned to me and asked me to go out and make sure that the women "out there" were readying the coffee and danishes. My associate quickly got up from his chair; *he* would go, he said. "But why can't she?" the man asked him. "Because Miss Schapiro is our lead negotiator," the associate replied very simply as he left the room. The men on the other side were embarrassed.

Such incidents still happen, of course. When preparing to negotiate with people or organizations that are inherently chauvinistic—respecting only what men have to say and unlikely ever to change—consider the probable benefit of adding a man to your negotiating team. Achieving your goal will outweigh your personal objections to gender discrimination.

When you're negotiating, slights may be deliberate to unhinge you. Prepare for sexist behavior. Plan to spot these remarks and behaviors as they occur, and handle them in ways that won't sandbag the negotiations. It's another aspect of the depersonalizing process. In negotiating, your primary goal is to gain what you want, not to argue with someone about his attitude toward women. I call this tactic *planned invulnerability*. Build it into your preparation for negotiating.

Women are partnership negotiators far more often than are men. After all, we have usually been reared as Ms. Nice Guys and Butterflies. You can reasonably expect the majority of women to start negotiating in one of these styles, but you must be attentive to underlying motivation. Ms. Nice Guy may undergo a sudden and dramatic change if things are not progressing according to her hidden agenda. Since we have been socialized to "put on a happy face," we women often obscure Steamroller personalities underneath a Chatty Cathy exterior.

Age and Generational Issues

Age often has a lot to do with how you negotiate something with somebody—your age and their age, and the different generations you represent. We've grown up with widely varying popular standards and models for negotiating—with our parents and siblings and other relatives, with friends and enemies at school, with teachers and other authority figures. We have standards within ourselves also. For instance, younger people often are exposed through the media to more psychological information than older generations were; they are more sophisticated about thoughts and feelings. They may not censor and ostracize others from their own consciousness, and therefore tend to be less judgmental and more accepting of other people. That makes them better partnership negotiators.

Expect more people—especially men who are middle-age or older—to follow the old confrontational negotiation method (Steamroller style) rather than the partnership approach. Women of middle age long accustomed to business negotiating may also subscribe to these hard-line tactics. Men raised after the 1960s—when society began honoring alternative standards for male behavior—may be less aggressive and more cooperative in their negotiating styles.

Between-generation negotiating can be tricky, at home and on the job. Older people customarily feel they've acquired experience and wisdom over the years, and that they're entitled to respect, even deference, from the young—like the tribal elders in simpler societies. An older male with a young female boss has a doubly hard time with his self-image; after all, he grew up believing that men are better than women, and that older is wiser than younger. His superior will have a difficult time being authoritative without offending him.

Motivational Issues

We always negotiate for an underlying purpose. There's our purpose, and there's the other side's purpose, and the two may not be the same. It will make a difference in the negotiating process whether we and our negotiating partner are motivated by power or control issues, profit- or pleasure-seeking, fear, vengeance ("I'll show them!"), a sense of fairness, or just because we've been cornered to do so by the other side. The negotiation goals we set will partly reflect those psychologically keyed purposes.

If we know well someone we'll be negotiating with, or can trust another person's report about the person, we can be fairly sure about personal motivations that may affect the negotiation ahead. Occasionally, however, it turns out unhappily: we did not know this person quite as well as we thought we did. For instance, we expected just and ethical behavior, and instead were torpedoed by greed, power lust, revenge, or obsession with control.

Companies and other institutions acquire reputations as do people. These reputations also can change through time as management changes or as a once-ambitious business matures and possibly declines, moving from cutthroat competition or keen risk-taking to fair, confident, yet conservative deals to retreat positions tainted by fear or uninspired leadership.

Look for the Motivational Factors

Apart from knowing the personality types for the people you'll be negotiating with, consciously determine what motivational factors might underlie their dealings with you and the goals they have set.

What do people want for themselves in negotiating? I believe there are six primary desires. Some people are always activated by a single need. Others may consistently combine several needs. Still others—maybe the majority of us—vary our main desires from one negotiating situation to the next.

An individual's primary motivational needs or wants are as:

- Power Monger: power over other people
- Control Freak: control over circumstances
- Pie Slicer: fairness, cooperation in outcome
- Cookie Grabber: materialistic acquisition
- Avenger: revenge or "proving something"
- Foot Shooter: sabotage, self-defeat

Each of these motivator types *wants* something from the negotiation in terms of the above. For instance, people who are after top control may not be very interested in money, and people who are into power may be very willing to cooperate in every way so long as they are put in charge.

And do take note of the Foot Shooter (as in someone who always shoots him- or herself in the foot). This contrary personality needs to arrange for things to fall apart so he or she won't be successful, won't realize any benefit or reach any goal from the negotiation. That person's hidden agenda—of which he or she is unaware—is actually to be victimized, punished, defeated. For whatever reason, the outcome must be negative for the Foot Shooter to be satisfied. Usually inaction will take care of self-defeat, but when forced into a negotiating situation, some form of sabotage is invariably contrived.

Positional Power

Most job situations, structured around supervisory and managing functions and chains of command, involve perpetual hierarchies of power. People move upward if they advance in their careers, or remain in place—even recede—if they do not; or they come in from other places to occupy elevated positions with power over people already there.

People in nondominant positions traditionally use negotiation when approaching more powerful persons or groups with requests for changes that they believe are essential, merited, or beneficial for themselves or others. Successful negotiating produces some benefit or favor they probably would not have got otherwise.

However, negotiation can also work against you with people in positional power. If you ask for particular consideration—such as getting a raise—you risk getting turned down. Also, if you do not handle the negotiation deftly, you might damage your own position. For instance, by requesting some improvement in the workplace in behalf of everyone, you draw attention to yourself. Your boss could then regard you as a troublemaker, which might be worse than not being noticed at all.

Sometimes a stronger, more assertive person or side will dominate and browbeat the supplicant. The purpose and spirit of negotiation is nullified by someone with power who is unwilling to make even a small compromise to partly satisfy a request, or at least explain why the request cannot be granted.

When approaching negotiation with people in power positions, we should consider the very tone of our own regard for persons and their associations. Though sophisticated otherwise, we may actually be in awe of certain individuals, in awe of their reputation and persona. Feeling flattered to be permitted in their proximity, we might not think clearly when negotiating.

If you admire someone—which can include a company's image—with whom you're going to negotiate, watch for any tendency to be adulatory. Work on becoming purely businesslike.

If you are preparing to negotiate with someone with obvious positional power, try to find out how this person negotiates with employees and business associates. If he or she has a reputation for being rough and tough, you can prepare accordingly.

Those truly secure in a positional power place are often willing to share some decision making and other power-connected responsibilities. Less needful of winning over the other side— whoever it may be—they invite cooperation, not competition, and so make good negotiating partners. You can look forward to a challenging negotiating climate with such persons. If the person you're going to see is powerfully positioned but is known to be fair and pleasant, go in fully prepared with all the information you can muster.

We are shaped by our upbringing. Among Anglos, a lower-, middle-, or upper-class identification may remain within us throughout our lives. Whether a parent is a blue-collar or a white-collar worker can profoundly affect a child's sense of family identity. Work and play styles of the past provide indelible images of negotiating with others. Recalling perpetual family anxiety over joblessness and low income may translate into a lifelong pursuit of stability that rules out riskier positions in negotiating.

Do not prejudge anyone who will be your negotiating partner. You may listen to adverse reports from others and use that information as part of your strategy, but always consider the possibility that your opposite's customary negotiating style may be layered. There could be a very different personality underneath a brusque, hard, or belligerent demeanor. Or there might be an impassioned, intelligent, and resourceful person beneath someone who acts obtuse or flaky.

It will be your job to scout out the full human dimensions of the other person when your partner appears to be so difficult. Just because others have not succeeded in negotiating matters does not mean that you cannot do so. With good preparatory thinking and special skill during the negotiation process, you may be able to contact the hidden person beneath the negotiating persona.

Cultural Differences in Negotiating Styles

Cultural background—yours and your negotiating partner's—is a major consideration when you prepare to negotiate. The more diverse we are from each other, the greater the preparation we need to understand the other side and to plan how best to present ourselves.

Acquiring culturally sensitive negotiating skills is no longer just for tourists in foreign lands, state department officers and diplomats, and international business people. The increasing global involvement of American companies in import-export trade or setting up investments and manufacturing abroad has roused sensitivity to intercultural negotiating. The abundant presence of foreign investors, employers, and employees within the United States also requires new negotiation skills. Part of it involves courtesy— simple good manners in knowing others' way of doing things.

And we are daily reminded of how our own population has become greatly multicultural. Our new "multiethnic pot" contains an amazing collection of cultures, races, ethnic groups, languages, and religions. To add to the confusion, large ethnic or racial groups comprise a multitude of subgroups with sometimes widely differing cultural attitudes, behaviors, and political beliefs. Good examples of such diversity are among the Hispanic or Latin cultures, which include Mexican, Central American, South American, and Spanish people. The same divergence exists with large immigrant groups we tend to lump together, such as Asians, Middle Easterners, African Americans, and Eastern Europeans.

Try to get insight into your negotiating partner's life experience. Prepare yourself for various attitudes and responses based on it. He or she may act tough, angry, suspicious, hostile, shy, cold, withdrawn, or belligerent. Allow for these or other possibilities, and if any happen as you negotiate, you'll just take a deep breath and handle the situation in whatever calm, nonreactive way you've prepared for it. Put your time and energy now into finding approaches for partnering with this person, in helping him or her feel at ease with you.

Or perhaps you yourself come from a non-WASP, non-Anglo background. Maybe you are a woman of color, or a woman whose first language is not English. If so, you surely have already thought a great deal about who you are, what you want to be, and how you can best achieve what you want within a culture that may not totally welcome you, or that possibly treats you as an exotic, if not an alien. Whether born in the United States or having arrived later, you have already had to protect your own interests many times by negotiating with people who act hostile or condescending toward you.

Plan to speak authentically when you negotiate—to be who and what you are. Prepare yourself always so well that if any negotiating partner somehow fails to treat you with respect, you will know that the treatment reflects that person's own ignorance, incompetence, and unworthiness—not yours.

Language Considerations

What language will be spoken when you negotiate? Will your negotiating partner be as verbal or even more verbal than you?

Just as Americans, British, Canadians, Australians, New Zealanders, South Africans, and other English-speaking nationals often seem to speak radically different languages, so are Americans themselves divided regionally in the way they talk—in the words they choose and how they pronounce them.

To compound matters, we negotiate often with people for whom English is a foreign language—maybe the second, third, or fourth one they've had to learn. If we or our parents are in that situation, we know all too well how complicated and frustrating accurate communication can get.

If English is your native tongue and you're going to negotiate with persons not as fluent in it as you, allow for hesitations, struggles to find the right words, and linguistic mishaps. You may wish to bring a dictionary to help you both find the words you need for important things. Help them without offending them or jumping in to put language in their mouths.

After all, the tables will be turned whenever you negotiate in a foreign language. Nowadays, whether we stay at home or travel abroad, we try to talk with people who have at least a minimal grasp of English. But if we can try to talk with them, however imperfectly, in their own language, we help break down social barriers. (And as you struggle with your ineptitude, think how others feel when attempting English with you!)

When coming to any agreement between two sides whose differing language skills may cause communication difficulties, be absolutely sure that you both understand exactly what the terms are. That's part of your preparation. If necessary, bring in an interpreter. Get a translator to convert documents into your negotiating partner's native language.

What Are Your Own Personal and Situational Variables?

While considering what the opposite side's variables might be, always be conscious of and attentive to the variables that you bring to the negotiation. And just as you tactically work with aspects of your negotiating partners, so they will respond to who you are, to your self-presentation and circumstance. Negotiation, after all, is an ongoing interaction between two sides, two differing positions. It is the coming together in productive discourse that moves toward agreement or resolution.

Sometimes you may intend to negotiate with a person or group known to have prejudices against or divergent attitudes from your own situation. For instance, you may be an accomplished business woman and have to deal with men from a culture that keeps all respectable women behind walled homes, or wearing veils and floor-length garments in public.

How do you steer a course between being honestly who you are and avoiding giving offense? Probably it is wisest to acknowledge openly the differences between your two cultures, but then swiftly find those similarities and mutual interests that put you together in a negotiating situation. Build bridges, not walls, when you meet. But all the while, be sensitive to the differences that may add problems to the situation if utterly ignored, or if handled insensitively and judgmentally by either side.

Cultural Differences Among Diverse People

There's always an element of education when you're negotiating—educating yourself, educating others. I feel that being an administrator in an urban community college with a large, multicultural student body requires me to have the wisdom of a master teacher. I must be well prepared, with my homework alerting me to all the pros and cons involved with all sides. And that's not just my position or the school's, or two opposing positions, but dozens of positions, each with its own needs, demands, and expectations that collide with others'.

Then I've got to know about the people I'll be negotiating with. I should know their special values; how they think and feel; their motivation sources; their priorities; above all, maybe, where they hurt. I should speak their language, not just my own, using words that really communicate to them. And I must always listen closely to them when they talk.

Because I'm a woman of color, fortunately I have a cross-cultural perspective. I don't lump people into huge groups. For instance, I know how someone from a Central American family differs from a person with a Latino background; they speak and even think differently. And that a woman or man who came recently from an Asian country is almost a half-world apart from someone in the second generation, even from the same homeland. Then there are all the class, age, and gender differences. . . .

Inevitably, many negotiations get off on the wrong foot because one or both sides are insensitive to differing cultural factors. Partnership negotiation absolutely requires awareness of the personal and situational variables inherent in such multicultural relationships—the business, professional, and interpersonal dealings, along with more casual contacts in everyday living and travel. Implicit mutual respect for one another's value systems is a basis for initial trust in any dialogue.

Good negotiation is always a mutual education process. Especially when it involves different ethnic groups. Everybody starts out feeling uncomfortable. We shouldn't make any assumptions, but get the stuff out there on the table—and don't judge it. Brainstorming, talking through the misunderstandings, getting things down on paper—these are all critically important processes when there's conflict between cultural groups.

In this country, women of nonwhite ethnic groups may sometimes feel doubly handicapped in negotiating situations—professionally and socially. But many can find their own routes toward
self-empowerment.

Before I go off to negotiate for the day—which is every day—
I do my morning imaging. It's like a ritual. I call upon
my Indian ancestry and visualize my ancestors. My maternal
grandparents were *mestizos*, and I feel these Indian roots live
deeply in me. I believe we've all lived other lives within our
ancestry—male lives too. Sometimes I see myself as a warrior,
sitting with nature, in prayer, knowing the Truth. When I put
myself into this strong identity, I no longer am my vulnerable
self. It often stays with me throughout the day like a shadow
companion.

In the multicultural situations that now prevail in many cities,
women of color can also consciously support each other as they
negotiate life. They will often understand each other's experiences
and share much the same feelings.

In spite of everything I've done professionally and out in the
community—becoming a high-ranking Latina in my field—I
find myself still driven for approval. This gets me into trouble
in negotiation. I have to fight it on a daily basis. It takes a physical form, with my stomach churning and heart palpitating. I
hide this vulnerability well, but it's taken a toll on my health.
     It's often difficult for me to negotiate with men. As a child I
was taught that they have the real power, that they are correct.
I was socialized in the United States, but in rural Central America where I came from, the women have a lot of power because
their men aren't around much. Also, after my father left us
when I was twelve, I really took charge of my mother—who
couldn't speak a word of English—and the younger kids. So
this thing about male power confused me and created conflict.
     White men especially create fear in me, so I must be careful
not to back down from my position in order to avoid their
disapproval or to please them. When I'm feeling like this, I

look for support from others in the room—from other women, mostly.

Negotiating Sprites

There's another class of internal variables that we must account for within ourselves and our negotiating partners. I call them *sprites* because they can pop up suddenly in unaccountable ways.

Have you ever been right in the middle of discussing some conflict or problem when the person you're negotiating with suddenly turns into someone else? Or maybe you find you're turning into someone you really don't want to have around—but here she is. She's just come onto the scene as if she has as much right as you to be present. And once she's out, you won't easily get rid of her. You've lost self-control.

What's going on here? Whether you've changed, or the opposite side has changed, or you've both changed, you've got to deal with a new and unexpected element. Maybe fast. But before you do, try to understand what happened to alter the script you intended to play out. Stay with it for a short time and observe: Could this be a useful character?

As mentioned before, my image of a person, any person—certainly myself!—is a composite of many different people. A character mosaic. We consist of pieces of different personalities. As we shape the persona we present to the world, we edit out aspects of ourselves that we don't like and believe others won't like either. We constantly reshape our behavior as we try to form a cohesive, consistent, and effective personality we feel comfortable with.

But guess what? Those people, or parts of people, are still there inside of us, just waiting for a chance to pop out. And at times they will, perhaps when you least want them to—particularly when you're tired or stressed. And just as this happens to us, it happens to other people.

Just as we've looked at the four principal personality types and how they are likely to interact with other people, we can consider different minor characters who may barge in when you're negotiating. A button gets pushed and we—or our partner—react.

Both to amuse yourself and to start recognizing them early on, you could assign these characters names that befit their single-minded identities, like:

- The Reverend Righteous: Is holier than thou, and lets you know it
- Vesuvius: Is suddenly eruptive, blows his or her top sky high
- Mole: Digs a little hole to flee from confrontation
- Poor Little Me: Turns your empathy into one-sided advantage
- Pit Bull: Grabs, bites, hangs on without letup
- Pouter: Signals displeasure, hurt
- Complainer: Gripes incessantly but offers no solutions, or Blamer: Accuses others of causing the problems
- Door Slammer: Gets up and noisily departs the scene
- McNasty: Loads every sentence with spite and venom
- Sharpshooter: Zings away at you while hidden in the foliage
- Slugger: Verbally bangs away at you
- Ditto Machine: Repeats and repeats and repeats
- Waterfall: Pours down copious tears over almost anything
- Thespian: Is the consummate actor and scene stealer
- Martyr: Is nobly self-sacrificing for The Cause
- Joker: Detours the negotiation process with puns and forced funnies
- Don Juan: Indiscriminately courts everyone
- Delilah: Seduces with an agenda of her own

As with the four personality types, such names describe their functions in a plot. Seldom will these caricatures benefit the negotiation process. They offer distractions and derailings, and probably will be dismissed by the other side.

Be prepared for the entrance of such unwanted, unexpected extras in the negotiating scene. They are symptoms of fear, of a sense of poor control, of a lack of self-esteem, of a one-track concern, of isolation and rejection. When it happens with your negotiating partners, deal with it by talking with them calmly, asking questions, letting them have their say and then departing, so you can go back to the real negotiation.

When your own internal bit players start stirring, recognize that they might have something valuable to say. Find out quickly how you feel inside. Your intuition or unanswered needs may have pushed them forward. They can offer insights into your feelings, and you may convert that energy (which can be considerable) from negative to positive to suit your negotiating purpose. Tone down these sprites to make them acceptable parts of you, not caricatures. Consciously and competently directed, they can work for you.

▬ EXERCISE ▬

1. List the situational variables that may affect the style in which you conduct negotiations.

2. As you list each variable, think of negotiating partners or circumstances that would be (a) comfortable or easy for you; (b) uncomfortable or difficult for you.

3. Get tough with yourself and confront your biases, prejudices, inexperience, or ignorance of certain regions, cultures, or generations.

PART II

STRATEGIES FOR PREPARATION

"It is thrifty to prepare Today for the wants of Tomorrow."
—Aesop, "The Ant and the Grasshopper"

6
SETTING GOALS

"Live deliberately."
—Henry David Thoreau

The most successful negotiation I ever did took place immediately after I was offered a top position in a publishing company. When asked to come in for a meeting, I assumed I would be hired; if I wasn't, there would be nothing to negotiate anyway! I wanted to be ready to discuss the compensation package. Not just my salary requirements, but also what I was willing to exchange—benefits, vacations, car allowance—in place of the salary I wanted. To prepare, I called a few people. (We're usually only one or two people away from the person who has the answers.) I found out what my predecessor's salary had been. I also learned the company's sales figures in the last two years, as well as some other financial and political background that might affect what the company would offer me. Going into that meeting, I knew exactly what they would agree to. Then I asked for slightly more—so I could appear accommodating when, needing to appear authoritative, they'd whittle it down. It was a good way to begin a new job. I felt well compensated while they could feel in control.

My best negotiation went on a few months ago, when I bought a new vehicle. In advance of visiting showrooms, I fully prepared on the base price of the car and the cost of options by shopping around. I set up my own financing, and negotiated with myself to be willing to "walk" if I didn't get the deal I wanted. I also educated myself on dealer value packages that were available, and when the deal approached closing, stood my ground with the salesman as to what my top price would be. The manager then okayed my offer. I haven't heard of anyone getting a better price on that model.

Preparation is the critical first stage of negotiation strategy. Many negotiations are doomed, or are lost on one side, because of the failure to prepare. It's often said that at least 80 percent of success in negotiating is due to excellent preparation.

If you remember only one thing from this book, let it be this: go into negotiation prepared. *Fully prepared.* Never undertake any negotiation without first doing your homework. The more experience you get at preparation, the better you'll become and the easier it'll be. Try to think of it as fun—an adventure as a professional investigator.

Can't I Just Wing It?

Sometimes we feel that we know enough and that we can trust our gut feelings on the rest of it. But preparation is crucial to your success for several reasons.

Obviously, you will want to appear confident, as if you know exactly what you are doing. You want—from the outset—to be in control of the situation, though willing to share control with the other side if it will meet you on equal intent and in good faith. Any uncertainty you feel about your position, owing to insufficient preparation, is bound to emerge some time during the negotiation, probably even at the start as you walk into the room. You'll feel defensive, even threatened. The other side will sense it, picking up a variety of unbidden clues from you. And you'll be perceived as vulnerable, unprepared, or uncaring. Your negotiating partners might even feel insulted that someone in your organization wasted their time by sending an ineffectual negotiator.

The preparation period gives you time to assemble for study any situational variables that will enter into the negotiation process. You can envisage different scenarios and imagine possible ways the negotiation might go, particularly when you know the other person's personality type and likely negotiating style. You can anticipate both certainties and surprises in the actual meeting. Being prepared for both circumstances will prevent you from getting rattled. Instead, you will stay in control of both yourself and the situation.

Being in control, however, has a price. You must gather information; prepare reports, summaries, and graphics; and anticipate, at times even rehearse for, the negotiation ahead. You won't feel in control if you don't have the information needed to establish and maintain the authority that creates credibility and trust, leading to agreement.

Initially, ask yourself the obvious: Why is this negotiation going to take place at all? Is this the right time, with the right people? Is it a conflict between individuals or groups that needs resolution? Or a business deal involving a possible exchange of products, services, property, and money in a yet-to-be-determined way? Or is it some other transaction or situation whereby one side hopes to persuade the other to believe or do something?

Some people caught up in details actually lose sight of this large purpose, thereby missing out on the implications. In negotiating interpersonal problems, defining your part at least is perhaps even essential in resolving a conflict.

Is it *you* who have chosen to discuss a prospective business arrangement or seek some resolution to a problem? Or has someone else approached you—the other side of a conflict or prospective deal. If you're the person who has proposed, or will propose, be sure you can write down concisely—a sentence or two—the basic purpose of the discussion. If you cannot do this, it's probable that you aren't ready to negotiate. You'll simply waste somebody else's time and test the person's patience. Delay presenting your case until you have done careful preparation and can be clear about what you want to accomplish.

When the other side initiates a negotiation, you should want to know in advance what the matter concerns. Separate intent to negotiate from intent to argue. If it's a business situation, ask for materials to review in advance, to prepare for the negotiation and also to save your negotiating partner's time. On the basis of information made available to you—ask them to send you what you need—you can then set your own goal for negotiating.

Setting Your Goal

Within the large context of the reason or purpose for negotiating, then, you will carefully define your *goal*—your explicit objective within this particular upcoming process. It's what you will strive for as outcome. If you don't keep the goal always in mind until you achieve the desired results, you're apt to get distracted or derailed and lose your purpose.

For example, you might want some specific thing for yourself, whether or not it can be translated into material terms. On the job you might want, variously, a salary raise (money), a desktop computer (work asset), a new position and title (conveying greater responsibilities, prestige, power).

Or you could be seeking a more personal, intangible yet meaningful result: improving an intimate relationship, perhaps, by working out better communication about feelings or establishing certain ground rules. Or you could be seeking neighborhood acceptance of a plan for taking cooperative action in halting crime. Possibilities for daily negotiation are endless, and so are goals you can set for them. When you set too many goals to be done at once, however, few get accomplished. It is best to prioritize goals and also establish short- and long-term goals.

In setting a goal for negotiation, avoid becoming too global and all-encompassing. This kind of goal (such as peace in the world for all humankind) is a purpose or a wonderful vision but impossible to carry out satisfactorily unless you reduce it to specific action goals that you yourself can achieve. Your goals can, and often should, relate to a much larger or higher purpose ahead of you, or waiting inside you in potentiality, hoping for attainment. A grander goal can only be accomplished in purposeful increments: step by step, or piece by piece.

Your Goal vs. Their Goal

Initially, you probably won't have the same goals as your negotiating partner. For example, you may want to retain the status quo in business or in a relationship, whereas your negotiating partners may want changes made, and must get you to agree to them. If you can be persuaded to share their vision and participate in seeking a mutual goal, which perhaps modifies theirs enough to satisfy you, you're obviously going to alter your original objective, which was to hold tight. And you'll end up with a finale that pleases and benefits both sides while preserving your partnership.

In some situations, though, both sides already share the same general goal at the outset, such as ending a disagreement between them or making money together through a manufacturing and marketing arrangement. Each negotiating partner could have a radically different plan for how to do this. But the fact that they both agree on the goal itself will make negotiating easier, so long as both maintain open-minded flexibility and a respect for the other side's integrity. Under such circumstances, the negotiation is unlikely to blow up. In my experience, however, the *how* is often more difficult to negotiate than the *what*.

Not always will your opposing partner's goal be clearly evident at the outset of a negotiation, much less before it at the preparation stage. If you sense a hidden agenda, you'll have to gather all the facts and information you can, and from them deduce the other side's likely goal and other relevant issues (such as negotiating style and bottom line). You then end up with a goal that involves taking a calculated, educated risk, whereby you know precisely how much you want, what you want, and what you are willing to pay. Keep your "walkability" in mind.

What Can Goals Do for Us?

Goals give direction to our dreams, harness our energy, and create urgency. They also help to manage attitudes and measure success. When we are excited by a goal and make plans to achieve it, we are motivated to initiate an action. Goals force us to realign our resources to work harmoniously. Achieving what we set out to do makes us feel productive, fulfilled, on course.

What Do You Want Out of the Deal?

There are good and bad negotiation deals, just as there are good and bad business transactions. (Don't forget the word *negotiate* comes from the Latin *negotiare*—"to do business.")

Make sure you know what you want or need to come away

with from a negotiation, what the ideal outcome is. If it's a materialistic goal, name it, quantify it—at least to yourself. If it's something intangible, describe it sufficiently to give it substance. Whatever it is, you want it to become *real*.

You can pinpoint a goal using the "one question" technique with yourself—such as, What do I want more of? Or less of? . . . more profit (by 20 percent), fewer interruptions, more critical feedback, fewer meetings. People are often more willing to give us what we want if they know exactly *what* we want, instead of being confronted with general dissatisfaction.

Set your overall aspirations high. We don't do better than we aspire to, whether we're talking about reaching goals, making deals, or having satisfying relationships. Falling a bit short of the destination you've set for yourself may be disappointing, but in retrospect you probably went further than you would have if you had set more modest goals.

Be clear about what you want whenever you enter into negotiating. Also be clear about *why you deserve it*. Aim high, yes, but be realistic about your expectations. Gear them to what you are actually offering in the deal to the others involved—the benefits to your negotiating partners.

What About "Negative" Goals?

Sometimes you may need to negotiate over something you *don't* want (to have, to be, to do). Life comes up with plenty of those situations.

If a negative negotiation is over some minor issue, it usually isn't worth getting into a big hassle over it, unless there is a pattern of expectations and demands upon you that needs to be addressed and altered. However, if it is a serious matter—somebody trying to get you to do something unethical, illegal, or potentially harmful, for example—you will want to take care of the issue promptly, firmly, briefly, and carefully.

Remind yourself, when you go after what you want, that you won't win all the time even if you believe you deserve to. Deserving is a key feeling in negotiating; we rarely negotiate effectively if we basically don't feel we (or the side we represent) truly deserve to win. Stress comes when expectations and reality don't match, and we do nothing to correct the mismatch.

Here are some examples of everyday negative situations that confront many of us, and which we could correct through conscious, competent negotiation:

- Getting last-minute projects the boss dumps on the desk
- Always having to clean up the coffee area
- Planning all the social events because nobody else will
- Being informed at the last minute
- Being asked to take on new jobs we're not qualified to do
- Being told to give up hard-earned client relationships
- Getting hurt

My first successful negotiation was talking the neighborhood bully out of beating me up. I convinced him that beating up a girl would make him look bad, and even weak. (I was also much younger and smaller.) I advised him to show off by doing something really scary, like riding down the steep hill by our house. I told him only one kid had ever had the guts to do it before. So he did it, and everybody now thought he was hot stuff!

Michelle had to decide: (1) What she didn't want to have happen to her (to be beaten up). (2) What the boy's need was—to look like a big shot? Establish credibility with his peers? She had to separate fact from assumption from hope, and to shift perceived benefits. (3) What acceptable alternatives she could offer for both herself and the other side.

Her solution was a real winner. After all, partnership negotiation is a process with each party willing to learn from the other and shift a solution to a mutually desired common goal. He looked good, and she was "unbeaten."

What If the Goal Isn't Yours?

In the professional world, we frequently adopt goals that aren't ours; they are the products of other people's decisions. Nevertheless, we are expected to adopt them, defend them, negotiate for them.

You may not agree with your employer's position on something, such as denying an employee a requested raise or promotion, or, in a more negative form, firing that person. How the outcome of the negotiation is handled will be up to you.

If you are asked to represent a negotiating side (as part of your job, say) and don't agree with the position you've been asked to take, you can try—in the preparation stage—to get your superiors to modify their instructions and expectations. If you don't succeed in getting that agreement, your only options are to ask to be replaced as a negotiator or to prepare to negotiate as best you can.

Drafting Your Negotiation Plan

In fleshing out your goal and the means of achieving it, you'll find it useful to start writing a negotiation plan. Writing your plan at the start will alert you to what you need to learn, whom you need to talk to, what teams you need to build, and what decisions you need to negotiate with others. It brings the real world into your plans.

Think about the following questions:

1. What situation exists that needs to be negotiated?
2. Will your side or the other side initiate the negotiation?
3. Is there any element of urgency that will pressure the decision making?
4. What are your proposals to accomplish the resolutions?
5. What do you intend to accomplish—what are your goals— that will benefit your side?
6. What does your negotiating partner see as benefits in the negotiation (your perception of the other side's goal)?
7. How might these mutual benefits be reached?

The *What* issues relate to goals. In this first stage of planning, be creative. Keep your mind open to at least several alternative ways of solving a problem or accomplishing your objective. Don't get locked in to one way. It is later on, for the purpose of "getting it all together," that you will want to be cohesive and focused on your solution plan.

Once they've jotted down various ideas, many people find it helpful to start making diagrams that show movement from the problem or situation toward resolution and destination. It's the in-between routes that become important to look at: how to get there from here. When set down graphically, usually the most efficient and effective way becomes quickly apparent, and you can begin seeing physically what's involved in the journey.

When you've mapped out a satisfactory visual plan, start converting it into words, phrases, sentences, paragraphs, units. Establish a logical sequence for grouping your ideas, and then turn the ideas into actions to be taken. The more specific you can be about how this will be done if agreement is reached in negotiation, and the more genuinely enthusiastic you can be about your proposal, the better your chances for success.

If you will be negotiating on your own behalf, such as getting a raise or promotion, you can prepare in much the same way, but downscale it to focus on you: your expertise in education, training, and on-the-job experience; your current responsibilities and contributions; recognition of your merit for a higher salary or qualifications for filling a position opening (naming people as references); some of your ideas for company improvements; an indication of your ambition to move ahead in service. Back up what you can with paperwork. People believe what they see on paper better than what you tell them. It can also be reviewed and shown to others.

People also know that you know when you ask the right questions. So prepare those, too, when relevant.

Never Lose Sight of Your Competition

In preparing a negotiation plan, don't lose sight of the possibility that you will be compared, explicitly or implicitly, to competitors. Surely there are other companies and people who offer products or services or solutions similar to your own.

If you're determined to go after what you want, figure competitors in your strategy. Know exactly how you're going to deal with actual or potential rivals. You'll need to research who they are and what they might offer. You and your competitors, after all, share the same general goals and objectives; to do business through negotiation. Then figure out how you can deliver more satisfactory service or goods to your prospective client or customer.

In designing your presentation, never neglect a brief opportunity to discuss any significant competitors—especially any who already work with the place or person you'll negotiate with. Expect your negotiating partner to ask you to comment on a comparison between you and one or more others in your field of work. If he or she does not, you could bring it up yourself, as in, "I assume that you are also discussing your needs with Y Company." If the firm is not you'll hear so; but also perhaps learn of other competitors.

Plan what you say to be brief and positive, not critical. Mention things that you know about or like that probably aren't important to this particular client. For instance, if you are negotiating to get a consulting job in handling public relations for a charitable organization, you might mention that a close competitor is well known for his or her promotion of sports events—which is true but not at all relevant to the work they want done for them.

Plussing

Plan never to "but—" your competition during the negotiation by making a direct statement that reflects unfavorably on them, such as "But I've heard they don't meet deadlines"; or "But they're not as dynamic as their reputation makes them out to be." It will reflect poorly on you. Instead, use a technique I call "plussing." Employ the word *and* to precede whatever you might say about your own company or skills that is highly positive and contrasts with what you previously said about the competitor. You could say, "X Company, I know, has a good reputation in the business community, and though we are a new company, we are aiming hard to achieve an even better one through our innovative approach to publicizing clients."

Anything you say that acknowledges your competitors' existence should probably be written out carefully, with its substance committed to memory. It's a sideline of goal setting because, if you don't acknowledge that it exists, you may never get a chance at achieving your goal. Don't leave it to spur-of-the-moment improvising. You want to sound knowledgeable about how your business compares favorably with others, and confident of its superiority.

Plan How to Put Yourself in the Other Person's Shoes

In the process of going after your own goals, never forget that your negotiating partners will have goals as well. They may not necessarily be able to verbalize them, but they're apt to reject any proposals you make if they feel that whatever you offer is not really what they want.

Years ago, after becoming a vice-president at Citicorp, I was eager to try pitching big accounts. One after another, my colleagues had for months been courting a tough CEO at a large New York corporation. When I asked for the president's permission for my turn in going after the elusive prize, he said, "Sure, why not? It will be good exercise for you. But don't expect anything but a hard time. Several of our VPs have bombed out ahead of you, and this guy's really fed up with us by now."

What could I lose? In any case, I'd get valuable experience. As I gathered all the information I needed, in my imagination I virtually put myself in his place; I became him. So what do I want? What am I concerned about? What am I not finding right about these Citicorp suitors? And as I pondered the answers to these questions, I developed my whole approach to the meeting.

"You're the last person I ever want to see from Citicorp!" was the greeting I got from my negotiating partner. "You look better anyway than the rest of them." (Of course I ignored his sexist comment. In winning a negotiation, you shouldn't fight the small stuff.) "Hurry up, you only have nine minutes left," he said. "No problem," I told him. "All I need to do is just sit in your chair." "Sit in my chair? You're nuts!" His amazed look delighted me. "That's possible," I said. He got up and in a gentlemanly way gestured toward the vacated seat, and then sat down in the chair that was intended for me.

"Now," I said, deliberately deepening my voice, "I want to ask

Citicorp what it can possibly do for us here." He listened closely, with astonishment on his face, as I posed a series of sharp questions that demonstrated that I had looked at the situation already from his point of view. Why should I change banks? Was there anything better in the services that Citicorp offered me? In this role playing, I was asking rhetorical questions—the questions he could be asking me. I was him-focused, not me-focused. After three minutes, I got up again and motioned for him to reoccupy his chair, and sat down in my assigned one. In not much more time than the questions had taken, I had concisely provided all the answers he needed. Visually and creatively, by sitting in his place, I showed him I had thought about his issues and problems.

My ten-minute appointment with him was almost up. "Please think over what I've said," I told him, giving him my business card as I stood up to go. We got the business. And I managed the account.

Of course I had strategized for this crucial meeting when anticipating scenarios. And just in case he wouldn't let me sit in his chair, I had other alternatives—none of them so dramatic or effective.

The Other Side's Goals

In negotiating anything fairly, there's got to be something in it for both sides. Your preparation should *always* consider what your negotiating partners would get from any deal you are proposing. When you're seeking their agreement or involvement, turn the matter upside down and inside out.

- What do they want?
- What might they be willing to contribute or concede in order to gain that benefit?
- How will they view you and your position?
- Will they trust you?

Then go back to your own position. To what extent are you going to be able to accommodate their needs and wants along with your own? The answer to that question is important because it will help you refine your goals and allow for concessions when negotiating. This is where you set your own limits: the lowest price or least number you're willing to accept; the highest amount you're willing to pay, etc.—what is really your absolute bottom line. Unless you are willing to risk or take an actual loss in order to set up a connection with someone that promises to lead to profitable future dealings, you want to stick to this bottom line.

At this time you also estimate your partner's bottom line. Write down the answers to these questions:

1. With whom will I be negotiating?
2. How much do I know right now about them?
3. What do I *need* to find out about them?
4. How can I learn what I need to know?
5. What might they want to get from the negotiation? (Or, what are their goals likely to be?)

To design and strategize an upcoming negotiation, you'll need as much information as possible about the other side. This will be just as important as having a full awareness of what you want and devising a plan to get it.

Sometimes a deal might initially look quite promising, but as you start investigating it you'll begin picking up indications that something could go wrong, very wrong, between you and your partner-to-be. Your goals and their goals may be similar, but there's a bad match in underlying values. If there's a chance that the chemistry between you isn't as it should be, it's better to get out before you're committed to anything. You may operate partly on intuition, but usually as you scrutinize your feelings you'll see that you've picked up on particular indicators of serious differences between you.

How to Accommodate the Other Side's Goals

If you imagine yourself stepping into your partners' shoes, putting on their clothing, and sitting in their chairs for a bit, you'll be looking at the world, and the negotiation, from a different set of eyes. If you start that tactic in the preparation stage, when designing your strategy for negotiation you will greatly improve your chances for anticipating the concerns and questions your partner will have.

As director of a new training school for service people in restaurant and hotel work, I've got to persuade people in management positions in the tourist industry to believe in what I'm selling. I have to show them how paying for employees' education will eventually pay off for them. When I approached the owner of one of the city's largest hotels, he told me bluntly, "Look, I don't want to buy into this stuff." He had the traditional view that staff should just train the newly hired people.

But I wouldn't give up. Perseverance is the life blood of good negotiation. "Let me sit down with you for a half-hour and talk with you," I proposed, and he gave me an appointment. Then I began preparing a plan for influencing my hotelier partner to do what he resisted doing. Why didn't he want to buy into the training? I asked myself. And then considered the barriers he'd see: the cost, no return on investment, likelihood of losing trained staff, no reduction in turnover, the nuisance of disrupting set schedules and procedures. And even, "They'll want my job if they're too well trained!"

Also, I'm all too aware that in our industry men tend to look at a women and think, "She works on the soft side—in human relations, promotion, sales—so she really doesn't understand the business. So I had to be really crisp in negotiating this deal. Nobody was going to make an emotional decision over a rational investment issue. I must be articulate and assertive, and come in with facts.

I knew his position well enough from having worked in the industry for years. So I could anticipate: If I say this, he'll say that. Walking in his shoes and putting myself in his mind-set influenced how I approached the whole topic. So when I went in to see him next week, I could say this: "Costs are rising, your profit margins are shrinking, you're trying to keep heads on beds and pillows, and your market share is declining. Now here's how the training we do will increase the number of guests you have, improve your staff morale, and contribute to your profit margin."

I used very specific examples of benefits. Moreover, I

brought in proof of how training had paid off with another hotel operator. A recent impact study had interviewed the restaurant staff before and after they were trained and certified according to the industry's competency standards. The study also contrasted past with present: gratuities earned, the average bill per customer, productivity measures (like the number of tables served in a given time frame), staff turnover rates, other data. The study showed a definite increase in all facets of competency, which resulted in higher net income and greater staff satisfaction.

The hotel man was amazed. He said he didn't think that the return on his investment would be that tangible, or so quick. Well, the outcome of that negotiation was that his hotel bought in, in a big way, about $20,000 worth, initially. Its large staff— over a thousand employees—are now in training and certification in our program.

This barrier breaking is just the start of a long-term association that will be profitable for both sides. And it all began because I took a long and thoughtful walk in that man's shoes!

But you have to know a lot more about them—your future negotiating partners—to be sure about what they want and how they might go about getting it through negotiating. And that's for the next chapter.

▬ EXERCISE 1 ▬

Negotiation Homework Checklist:

1. My goal in two words or less is:

2. My partner's primary goal in ten words or less is:

3. My partner's goal(s) may also be:

4. I am meeting with:

5. His or her title is:

6. His or her responsibility is:

7. Other people who may also be present:

8. Their responsibilities are:

9. Two questions each person may ask me (and my answers):

10. Three distractions or surprises that may occur during our conversation and how I will handle them:

11. The personality type and negotiating style of my partner most likely is:

12. Accordingly, I shall emphasize this facet of planning in my preparation for negotiation:

■ EXERCISE 2 ■

In preparation for negotiation, information I need about:

THEM

1. What do they want?

2. What are they willing to give up?

3. What are their risks organizationally and personally?

4. What are their perceived needs concerning the project, politics, etc.?

5. What kind of future plans do they have concerning this project?

6. What historical data might they have about me (positives— to build trust or credibility, negatives—i.e.,blockers)?

7. What are their fears?

8. What unmet interest might I satisfy? (need vs. position)

9. What could be some low-cost, high-benefit items that I might offer them?

ME

1. What do I want?

2. What am I willing to give up?

3. What are my fears about this situation?

4. What or who might support me to achieve my goal?

5. What price am I willing to pay to get what I want?

6. What is the worst-case scenario if I don't achieve my desired goal?

7. What questions can I ask to get three yes answers?

8. What might they offer me that is low cost to them but high benefit to me?

9. What kind of history do I have in this situation to increase my credibility?

THEM

10. What are their hot buttons?

11. Who could be my advocate?

12. What don't I know about them or the situation (style, timing)?

13. Who could give me information about the situation?

14. What do they think of their available power?

15. What don't they have control over?

16. What are the consequences to their actions?

ME

10. What's in it for me?

11. What is most risky for me in this situation?

12. What do I need to practice in order to act versus react?

13. What are my alternatives if I don't negotiate?

14. What style of negotiation do I have?

15. What don't I have control over?

16. What are the consequences to my actions?

7
LEARNING ABOUT YOUR NEGOTIATING PARTNERS

"God provides the fish. We must dig for the bait."

—Virginia Satir

The person across the table—or at the end of the telephone line—with whom you are negotiating is your negotiating *partner.* This is true whether you are arranging for after-school day care for your child, a payment schedule for a medical bill, the hiring of a new employee, the site of a new regional office, or the cost of printing a brochure. The process and the necessary preparatory steps are the same.

Crucial to the preparation of your negotiating strategy is the amount of information you can assemble about your negotiating partner. First, as yourself, consider:

- Who is your negotiating partner? What is his or her point of view?
- What is his or her negotiating style?

If you don't know the answers to one or both of the above questions, where will you go to learn the answers? If you don't know your negotiating partner, talk to people who do. Use your contacts and your networks to discover as much as you can about their personality types and negotiating styles. For example, in the different situations listed above, you might talk to:

1. Other parents who have children enrolled in the same program.

2. A staff person in another department of the health facility.
3. "Off the resume" references—people who still work at the potential employee's former jobs.
4. Managers in corporations already located at the potential site.
5. Other printers.

Some of the questions pertinent to your investigation are:

• What is the history of your negotiating partner? Is he or she long established, trustworthy?
• What do you need to know or can you find out about the partner's financial situation?
• What are the goals of your negotiating partner?
• What is your best guess about his or her underlying motivation?
• How much might your partner be willing to risk in order to achieve those goals?
• What might he or she concede to make a deal with you?

Now, make a shopping list. Note the responses that are blank or uncertain. These blanks must be filled in with information, or at least educated guesses. Identify how you'll seek the information you need.

Please note that while some of the questions sound very high-powered for, say, a negotiation for after-school day care, they are exactly the same questions you must answer if you were negotiating for a new site for a regional office. On the other side of any negotiation is a human being who has needs, wants, desires, curiosities, humor, anger, and fears—just as you do. The more you understand the unique nature of your negotiating partner, the more successful the deal will be for both of you.

For a formal investigation, here are some of the resources you might use:

• Reference departments of public libraries, with back issues of magazines and newspapers
• University libraries
• Local newspapers

- Libraries of local or cable television stations
- Chambers of commerce
- Tourist bureaus
- Trade associations
- Professional organizations
- Financial and business libraries
- Historical societies and museums

While researching information on business leaders and their organizations, learn as much as possible about their financial health: budgets, stock value, corporate assets and liabilities, actual or potential management problems. Watch for other issues related to economics. For instance, you may find that some company you intend to approach to sell a product or a project already has a full plate of ongoing projects. What would prompt it to take an interest in your idea? These early preparations spent considering prospective clients might turn up alternative negotiating partners—new leads, in other words—that may be potentially good business for you.

To obtain more information about a particular company, you can even "case the joint"—do some direct sleuthing to find out what you want to know. Be inventive here. If you know a person who works at a company you want to do business with, get invited to lunch in the cafeteria, where you might meet people you'd like to talk with further. Have your friend point out who's who. If you see some key managers there or in hallways or the parking lot, watch how they walk and talk and treat others. This will indicate how they'd be if and when you negotiate with them. However you do it, discover the personality types of persons in key positions because they are the ones who will surely make the ultimate decision for or against your proposal.

Always Use Your Networks

What contacts do you have to help you find out what you need to know about your future negotiating partner? If you lack direct contacts, reach into those social and business support networks to find out how you can get better connected. This communication advantage is a big reason for developing an extensive network of people around you where you live and work.

Remember, successful networks include a diversity of people. As one magazine editor told me:

> I've always tried to network *down*. That's contrary to the myth we were all taught about not going out to lunch with the secretaries; that we're only supposed to network up, and not waste our time being nice to underlings. Every bit of success that I have had in this world on the job is due to the fact that this is the only mistake I *never* made in my working life! What I do when first on a job is hang around the mailroom, the water cooler, the ladies' room. The secretaries and typists, the mail clerks, and bookkeepers are usually my key alliances in any workplace. They have often proved invaluable when I've had to negotiate something on the job. They can have a lot of information, and will share it if they like you. Information, remember, is power.

Who really knows or has negotiated with the person, the company, the association? Ask within your networks. One lead takes you to another, and then more. Find out exactly what you need to know by asking questions about informants' impressions, experiences good and bad, or what they might have heard from others (though watch out for idle gossip). Call a variety of people to get different reports and information; don't rely on just one or two opinions and experiences unless that's all you can get. The more varied the sources of knowledge you acquire—including the negatives—the more empowered you will be for the negotiation ahead.

Identify the Decision Makers

When you ask around for information, find out who the real decision makers are on the other side—whom you will be negotiating with. People's titles and positions may not have any direct bearing on their true place in a chain of command or power structure. As one executive trainer learned:

I spent four years thinking up proposals, developing them, and presenting them to the president of a company to whom I had been introduced through mutual friends. He turned down all my ideas, although often I saw him grab similar ideas from other people. I was bewildered as to why I was failing to make a deal.

Then one day I was talking to someone who knew the company well. She said, "Oh, he never makes any of those kinds of decisions. He completely trusts his department heads to make those decisions, and he practically rubber-stamps them. He'd never go around them and make a deal. The person you need to be talking to is Louise, his marketing director." I met with Louise, and we had a deal within an hour. What a lesson.

Realize that the person in a company who makes the real operational decisions may not be its president or chairman. Also, you may have to go through several presentations and negotiations until you get to the top and final stage, particularly if what you propose requires a sizable investment along with a risk from the other side. Don't discount someone assigned to see you who is not in the highest corporate echelon. This person may be the first stage of an important negotiation. He or she may make the preliminary decisions that winnow out undesirable proposals, passing the likely ones upstairs to a higher-up decision maker.

Thus, if there's the probability you'll be going up a ladder in negotiating something large, you will need to present your position effectively at each phase of the total negotiation process, being well prepared from the beginning. You may start out with a Datacrat or Mr. Nice Guy, for instance, and end up with a Steamroller. It's wise to prepare a major presentation for all negotiating eventualities.

■ NEGOTIATING WITH STEAMROLLERS

Rule of thumb: If you cannot write down on the back of your business card the goal and purpose of your negotiation with a Steamroller, you're talking too much. Tell the person what you want to achieve; don't go on and on. If he or she likes what you say, the

Steamroller can make a quick decision in your favor; somebody else will handle working out the details.

Among benefits you can give is speed (in delivery), no details ("We'll take care of it"), and expertise. You'll reduce the Steamroller's defenses if you say, "I only need three minutes of your time." And tell him or her, "This is what I want to talk about." The individual then knows the *what* as well as how much time you take. With Steamrollers, negotiate time before negotiating position.

Figure that Steamrollers will lose every piece of paper you give them, no matter how valuable it seems to you. They don't read long letters. Single-paragraph memos are their limit, for either reading or writing. They may not read contracts either—and certainly not the fine print. They hire lawyers to do that for them.

Prepare to provide Steamrollers with summary sheets at the meeting itself. Don't send them a hundred pieces of paper in advance and expect them to read everything. Highlight what you want them to read and put yellow stick-on notes on pages if it's a long document. Tell them they shouldn't waste their own time reading the little stuff but that they *must* read what's marked for them.

In your planning, figure on giving at least four solution choices as you near decision time. Put your own favorite third—the one that would work out best for you both. (The others should be so slanted in your favor as to bother them.) They'll usually respond to this menu by saying, "Reject . . . reject . . . accept . . . reject." By giving them a range of options, they'll be happy turning down all but the one that makes the most sense. What they really want is apparent control over the negotiating process. They empower themselves by rejecting while they are looking for a quick workable solution.

Keep in mind that Steamrollers are high-risk negotiators. So calculate out how a quick negotiation can work for you. If you're a Datacrat, you're going to be pushed hard and fast; you won't have time and space to think.

Also, prepare yourself for dealing, inevitably, with a variety of aggressive, frontal attacks. Do this by depersonalizing the issues and desensitizing yourself well ahead of time. Practice this over and over. Remember, Steamrollers don't mean to savage you *personally*; it's simply their normal tactic for winning the negotiation. They don't really want to overpower you. It's just a game with them. Negotiation provides them with a source of energy.

The danger is that if you haven't desensitized yourself before negotiating, you'll "go with your feelings." If honest feelings are not kept in tight control, those who get emotional are going to lose, especially with a Steamroller. They are comfortable with anger. Are you? And is that the way you want to spend your energy? Probably no. So defuse them. Let them wind down. Call out their name and say, "Let's look at this." Do *not* say, "Now, let's not get excited!"

Most important, *be clear on what you want in advance of going in.* Know also what the Steamrollers want and why they want it. With Steamrollers, the negotiation will go fast and there is usually no way to reverse the direction and sequence. It may be a one-time deal.

Figure that they'll always ask for a little more once the contract is drawn up. If you want to indulge this habit, during your preparation figure in something that is of little value to you as a calculated giveaway that will give them the illusion of being king of the heap.

The Three Yes Questions

Anticipate that all your proposals may be rejected. Therefore, prepare in advance three questions to which they are certain to say yes. For example:

1. Did we meet the last delivery deadline well ahead of time?
2. Was the total order completely filled?
3. Did it arrive in satisfactory condition at your warehouse? "If so, then we agree."

Then try to close them after their three yesses. (The Three Yes Questions scenario is discussed further in Chapter 8.)

Don't listen to their first no; just ignore it. They probably expect you to, but think maybe you'll fall for it. Steamrollers want you to push back, constantly and hard.

When the negotiation isn't getting anywhere, Steamrollers attack even more. Or they'll throw more issues onto the table, trying to find out where you are right now. Pull back and say, "Wait a minute. We were negotiating about X, and now we have here

ABCD. We're losing time. . . ." That should do it for them. If they're still interested in continuing the negotiation, they'll get back to issues that are stalemated and together you may find a solution.

Outbursts of anger and attacks are Steamroller negotiation strategies. They are more comfortable with force. If you need to use force—and you may want to with them—do so unexpectedly and fast. Justifiable anger is a great weapon as long as you control it and direct it consciously to serve your purpose. But remember, Steamrollers are very good at retaliation. So unless you want to fight their fire with your own fire—which may result in ashes—try to shift them off the attack mode. Hold up your end of partnership negotiation by giving them lots of choices and solutions.

Match their voice energy without attacking or counterattacking. Stay calm, reasonable, pleasant, and firm. Set definite limits if they become abusive, such as, "I'm willing to talk about the issues, but I'm not willing to be called names." Always depersonalize their insults, which come from their energy, impatience, and need to compete.

Never back down to the bottom line the Steamroller tries to push you to. Stand your ground while offering new solutions. Offer time savings as one benefit of the negotiation: This way it will be faster; you can get it with less time investment.

If they threaten to walk out, let them walk. But offer an alternative that will help them save face if they decide to stay. Say, "I don't blame you. However, we could do it this way and get better results."

Do's and Don'ts

DO:

• If you have positional power, whatever it may be, tell them upfront about it, even if they may already know. That's how you gain credibility, since they like to deal with someone with similar or equal power. And they like to deal with people who look and act competent.

• Speak audibly and forcefully. Try to match their speaking speed and tone.

• Use the word *results* often, along with *benefit, leverage, done, gain.* Words create attitudes.

• Pick a phrase they often use and reflect it back at them: "to hit the target," "to close the deal." (But don't use any expressions that are against your own style in a major way; you want to stretch but not abandon yourself.)

• Remember that timing with a Steamroller relates to the present and future. Deal first only with what happens now in the short term, from right now to several weeks ahead. Then get into future outcome and results.

• Expect Steamrollers to do various other things while talking with you. They'll take phone calls, bring the secretary or associates in, sign letters and documents, and even read the newspaper. (When you're on the phone, you'll hear the papers rustling.) Don't feel they're not interested in you; that's just the way they do it, since they try to cram as much as possible into each minute of their day.

• Recognize the Steamroller's need to pack each minute with action. Sometimes it can be dysfunctional; know when this occurs. Respond with a matching sense of urgency: "Of course, time is of the essence." (On the other hand, as a general rule avoid letting negotiating partners know of your own sense of urgency, which puts you at a disadvantage.)

• Turn the Steamroller image around in your head. Rather than think that this is a pushy, terrible person, tell yourself, "What an opportunity!" Because it is. (Steamrollers are always challenging. You'll learn a lot from negotiating with them. They'll treat you with respect when they discover that you are equally powerful, equally prepared. Since they like to know they're dealing with someone with equal or similar power, they will put you to frequent tests just to see how you'll react.)

• Always expect them to ask for a little more from you once the contract is done.

DON'T:

• Try to contact them in the morning, when they're busy with seventeen phone calls and six meetings to go to. Catch them in mid-afternoon, for they're likely to be ready to halt and listen by then as they count up the day's winnings.

• Get emotional. Keep your strong feelings—anger, hurt, irritation, upset—under control. They hate weakness. If they test you, don't go into a Nice Guy mode; just stay centered.

• Give them less than quality stuff, and always do it fast and efficiently.

• Bother them with details. They expect other people to handle them. This isn't the way you get buy-in or credit.

• Expect them to bring any papers you sent them. Come with an extra set, and when they start rummaging around in their briefcase, just hand it to them. Say, "Here it is. Let's not waste time looking for it." And don't move into a parental role: "Who knows where you put things?" Avoid any put-downs.

• Propose to meet them for a lunch when you can talk business, since they rarely make time to eat. If they suggest it, let them order first if speed is a factor, and maybe follow suit. But whatever you order, don't take long with it!

• Ever apologize. What they hate most is a sweet little voice saying, "I'm so sorry." And don't expect them ever to apologize, either.

■ NEGOTIATING WITH DATACRATS

Datacrats love details. They always read the fine print. If you want their business, pay attention to details and load them with information. Know the intricacies of history—your own, your company's, the issues—so that you can respond accurately and fully to their questions. Written or visual materials submitted to them should reflect the past, present, and future line of presentation: past (how we have done it and how it was), future (how we will do it for you), present (how and what we need to do now to create action). In that order.

Since they are thorough, they probably are conducting their own separate investigation before negotiating with you, so be careful about what you claim.

You can expect them to ask probing questions starting with *how*: How can we be sure you will deliver the merchandise? How do you plan to make your payments? How many cubic feet are in the storage containers? Prepare your background information accordingly. When talking with Datacrats, plan to use reflective strategy using that key word: *how* you will implement the program, how you'll deliver the goods, how you will provide warranties, and so on.

When I am going to negotiate with Datacrats—and many of my clients are in areas such as finance where they abound—I know that I must modify my own supercharged, extroverted style that works in other situations. My right-brain manner must shift to accommodate a left-brain partnership. I need to stay consciously competent and observant, however, since Datacrats can shift their own style (often to Steamrollers), and I must move with them to create a comfort zone—unless I choose a hard-nosed, rigid strategy.

I practice in advance to achieve a presentation that will look, feel, and sound authentic. I don't want to pretend to be someone I'm not, but I must work at being calmer, quieter, more analytical. Datacrats stroll in to a meeting on time, or even come in a half-hour early. They look cool rather than formal in demeanor. They are organized and prepared, their briefcases stuffed with paper: reports, charts, analyses. (When a Steamroller is prepared, it's because a Datacrat has provided all the information.)

In the opening, they need time. They won't want to be rushed. Your presentation timing should go like this: past, future, present. If you're more of a Steamroller, you may miss the major piece of giving them past information and other details that may seem irrelevant and time-wasteful to you. But they need and want to hear how you've been in business for forty-seven years, have 153 employees, sold $1.6 million in goods last year. Give attention to detail that provides all conceivable evidence for persuading them that you are a reputable and responsible person or company, here to stay. You won't sell them today and be gone tomorrow.

As soon as they feel pushed too fast or even attacked, as by Steamrollers, they begin their retreat. Withdrawal from active engagement, whether it's negotiating or direct combat, is the Datacrat's typical response. What is seen as lack of empathy or interest may actually be fear or discomfort over no evidence of trustability, and that is negotiable.

When you do not know the answer to a question they ask, say so honestly and promise you'll get back to them after you've looked into it or researched it thoroughly. Such an experience can be a benefit if you handle it right. They will have a good opinion of you for it, because you've shown respect for their need to have detailed information.

Don't rush your information-giving. Datacrats don't trust fast talk or quick responses. You will build a good negotiating climate if you remain patient and always have documentation to support your facts. Like many people, Datacrats have great respect for the written word. (Years ago, the TV program "Candid Camera" demonstrated that when they put the sign *Delaware Is Closed* on the highway, drivers turned around and went home.)

If they are the ones coming to you with details they've assembled and you don't have time or patience to deal with details (and can't see the point of them anyway), you'll have to educate and manage the Datacrat. After all, none of this is getting you any closer to closure. Just say, "All this information you're giving me is rather confusing to me." Announce that this is obviously their area of expertise, not yours. "I might make a mistake when going through them." Datacrats never want to make a mistake—even cause you to make one—so you're playing into this.

Ask them to summarize the things that are really crucial in any agreement they will make with you. And set it down on a single piece of paper. Usually they are trustworthy people; when asked to come up with a big picture minus the tiny details, they'll do it.

Never give Datacrats more than two choices at any one time. If you pile more on them, they'll get overwhelmed and start procrastinating. You don't want to interrupt the forward-moving thrust needed in negotiation. So gently apply a time frame that sets specifics on the road to progress while giving them freedom to choose: "We can talk about it right now, or we can talk tomorrow at 2 o'clock. Which do you prefer?"

Realize that any negotiation with a Datacrat could require four or five meetings before anything gets settled. They simply won't make decisions on the spot, as Steamrollers do.

Expect a lot of silence when you talk on the phone. For example, if you ask them, "Have you read the last batch of data I sent you?" there may be a long pause. Keep reminding yourself that they don't respond rapidly because they are incessantly reviewing, reconsidering, and rereading whatever the negotiations are about. Be assured that things are going on in their head, and since they don't like chaos, they are putting them in order. Don't interrupt them, no matter how much of a hurry you're in.

Datacrats are notorious procrastinators. You have to work hard to speed up the negotiation process in order to reach closure, to make some agreement. How might you do this?

- Summarize often whatever you both have already agreed on or given up as concessions.
- Write down whatever you can and review your notes with them.
- Provide statistics and graphs that will help convince them.
- Speak slowly and firmly.

When you think you've arrived at an agreement, consider their need not to feel pushed. Give them time to consider the agreement: "I am sure you will want to look this over again." But all the while bracket them: "And I will expect to hear your decision by 10 o'clock tomorrow."

Do's and Don'ts

DO:

- Send them lots of documents, graphs, statistics, but since they're always looking for mistakes, if they find you've made any, they won't trust you and may well turn you down because of it.
- Give them historical data to give credibility.
- Stress the *how* process, not the *what* (which Steamrollers like): how we will coordinate the loan; how you will obtain the permit; how they could improve the landscaping around the plant.
- Give them lots of written information. That way, you'll minimize their need to have much personal contact with you.
- Exercise patience and restraint as you wait for their responses, their decisions.
- Give them a sense of participation in designing the negotiating process and putting together information that leads to their agreement and thereby produces a positive outcome.

• Tell them how you handle any unforeseen circumstances (surprises) that might occur, so that they will be assured that you are prepared and willing to solve any possible problems.

DON'T:

• Ask unnecessary personal questions, but do treat them as people, not machines.
• Ever say the word *approximately*. You will lose credibility. Do say, "I will find out for sure." Then have all the facts, as up-to-date and accurate as you can get them.
• Wear bright clothes when you go to see them. They are overwhelmed by energy.
• Ever set up an exciting event full of surprises, such as a big birthday party. They won't be touched or grateful.

■ NEGOTIATING WITH BUTTERFLIES

Most Butterflies have a short attention span and high energy. In strategizing any negotiation with Butterflies, you must figure how to get and *keep* their attention for at least five minutes before they introduce a new issue, position, or side story. Open the negotiation with personal comments before marching toward the bottom-line hook. Ask, "Didn't I read an article about you a few weeks ago?" Then you've got them. They love to talk about themselves. Just listen genuinely and let *them* tell you about them. But set a time limit: "In nine minutes I do have a call to make."

Butterflies usually won't negotiate seriously, or agree to get into some future negotiating, unless you feed them. Proposing "Let's break bread together" will build trust.

Who is the key word when you're trying to lure a Butterfly into some agreement. Their questions are about people, and your responses should be as well. Who has bought this property . . . who has done it this way . . . who has worked with you before . . . who is in on this deal too with you . . . who will be responsible if we agree.

This relationship building may be essential if you need to be associated with them in a future transaction. You're setting up the climate for the negotiation's second stage, which should take place somewhere where they cannot be distracted. Either lure them to your office (and turn off incoming calls routed to them), or trap them in your car and drive to a picnic in a nearby park so you can talk quietly, without interruptions. (Butterflies are always sure to find distractions wherever they may be, so provide dull vistas with few if any people around.)

To negotiate with Butterflies successfully, find the thing that excites you most about what you're proposing and let it energize you. Hold that feeling and bring that energy to the table while maintaining a sense of humor and a certain playfulness. But if you can't match their energy and flair—if you're an innate Datacrat, say, but absolutely need their involvement or cooperation—find someone else to talk to them for you. For if you bore them, or they pick up your disapproval of their style, you're sure to lose—unless they calculate that they *need* you almost as much. (And sometimes they do.)

Butterflies usually do business in a cooperative relationship mode rather than in an up-down competitive one. But if they ever think you've done them in, then watch out for "I'll get you before you get me!" And since they have connections, staying power, and passion, when they stop cooperating they can be tough and unfair competitors.

If you're a Butterfly yourself, make sure some Datacrat will be around to handle the details properly.

Be forewarned about this: Just before an agreement closes, most Butterflies will expect some extra benefit. If you want to create goodwill, prepare to throw in something extra before it's even asked for. If you do this in advance, you can even build it into the cost figures. Just say, "I know that it's not in the contract, but for you. . . ." Then they'll go around telling everybody about this marvelous thing you have done for them. Which gives you good publicity and you've remained in control of the negotiating.

Start off your negotiations in a purely social way, as if you've met only for the pleasure of seeing them. Ask about children, grandchildren, partners. Talk about jobs, the gym, cars, the weekend. Part of your preparation is to know something about their interests. Find common interests and use the "we" technique.

Make a strong personal connection, and only then move on to

a proposition that is almost guaranteed to interest them. In other words, don't start with an impersonal bottom line: "I brought a copy of the contract for the deal I'm proposing." That will offend and upset them, and you may get nowhere. Start with bonding, one human being with another.

Because Butterflies have a real need for inclusion, they require a lot of attention and reassurance from others about their personal strengths and attractiveness. During negotiation, you might consciously compliment them about how many good decisions they have made before. Say how many people you know who think well of them.

Realize that they'll negotiate with you, buy from you, agree with you, make concessions, and say yes if they like you and trust you, and if they sense you truly like them and will be loyal.

Since Butterflies make intuitive decisions, speak on emotional terms with them when you're guiding their decision making, such as, "I feel this would be the best decision for you."

Take time to brainstorm with them. They love it when you ask for their expertise or ideas. But stay alert. Though they may have some wonderfully creative ideas, they are equally excellent at putting several issues on the table and shifting from one to another, without anything ever getting settled. They need to be bracketed. Summarize agreements and concessions and review goals: "We want to use your service and you want your service used"; "We agreed on price and now we need to clarify terms."

Make sure you negotiate by the agenda. Otherwise, by the time your part of the agenda comes up, they are mentally and emotionally "gone"—even though they are still there physically. Your attentiveness and obvious consideration will increase their willingness to get off any positions they've stubbornly taken up and to make concessions.

Note that although Butterflies may come into negotiating in a very social manner, because their time management is bad, all of a sudden they take up a fast and tough negotiating style because they're frantic to finish the job and move on. Here's how to watch for that. Note their initial body language: maybe leaning over you, pointing a lot, chatting about this and that in a very animated way. Then they look at their watch. That's the shift. Get in there before they do. You should quickly say, "Bottom line, this is what we talked about." Summarize and push for an agreement right then and there, and you may get it.

Butterflies may have to modify their scatterbrained style in order to do business with Datacrats. They must be very careful, then, about assembling details and preparing properly to negotiate, and they must curb their freewheeling exaggerations, which to Datacrats become downright lies.

Separate fact from fiction for them, and for yourself. Butterflies tend to distort for dramatic effect and then begin believing some figment of their imagination. "But you promised me this . . ." they might say accusingly to you. If you still want to hang in there, you'll have to go back to small, definite agreements and then re-create a positive relationship. It's important, therefore, to set definite limits on the negotiation all along the way by stating exactly what you have already given to them and that you are not willing to give more.

Some other bad news about the Butterfly type is that although they might quickly agree to everything, they won't do the same thing when finalizing the agreement and attaching their signature to it. When that happens, you must really bracket them by saying something like, "By 12 o'clock today you've got to make your decision." If you are kind and firm at the same time, and they know the deal is to their advantage, you'll get it.

Some Do's and Don'ts

DO:

- Publicly compliment them.
- Acknowledge their civic visibility: You saw their picture and the article in the newspaper, heard about them from important others (name dropping is to be encouraged with them).
- Always use who.
- Expect them to push to the limits, asking for as much as they can possibly get. "By the way—" they'll start in. If you haven't prepared for this by planning to throw in a little bit extra at the end, just tell them firmly but kindly, "The answer is no."

• Create a positive relationship by sending them notes, flowers, birthday cards.

• Use their names often. They like this, and it helps ground them, keep them from flying off on tangents. For example: "Mary, this is what I think we should do."

• Work primarily on building a relationship when first negotiating with them.

• Remember them when you don't need them, so that they'll be there when you get back into the negotiation process. (All people like this, but Butterflies especially!)

DON'T:

• Rush them.

• Get thrown by their fluctuating ups and downs. Depersonalize their moodiness: it's about them, rarely about *you*.

• Expect them to be consistent. This type, above all others, will suddenly shift on you—become a different type or undergo an extreme mood change.

• Ignore them or belittle them if you aim to keep doing business with them! If you do ignore them, they may turn and attack.

■ NEGOTIATING WITH NICE GUYS

These are the caretakers, the Nice Guys. Let us take good care of them, by respecting their special integrity, by talking to them as if they matter, because they *do*. Before, during, and after negotiating, try to get to know them as individuals, as persons uniquely themselves. Show interest; ask questions and remember their answers; reveal some hidden things about yourself to encourage them to do the same. Get them to laugh. Make them feel safe and appreciated.

You can be less defensive with Nice Guys than with the other three personality types. They are natural negotiating partners. They welcome partnership negotiation. They won't bulldoze or nitpick or gush as the accustomed means to get at whatever goal they're expected to achieve. They operate aboveboard, carefully, considerately. They always follow the rules. And they often need a lot of time to make their final decisions, because they are not impulsive or risk-taking or egotistically sure of themselves.

Since they dislike and fear conflict, they are uncomfortable with any negotiation process that involves opposing opinions, particularly strong ones. Which means that they avoid negotiating directly about anything that cannot be solved by their agreeing to take on one more responsibility themselves. In fact, often they will automatically start doing the very thing that nobody else seems willing to do, just to keep peace. Which gives them a certain martyr's air. People then begin feeling guilty or resentful because the negotiation process, which should have resolved the issue, has been silently co-opted by Mr. or Ms. Nice Guy.

A word of caution: Be wary of some of the seeming Nice Guys out there. There are entire cultures that behave hospitably and amiably, in Nice-Guy fashion, when they really are preparing to negotiate on the offensive, like subtle Steamrollers. They wouldn't think of uttering a rude no when you make your proposals, and so may string you along.

That's what happened to me when I went to Japan, representing Citicorp as a senior vice-president. The trip, I figured, was a thank-you of sorts for bringing in a big account. Now they were sending me to Asia to pick up more business. So there I was, sitting for several days with Japanese gentlemen, discussing what our banking firm could do for them. All the while they smiled and said, "Yes, yes, yes." I wasn't sure they were hearing exactly what I said that they were agreeing to.

When I got back to New York, I told the guys how successful my trip had been. "Did they sign the papers?" they asked. "No, they're sending them." At this, they almost fell down laughing. "Ha ... they got you good, Schapiro!" they said. A few days later a long letter came from my Japanese friends, telling me in detail that what they said yes to just wasn't so at all. From then on, I've been cautious about people who forever smile and nod and say yes. I need to see their signatures on the papers instead.

Nice Guys naturally tend to give away more than necessary upfront, so that you will like them. It may appear easy, then, to take advantage of them. During negotiation, remind them of concessions they have already made, then offer at least one to them. If you don't attend to their interests too, in the long run the imbalance creates a victor-victim situation. When Nice Guys start seeing that they're losing or being taken advantage of, their energy slumps and they won't budge. Then they won't make good workers . . . or good negotiating partners.

When trying to close a deal with Nice Guys, always give them the why. They need rational reasons for everything in order to process the information at hand and then reach conclusions. With Nice Guys who dillydally in decision making, use "I suggest . . ." to guide them toward your goal, which you are honestly persuading them could be a good goal for them as well. Figure on feeding them solutions, because they probably won't come up with initiatives of their own.

Protecting Nice Guys from themselves, as well as from others who might take advantage of them, should be part of your job in any negotiating transaction. If you're on a team with them, it will be particularly important to do this, discreetly. If you do it well, they'll be grateful from then on. This can be a smart tactic on your part because—quite contrary to common belief—Nice Guys actually often finish first in a great number of professional positions where they have considerable power.

Some Do's and Don'ts

DO:

• Regard and treat them as translators, peacekeepers, facilitators in negotiations, and set up situations where they can play savior.

• Use words like *nice, I suggest, why, fair, equal, sensitive, feel, care, helpful, disappointed.*

• Reinforce their decision-making risks by telling them how useful their decisions were to the whole team.

• Create a good one-on-one relationship: compliment them, send them little thank-you gifts, remember their birthdays with cute cards.

• Let them know what your expectations are of negotiating situations and how they might contribute.

• Inform them about the big picture, and how their decisions will affect it.

• Create opportunities for them to feel good about the human element in the negotiating—establishing a "we" and "us" climate.

• Let them know where and when they can reach you during the decision-making process, for they often need reassurance.

• Help them have some wins by showing them options that may be of low value to you but high value to them.

• Summarize and count the concessions they've made (they won't); they will then feel goodwill from you, not "taken."

• Explain that it will be helpful for them to tell you what they want and don't want.

• Help them say no when it's to their best interests, and assure them that you'll still like them anyway.

• Encourage them to speak up more by complimenting them when they do assert themselves.

• Tell them, diplomatically, that it is bad for you or the team when they agree to things they cannot follow through on.

• Commit to supporting them and protecting them from "furious" Steamrollers or conflict that might make them look "not nice."

• Set limits on time—when you must have their decision.

DON'T:

• Give them technical documents (CCRs, blueprints, etc.) to review alone; they won't.

• Make them the "lead" or "Boss."

• Ask them to take the "bad guys" role or be bringers of bad news.

• Start with bottom-line business when meeting them.

• Look angry without explaining if it's about them, for they will get stuck on what's wrong with them or what they did wrong instead of participating in the negotiation process.

• Let them get away with saying, when asked what they want, "I don't care," "Whatever you want," "It doesn't matter." If you say, "I want this—" you may shift them to the "tell" mode: "Well, I want. . . ."

• Allow them to participate by remaining silent to an option proposed, instead of saying no.

– EXERCISE –

PREPARATION WORKSHEET

Before we turn to our friends and colleagues for information and assistance when preparing for negotiation, it is often helpful to write out thoughtfully the specifics of the situation, determining both exactly what it is we need to know and who can help us in learning the answers.

SITUATION	NETWORK SOURCE
What do I understand?	Who in my network can confirm this information?
What more do I need to know?	Who can give me more information?
What do I have control over?	Who can help me gain control?
What more do they need to know about this situation?	Who, other than I, can educate them?
What don't they have control over?	Who can offer them more control that benefits the negotiation outcome?

8
ANTICIPATING SCENARIOS

"If you don't know where you're going, any road will get you there."
—L. Frank Baum, *The Wizard of Oz*

When preparing to negotiate for my first management position—I'd just graduated with my MBA—I asked my father, aunt, and boyfriend to take turns grilling me about all kinds of things, as a potential employer might do. They showed no mercy, and a few times were so tough or mean they were awful! But while I got through each session still somewhat intact, I did spot some places where I needed to do more homework. Anyway, when I went for the interview—actually, there were three in two days—I was well prepared and composed because of the role playing. The people were actually so much nicer to me than my home team had been that I felt I breezed through the ordeal. And, oh yes, I got the job.

A major piece of preparation is figuring out ways the future negotiation might go—all those "What ifs...." You set a basic meeting scene and a couple of characters with a problem to resolve or a decision to make, and take off from there.

Scenarios for what could happen are virtually no-risk exercises you can do inside your head, or enact with somebody else. Start imagining—anticipating—how your negotiating partner might act, what he or she might say, then project what may happen between the two of you, for better or for worse. Designing various game plans will greatly increase your chance for success in the negotiating process ahead. Ad-libbing or rehearsing different scripts will make you versatile and adaptable.

Anticipating scenarios also helps you protect yourself from being adversely affected by difficult behavior or predicaments, such as becoming browbeaten or embarrassed, feeling exploited, being unduly rushed or pressured, getting distracted or led astray, being surprised or judged ill-prepared, or otherwise adversely positioned on the negotiating gameboard. With preparation, it's as if you've heard and seen it all before.

How to Construct a Scenario

By picturing scenes that might come, you get a wide variety of negotiating experiences in advance of the negotiation. The possible scenes you play out show how every word and action has particular consequences, and those consequences lead to new actions. The negotiating that takes place in your imagination may have a thousand different forms.

Identify the scenarios that lead easily and directly to the goal you have set for yourself. These are the optimal or best-case situations. Then look at the elements that have helped this happen. Consider how you open the negotiating, how your imagined negotiating partner behaves, what he or she says, how you respond.

At the same time, create a few worst-case scenarios. There's always a chance that one might occur. Think of how you could avert it: what you would do or say to change the deteriorating situation, and how your partner might then respond so that together you rescue the process.

Let's walk now through several possible scenarios. You'll see from the examples below that this simple scene could be played out in a near-infinite number of ways, starting with the same initial lines from the character YOU.

YOU is an inspirational speaker who specializes in giving talks to high school students, motivating them to go on to higher education or vocational training. And she's going in to talk with the principal of a suburban high school about giving a workshop series that will be attended by all seniors.

YOU's preliminary research did not produce much information about the person she's scheduled to negotiate with. So she has sensibly prepared for meeting each of the four different personality types. That's because quite a lot of the negotiation's course will depend on the person she'll meet with. By anticipating any expectations, such as sending or bringing in materials about herself and her presentations, she'll be better positioned to negotiate. The mood or circumstances of the meeting can also be highly variable.

YOU [Holding hand out in friendly manner while walking into the office cheerfully]. Dr. D, it's good to meet you after our phone conversation last week about my giving the workshops here. Such a beautiful day out there, isn't it?

DR. D [Staying behind his desk, taking your hand limply and almost reluctantly, then turning to look out window]. Er . . . I guess so. [Silence]

YOU I brought you the papers you asked to see. [Puts folder on his desk.]

DR. D [Acting slightly irritated]. I expected to get them a day or two ago, since you said you would send them.

YOU I'm sorry. It took longer than I'd expected to put them together in a form that would show you exactly what I have in mind.

DR. D [Frowning]. I really have to study everything ahead of time, before meeting with anyone about something like this. So I am afraid I won't be able to make a decision today. It will be a waste of time for us both to meet now to talk.

YOU [Brightly, still hopeful]. But I am here, and at least you might look me over and ask a few questions.

DR. D [Somber and nervous]. No, I cannot possibly judge the feasibility of hiring you to give the program without first having the materials that substantiate what you do—seeing your brochures, your curriculum vitae, your professional credits, other institutions' recommendations, personal references, and so on. [Getting up now from seat and moving to door, to escort You out.] I regret that you have bothered to come by.

YOU [Accepting temporary defeat, gamely]. At least you now have those papers, Dr. D, so you can study them carefully. I will include a short video program too, which may be helpful. [At this, Dr. D looks decidedly dubious, as if distrustful of anything "showy."] I will call you on Friday afternoon to make another appointment with you.

DR. D [*Moving You out into the hallway*]. Yes, you may call me if you like. I will let you know at that time whether it will be worth while to discuss this matter further. Good day. [*Since he does not extend his hand in courteous farewell, you do not.*]

YOU [*Holding hand out in friendly manner while walking into the office, cheerfully*]. Mr. B, it's good to meet you after our phone conversation last week. Such a beautiful day out there, isn't it?

MR. B [*Glances behind him at window*]. I've been too busy to look. [*Phone rings on desk and he picks it up, converses in noisy grunts for a few seconds while he stares at you, then bangs down receiver. Remembering you had held out your hand, he now thrusts his out to you, and grips yours like a vise.*] You're here about . . . ?

YOU I'm Ms. Y. We have an appointment for now. I briefly spoke with you last week about doing a program here to motivate your senior students.

MR. B [*Speaking rapidly*]. Oh yeah, I remember now. Your proposal sounded good. How much do you charge per hour?

YOU I work on a fee basis.

MR. B So how much for the package deal?

YOU A thousand dollars.

MR. B Our budget for consultants doesn't have an extra Kay in it. How about seven-fifty?

YOU For that I could do three lectures to everyone instead of five workshops with small groups.

MR. B Let's hold that. Now, what exactly would we get from you?

YOU You can see for yourself. I have a video here you can watch that shows me in action. Your secretary said you had a VCR here in your office.

MR. B [*Smiling, pleased at the prospect*]. Okay. That's great. But don't show me more than a minute and a half. [*Looks at watch.*] Then I've got to leave for a staff meeting. What else do I need to know about you?

YOU Here's a portfolio you can look at. Keep it.

MR. B [*Shuffling rapidly through pages*]. You look good on paper. [*The video comes on, and he watches it attentively for less than a minute.*] You look good on tape too. Let's make a deal. Two lectures for five hundred. Two Tuesdays starting two months from now. If the kids get something from you, we'll bring you back for more.

YOU Right. I'll send out a letter of confirmation today for you
to sign.

YOU [*Holding hand out in friendly manner while walking into the office, cheerfully*]. Mrs. S, it's good to meet you after our phone conversation
last week. Such a beautiful day out there, isn't it?

MRS. S [*Taking You's hand warmly and at first forgetting to put it down*]. Oh, it's
absolutely gorgeous! I couldn't believe how clear the sky was
when I drove to work this morning. And how lovely the air
smelled. The hyacinths and crocuses are out. I don't remember
spring starting like this before.

YOU [*Trying to get on track*]. Mrs. S, you seemed very interested in my
proposal to do a series of workshops for your senior students—motivating them to prepare for future careers.

MRS. S Oh yes, what a marvelous idea that is! I am sure my admin-
istrative staff and teachers would love to have you come. [*Goes to
door.*] Dora! Sally! James! Come here at once and meet this wonderful speaker. [*The small group comes to doorway.*] This is . . .

YOU My name is Ms. Y. I've come to talk with Mrs. S. about doing
special motivational workshops for seniors.

MRS. S [*Coming very close*]. I simply adore that blouse you're wearing! It
matches all those flowers out in the walkway—pink, purple,
white, green . . . Mmmm. [*Pinches fabric to feel it.*] Do you mind
telling me where you bought it?

YOU Actually, I . . .

MRS. S [*Suddenly looks at watch; abrupt*]. My goodness, it's time for our
staff meeting. When we made this appointment, I didn't remember that Tuesday's always a bad day for me.

YOU I'm sorry to hear that. But I will leave my portfolio for you to
look over, and also a ten-minute video that you and your staff
can watch; it shows me in action with a group of teenagers.
[*Turning now to secretary, who had ushered You in.*] Please remind Mrs.
S to watch the video and look through my materials. I will call
the office on Friday to get your decision. We can discuss the
terms of the arrangement then.

MRS. S [*Rushing out door, grabbing You's hand warmly*]. Oh, you conduct
yourself in such a professional manner! My instincts tell me that
you have terrific charisma, so you may go away now assuming

that we're going to hire you. My assistant will work out the details with you tomorrow. I know all the students will just love you.

YOU [*Holding hand out in friendly manner while walking into the office, cheerfully*]. Ms. N, it's good to meet you after our phone conversation last week. Such a beautiful day out there, isn't it?

MS. N [*Almost shyly giving her hand quickly, then withdrawing it*]. Oh yes, it surely is. [*Anxiously.*] I forgot to mention when we talked, Ms. Y., that I am only the acting principal here. I was interested in what you told me about the special program you are offering for our senior students. We can chat some more now, of course. But I do want you to understand that I am not the final decision maker here.

YOU I understand. I don't expect you to be. These things usually have to be passed on by a number of administrators. Though when a principal is really enthusiastic, it definitely helps.

MS. N [*Almost recoiling*]. Certainly I can make my own recommendations, but because I am only temporarily here, I have no authority whatsoever.

YOU [*Handing her the materials*]. I'll leave with you my portfolio as well as a short video showing me in a workshop situation with students. Look them over yourself. I am sure you will like them. Then please pass them on to those who will need to consider them once you've told them that you would like to have me come here to do the project. The person who makes the contracts can then call me to discuss the details of our agreement.

MS. N [*Relieved that You has taken charge*]. It was so nice of you to come in and see us, Ms. Y. I'll give all your materials to the others and tell them how cooperative you are. And so very professional, too!

YOU [*Reassuringly taking her hand again before departing*]. Thank you, Ms. N. I know that I will do an excellent program for the students—which will reflect well upon your own accomplishments as acting principal here. Maybe they'll even make you permanent principal!

MS. N [*Terrified but pleased at same time*]. Oh, I don't think so. Not me. But maybe they'll ask you to apply for the position.

. .

Anticipate the Personality Types

Each scenario I've depicted here shows how the success of the intended negotiation changes according to at least one crucial variable: the personality YOU was dealing with. YOU meets here a Datacrat, who is uptight, cool and formal, unwilling and unable to do fast decision making; a Steamroller, who is hearty, busy, brusque, and decisive; a Butterfly, who is warm, overly sociable, even flighty; and a Ms. Nice Guy, who is amiable and agreeable, uncertain, unempowered. Each one requires from YOU a different approach and dialogue in moving toward her goal. Granted, the scenes exaggerate the types as they might play out in real life, but when anticipating scenarios we should do so to dramatize the differences that negotiating styles can make.

When anticipating scenarios, the most important aspect is to consider the personality types you may be dealing with as negotiating partners. Also, will you meet with one person, several people, or a group? If you don't already know them or else learn much about them from others, your preliminary investigations should try to find out what the players are like as people.

But not until you directly experience the negotiation process itself will you really be *sure* about what types you're dealing with. Then you might find yourself surprised. Someone may behave very differently from what you had previously expected, based on hearing a voice over the phone or from someone else's reported experience. (We take up the important issue of surprises during negotiation and how to handle them in Chapter 11.)

Don't take the information you've assembled about your future negotiating partner as absolute truth. Leave room for the unexpected. Then, by preparing for a variety of possible scenarios, you'll be ready to pull out a presentation and response you're sure are most appropriate for the particular circumstance.

Also, since sometimes known personality types can dramatically change their negotiating styles on you, especially when under pressure (such as Butterfly to Steamroller), you'd be smart to prepare for a whole gallery of different characters, including some of the surprise "sprites" we described in Chapter 5.

Like individuals, corporations and groups often have established, distinctive personalities or cultures that determine their negotiating styles. Some can be regimented and formal; others rough, tough, hardlining; still others unconventional, even zany (such as firms that still continue a youthful startup energy and style even when they've gone public and are listed on a stock exchange). Figure that into your scene-setting.

Since you cannot expect to modify their ongoing style much by anything you do or say, your scenarios should focus sensibly on how you can adapt your own personality to merge successfully with theirs. This isn't selling out; it is good strategy in giving a sense of comfort that will increase trust when you get around to negotiating. At a company where negotiating with others is a primary activity, you must match its outlook and values.

Remember that people working for companies or representing groups are expected to follow the set style as well as the party line. Sales personnel reflect this conformity, particularly if they received intensive preparatory training. When you're going to negotiate with them, whether over a business or a personal matter, take this into consideration.

> The thing that first really impressed me the most about the place where I work now is how they put a lot of effort initially in showing you exactly how they want you to sell their products. They expected us to represent them always as concerned, caring individuals who reflect the integrity and very human qualities of the corporation itself.
>
> They showed several training films, gave us audiotapes to take home or travel around with, and put on several day-long workshops using intensive role playing. By the end of that two-week period, I felt totally programmed to sell for them out in the world. I was comfortable with this persona they'd given me, and I liked theirs too. I knew I could now go out and negotiate with prospective customers in complete confidence.

The Negotiation Climate

At this stage, anticipate closely how any known or predicted personal or situational variables might enter into scenarios you construct. For instance, how the age, ethnicity, professional ID, and regional origin of your future negotiating partner might affect the climate of the meeting. Becoming highly sensitized now to significant differences between you and the other side enables you to construct scenes where things go right or wrong depending on your words and actions and responses.

Consider the possibility, for instance, that the other side is likely to prejudge you for whatever reasons and be cold and suspicious, or hot and angered—or believe that you're going to act that way. If so, you'll want to try to defuse prior misunderstandings and prejudices as soon as possible in the actual negotiation, if you're going to get anywhere. Your scenario anticipation should focus on contriving strategies to do this. Sketch out different combinations of variables and imagine how each scenario then might play out.

If the negotiation is over some tension-filled matter, it will be hard for both sides to be open and candid, especially if they feel hostile toward each other. On the other hand, if the meeting is to discuss a possible business deal, the climate can start out with pleasantries and overall accord.

Anticipate the negotiating climate as you might do weather forecasts. There are particular likelihoods of certain favorable and unfavorable occurrences happening. Be prepared for all sorts of eventualities.

Scripts

Contriving a variety of possible scenes gives you a good understanding of what consequences are most likely to come from particular actions. You must at all times know how you might react to somebody else's action, and how somebody else might react to some action of yours. It's an If-I-say-this-then-he-will-do-that kind of situation.

Before you strategize in detail the negotiation ahead of you, set aside plenty of time to play with all the known or anticipated elements. Construct the scenes that could be. Do some dialogue between you and an imagined person. Or write it down, which can actually be fun when you see how the words and "business" start looking real on paper, like a play or movie script.

Outline the plot and start filling it in. You can use a tape recorder to rehearse impromptu or written-out scenes to help you get into the role and discourse. Do your opening presentation, for instance. Answer questions that the other side might put to you. You'll acquire greater ease as you keep working at it. And play the tape back so you can listen to yourself talking. Watch out for repeated words and expressions (all those annoying, meaningless *you know* fillers), awkward pauses (the *umms*), uncertain pronunciation, and words you stumble over. Start cleaning up your verbal act so that you'll be smooth and polished when you go in—if that's how you aim to be. (In certain negotiations, you may want to seem hesitant, nervous, or upset.)

Ask a willing friend or relative—someone you feel comfortable with, who won't be uptight or judgmental—to portray either you or your negotiating partner in a particular manner. Describe the Steamroller, Datacrat, Butterfly, and the Mr./Ms. Nice Guy, and give them a choice in roles to start with.

It will be useful for you sometimes to enact the other side, to help you "get into their shoes." When someone plays you, watch and listen closely. Even if you haven't asked them to show you some weaknesses in how you present yourself or to point out undesirable mannerisms (including sloppy speech habits), they may do so now.

This is time well spent. By multiplying the number of choices in actions that might be taken and then increasing your understanding of probable consequences, you'll be able to spot the negative ones and pick the ones most likely to succeed, which you can then focus on.

You can have fun anticipating various scenarios. By the time your negotiation comes around, you should feel eager to go—and prepared for anything.

Know Thy Hot and Cold Buttons

People—sometimes even their very presence—can annoy us in a negotiation, often for no reason. Perhaps we already have an unpleasant history with them. Perhaps they simply remind us of someone else we dislike or with whom we are uncomfortable. Whatever the impetus, almost as soon as they open their mouths, what they say may trigger an angry or fearful response in us, and we may either feel like exploding or become remote and chilly. At this point, we can readily forget our goals and our agenda, and begin to lose control in the negotiation.

An important component in becoming a conscious, competent negotiator is reacquainting yourself with your hot and cold buttons. Realize that in any negotiation, but especially a tense one, your negotiating partner may deliberately or unintentionally press some of them and set you off. Use the preparation stage to desensitize yourself to possible verbal assaults and insults, outright or subtle, intended or not. Learn to note what was said but not to overtly react to it.

To be fully prepared to negotiate at any time for anything, make a list of various comments—perhaps things people have said to you in the past—that almost invariably elicit a defensive response on your part. Remarks, for instance, such as:

- "Oh, I didn't expect them to send a woman."
- "Aren't you too young to be handling a serious and complex matter like this?"
- "I really can't take anybody from California seriously, you know."
- "You should go home and talk this over with your husband and then get back to us."
- "Sorry, but we know from our experience in hiring women that blondes have a better record than brunettes in selling our line of goods."

In such circumstances you may feel understandably indignant. You want to shoot back after someone has tried to shoot you down. Two of my mental billboards come to mind:

> FIGHTING FIRE WITH FIRE ONLY CREATES ASHES.
> TWO PEOPLE CAN'T GO CRAZY AT THE SAME TIME.

In partnership negotiation, you prepare yourself for effective negotiating, not for combat. You do this in part by looking upon negotiation as an opportunity to reach an agreement to conduct future business or to resolve past grievances, not as a way to arouse or continue hostilities. And you do this also by steadying your nerves so that nothing the other side can say will make you furious or get you to feel and act wounded.

Also, prepare to watch for hot and cold reactions from the people with whom you negotiate. Unless you intend to create a victim-victor climate, avoid tampering with your partner's buttons.

Sometimes, though, we offend someone unknowingly. How would you know if you inadvertently push any of these reaction buttons in the person on the other side? Be sensitive to a sudden shift in climate, going from pleasant to adversarial, from warm to cold; to a difference in that person's face, perhaps becoming either rigid or trembling; to a voice changing in tone or eyes regarding you with a different look. The negotiation itself may become blocked, even seem hopeless, with your partner perhaps acting anxious to end it and depart.

Innumerable causes for hot-button pushing crop up in business situations. In your preparations, anticipate items in your presentation or discussion that are either guaranteed to perturb or else possibly may do so. Here are just a few examples of circumstances that you must now inform your partner about, and expect to get heat over them:

- Costs have doubled since your last meeting.
- You will be in Germany during the upcoming sales conference.
- The materials you promised are no longer available.
- You can't meet the delivery date.
- The favored assistant has left your firm.

In personal relationships, whenever there are conflicts hot buttons tend to get triggered, deliberately or not, because often there are intense feelings between the people involved. If you're negotiating some issue that's causing friction or disturbance, and start picking up indications that something has gone awry, you can attempt to amend the circumstance by asking your partner if you've said or done anything to cause concern or annoyance—and say that you did not intend doing so. Even if giving offense is denied, your very acknowledgment of the possibility may help get things back on track.

Don't Be a Judge; Be an Observer!

So often people put themselves behind the eightball by being judgmental—even prejudicial—figuring in advance how someone really shouldn't think this or do that or be in such-and-such a position. As you anticipate scenarios, be very attentive to any tendency in your thoughts or feelings to become holier-than-thou. You may see your way as the only way. Other people pick that up as a moralizing or a condescending attitude on your part. Not only will they probably take offense but they may wish to retaliate in kind by judging you and your position. And neither may look any better to them than they do to you. So what have you gained?

Remember that if you start judging people when you negotiate, you'll put yourself in a position without options. You're sure to lose, especially if you allow that person, or your righteous anger about that person, to push any of your hot buttons.

Your anticipating scenarios should take into account who you are. Base your knowledge on past experiences and feelings. For instance, ask yourself questions like these:

1. What personality types are easiest for me to get along with? Even though I mix amicably, how will I deftly direct my negotiating toward achieving my goal while making sure that I am also considering their interests and needs?

2. Which personality types are diametrically opposite to my way of thinking, of doing, of negotiating, of being? What sorts of things might I talk about with them?

What if you just can't like the person, no matter how hard you work at it? Come up with scenarios in which your negotiating partner just goes out of his or her way to remain unreachable or unlikable. If your goal is important to you, start directing your scenarios away from having an agreeable relationship and into a strategy that brings results you're after.

When negotiating with difficult people, keep in mind that you don't have to like them to negotiate successfully and thereby achieve your goals. Though partnership negotiation blossoms when there's rapport between the two sides, it also works when the focus is entirely on getting something settled.

A "Higher Authority"

When I was a college student earning money by selling book sets from door to door during the daytime, I learned something early about how the person you're negotiating with can put off or end any deal by appealing to a more potent person who's just not around at the time. I would show my samples to Asian women staying home with their children. They would nod and smile, and tell me shyly that only their husbands could make such important decisions.

At first I felt I was wasting my time. But then, to my amazement, orders started pouring in. It was obvious that when the man of the house came in the door that night, his wife would show him the beautiful brochure and simply tell him, "We are going to buy this set of books!"

So all is not lost, in other words, when someone begins referring to some higher authority when you're negotiating. But you have to sell them first. And then make sure you do the follow-up with those other people if you don't get any response.

Sometimes you will negotiate your fingers to the bone and find out at the end of all your work that the person you've been talking with is not the real decision maker. And you didn't know this ahead of time. Your homework somehow didn't reveal that important point. That's why in doing your preparatory research and networking, you want to make sure that you'll be talking to the right person or people. Or, if not, that the ones you talk to will have appropriate access to the higher-ups who actually make decisions.

Keep in mind that someone who fails to make an on-the-spot decision and defers to another's authority or authorization may not be telling the whole truth. So you may want to put your all into a presentation in the near-certainty that if you impress and influence this person, the word will get passed along or upstairs, and the approval of the person you met is the necessary key element.

In designing scenarios, always include one or several with people who listen to your brilliant presentation, thank you, and then say you'll have to go through it all again with some other person or entity with the power to make things happen. You will learn ways to find out as soon as possible when initiating negotiation whether this person has any clout or not, and if so, to what degree. You can devise gracious ways not to show your disappointment or irritation while making sure that your goal can be pursued further up the chain of command.

Sometimes you will want to use higher authority to your own advantage during a negotiation, especially if someone springs some terms or solution you cannot, or don't want to, decide right then. Higher authority also makes a convenient and nice way to say no later, over the phone. You can maintain a good working relationship with someone, and let the "boss" be the heavy. Therefore, one of your scenarios could be backing away with that exit line while holding on to your credibility.

Preparing the "Three Yes Questions" Scenario

Always expect that you could get a strong no from the other side. By doing so, you will arm yourself with what I call the Three Yes Questions—three questions about your own position that you can ask your opposite one after another in the certainty that you will get a yes response for each of them. These questions must be devised in the preparation stage, when you are anticipating scenarios.

For instance, suppose you are going in to ask your boss for a raise. In anticipating scenarios that might unfold, you must concern yourself with the possibility, or even probability, that he or she will resist your request. The litany of poor indicators begins: The economy is bad, the company's earnings are low, your job evaluation was not 100 percent perfect, you don't take enough work home, as others do.

Now you've got to build your strong case before you get a firm no. First, you must put your boss in the right frame of mind to regard you as a valuable asset. How will you do this? By coming up with three questions to which only a yes answer is the appropriate response. Make sure that this will be so. The questions could go like this:

1. Do you agree that I am at my desk to work every morning before 9 o'clock?

2. Do you believe that my work shows that I am wholly committed to the success of this company?

3. Are you sure that if you gave me a job to do, I would put in maximum effort to get it done on time, and turn it in in a wholly professional form?

If you get your three yeses, you probably have underscored your loyalty and the quality of your work. Your boss may also begin thinking of how the responses might go if the same questions were asked of associates of yours who may earn more than you now but are obviously less valuable to the company. (You may even design your questions with this contrast in mind.) You can now proceed to the issue of your meriting that well-earned raise. And maybe also be kept in mind for a future promotion.

Pre-negotiating over the Phone

Increasingly, people form important business associations wholly over the telephone, and then negotiate major deals. Conference calls and speaker phones joining two or more parties have become routine.

Initial interest and trust is established by your voice and the content of your message. This skill in negotiating over the phone is quite amazing when you think that, in meeting people directly, 65 percent of our response has to do with reading body language, 30 percent with the way people say what they say, and only 5 percent with the content of what they say.

In telephone negotiations you must concentrate completely on what you say and what you hear from the other side. You will also pick up other auditory clues: background music, asides to people coming in and out, coughing and throat clearing, breathing in and out, paper rustling, tapping, and pauses—those empty spaces between words and between sentences, both theirs and yours. You will learn a great deal about your opposite in any negotiation by talking with him or her over the phone, such as in calling to set up a meeting to negotiate. This initial contact can indicate the scenario likely to transpire when you finally meet with this person.

But using telephones also can pose a number and variety of

problems. When you're going to be negotiating over the telephone, you'll want to consider points like these as you anticipate scenarios:

- Being put on the speaker phone unexpectedly and not knowing who else is in the room
- Suspecting that people in the room are making face or hand gestures to signal the speaker about how to react
- Getting disconnected in the midst of a crucial part of the discussion
- Getting distractions at your end or at your partner's end that interfere with or interrupt the conversation flow
- Strange reactions indicated by silence or tone of voice that can't be interpreted without seeing facial expressions
- Incoming calls that compete for your or your partner's attention, including call-waiting beeps
- Being told "I'll call you right back" when you were halfway through an important pitch
- Being put on hold and then waiting for several minutes, only to get disconnected
- Having a bad connection with a lot of static or faint sound transmission, making it impossible to hear clearly and accurately
- Talking with someone who is hearing-disabled, or being yourself hard of hearing

Negotiating Just for the Hell of It

Sometimes you may know in advance that the whole thing is futile, you can't possibly get what you're asking for. You know it. They know it too (or some of them, certainly). But you're going to ask anyway. You'll go ahead with it deliberately. For a conscious purpose.

Under certain circumstances, you might wish to consider applying for a position, making a proposal, or undertaking some other negotiation in which there is clearly little if any hope for a favorable outcome. By doing so, you may get your foot in the door to places and people you might not otherwise see or meet. You simply regard this as a strategy for making connections. The down-side: be careful not to waste people's time.

I like the challenge of negotiating for almost anything. Even when I suspect I'll bomb out, I usually look forward to enjoying myself and learning something useful from the entire experience, from preparation through that final no. I tell myself ahead of time, "What can I lose?"

Laying the Groundwork

One of my interviewees for this book mentioned a highly useful image for a negotiating tactic. She called it nemowashi, which in Jap-anese means "preparing the soil." Before you're ready to plant any-thing—a seed, a flower in bloom, a shrub or tree—it's wise to get a tool and dig around in the ground, loosening up the soil and letting the air in. That way, whatever you put into the ground is more likely to take root and thrive.

In cultivating business or personal relationships with people, design some of your conversations so that you'll prepare the soil for introducing, subtly at first, the goal you have in mind. In a sense this is skillful manipulation, but if your persuasion allows the other person eventually to come around to your way of thinking, and even be unexpectedly happy in it, all the groundwork has been worthwhile.

In your scenario making, think of how you might try some deft nemowashi on people you deal with and want to influence, in the workplace or at home. You might even consider using some of this humanizing technique with hidebound bureaucrats enmeshed in rules and paperwork—by phone call or letter. You may be amazed at how well this paced, gentle persuasion can sometimes work in your behalf.

▬ EXERCISE ▬

1. Think of an upcoming negotiation. Write down a few sentences you might say on behalf of your side. Opposite each sentence, write two or three possible reactions or responses you might elicit from your negotiating partner.

   Keep in mind:

The most likely situation

The least likely situation

The most probable objection

The most likely counteroffer

Then, given each of these scenarios, what are your options?

2. Never end an "anticipation review" without imagining what I call "flying balls of garbage from outer space." What is the most unlikely, bizarre, or unforeseen circumstance that could occur during this negotiating session?

9
THE TACTICS OF
TIME, PLACE, AGENDA

"There is no right or wrong, only consequences."
—E. Morler

A few months ago I wanted to negotiate an important deal with a client company I'd worked with before. The human resource department manager who handles contracts for training seminars is a Butterfly. When I first tried to propose the new series, I took Beth out to lunch. Naturally, she loved that. But she had to keep checking out the people who came through the door, while she flirted with the waiter and chatted with the couple at the table next to ours. The meeting was hopeless.

The second time I got an appointment with Beth at her office. But her phone kept ringing and she kept answering it. Each call meant she had to discuss the weather, tell a joke, laugh at the caller's joke, and relay the latest gossip or a new creative idea. People kept wandering in with memos or special requests, interrupting her attention to anything I was saying. The entire half-hour scheduled for me was wasted.

I finally hit upon a solution: I'd ask her out for a picnic lunch. It was late spring and the weather was almost guaranteed to be pleasant. We had an hour and a half of quality time together, without social distractions and interruptions. It allowed me to propose in detail an exciting new program. Beth's enthusiasm quickly ignited once she could focus on what I had to say. Three days later, I got the contract.

. .

In this sequence, Judith, the trainer, didn't take Beth's distractions personally. Judith observed Beth's style and situation, and shifted her strategy to employ tactics that would gain her objective. Judith arranged settings where Beth could refuel her self-esteem by showing, at the restaurant and at the office, how many people liked her and how important she was. Probably, this was necessary to do for Judith to establish trust with Beth. If Judith had initially tried to isolate Beth, she might have failed to elicit Beth's commitment to the new program.

Scheduling the date, time, and location of a negotiating discussion is not a simple matter. If we act headlong, without carefully strategizing the logistics, we may schedule a meeting that will cancel out any advantages we might have had from our other preparations. Or, if we quickly agree to any and all arrangements the other side makes—happy, maybe, to be relieved of that responsibility—we may be stuck with a time and place that are wrong for our purposes and defeat our goals. Timing and environment can work for us or against us when we negotiate.

The Pre-negotiation Phase

When you arrange time, place, and agenda, what you're really doing is negotiating for the best climate. Who is in charge of setting up the first face-to-face meeting? The person or group that proposes the circumstances puts itself in a superior position. Expectably, that side will try to design and control the proceedings.

But wait a minute. Who wants to negotiate the most? Which side is more anxious to make a deal, resolve some conflict, come to terms? That party, rather like a suitor or supplicant, feels obligated to make things attractive to the other side. They make the big effort; they travel; and they pay the bills. However, even if your negotiating partner proposes the date, arranges for an agreeable meeting spot, constructs the agenda, and underwrites the cost, you are under no obligation to accord him or her more control over what happens at the meeting.

Supplicant negotiators can make deals seem sweet. It's like selling, where the eager salesperson pursues the potential, but reluctant buyer. Or the reverse, where the avid would-be buyer courts or hounds the person with some scarce and valued commodity she's not willing to sell. Consider this: when you accept to be treated, you accept the "owe you one" position. When you treat, you are in control; or it might say, "I know I need to convince you, and this is my first concession."

Every action will produce a reaction and consequences. Where there is unequal interest in negotiating, the power or trump card is held by the side that controls what the other side wants.

Equals as Partners

If the need is a toss-up—if both parties are equally interested or concerned—the dynamics switch. For instance, if you want to sell and the other side wants to buy, you'll probably have little problem working out where and when you are going to meet and agreeing on the agenda. If you are meeting in some neutral territory, you'll probably go Dutch, or treat each other to a round of drinks. You can ease into partnering negotiations naturally, as long as each side has honorable intentions. You can be open, but appropriately cautious.

Even partnership negotiation, however, has subtle struggles for control. Setting up a meeting's details can have symbolic importance from the very start. Do not be so desperate to negotiate that you agree to meet any time, at any place, to follow any schedule that the other side proposes. You will relinquish your control over the negotiation by allowing the opposite side to arrange everything without considering your suggestions or desires. They may appear to be overly generous. You may be flattered. In those circumstances, look for hidden agendas.

You may not be in a position, financially or geographically, to take charge of setting up the negotiations. You may wish to agree to their arrangements. If and when you do, consider how the choice of time and place might affect your position. In your preparations, find out as many details as you can. Recognize your own vulnerabilities. For instance, a breakfast meeting might be scheduled for the crack of dawn, and you're a night person—normally nonfunctional until mid-morning. Or you might be going to a place where the air will be thick with smoke, and you're so allergic to it that you'll spend your time coughing and wiping your eyes. Or you always have trouble hearing what is said in a crowded restaurant with lousy acoustics. If you do not set up the meeting, make your needs clear to those who do.

Consider the Time Frame

Keep in mind the length of time the negotiations will probably take. Consider your partner's style: a Steamroller may take only a few minutes to reach a conclusion; a Datacrat or a Nice Guy needs much longer.

Some negotiations take five minutes; others take five months or even five years. Complex corporate undertakings may involve wearisome months of haggling over terms and conditions, filling out reams of bureaucratic forms, conferring with lawyers about contracts, sending out bids, interviewing and hiring personnel, making inspection tours and quality-control decisions, and securing suppliers. Other deals are settled with a simple handshake and no forms, or even receipts. Don't forget the power of the written word. If a handshake is what they suggest, use "higher authority" and say, "I know your word is good, but I have this manager (or board) who must have a signature."

When you intend to negotiate, first make a realistic estimate of how long it will take either to reach an agreement or to call it off. Then estimate how long it will take you to prepare to uphold your position in the proceedings ahead. You probably should add some leeway to that figure, in case some unforeseen distraction comes up. A Butterfly, for instance, usually needs more time to "play."

Give your partner a choice of several dates and times. Don't offer a Datacrat more than two choices; she'll get into a "what if" mode and delay the negotiations. On the other hand, always give Steamrollers at least three choices.

Selecting the Place

Try to propose several possible meeting places appropriate for the matters to be discussed and geographically convenient for both sides.

Often, people like excuses to leave their own offices. Datacrats need to have a quiet place where there is little distraction and few, if any, interruptions. If too much is going on around them, they will be unable to concentrate and will become irritable and anxious to leave.

Steamrollers can negotiate almost anywhere as long as not a second is wasted. They will be happiest if they are able to do other things while talking with you. They might propose, "Why don't you drive me to the airport, and we'll discuss it along the way?" If this is your only chance, take it.

For Butterflies, look for a "warm climate"—a nice place where you can personally connect in your first meeting. You may not get a lot accomplished in this encounter, but you will establish a relationship.

Nice Guys may seem happy to be anywhere you propose. But you will score big with them if you give them options and ask them to choose. Because of their amiability, their likes and dislikes are often taken for granted. By showing them special attention, you will gain extra, subtle points.

The appropriate settings and climates for different negotiating styles can also change from the beginning of your business relationship—when your success is absolutely crucial—to the point of closure and agreement—when both partners should know and trust each other far better than at the start.

The Etiquette of Logistics

If you meet in a restaurant, who pays the bill? You, if you're the person or side who has selected this place for the meeting, who is seemingly more in need of a positive outcome. Your negotiating partner may wish to share the cost; you then have the option of accepting. It's a sign, possibly, of equal interest. If the other side invites you and pays, be sure you don't feel obligated to give in on a negotiating point—don't succumb to a business "seduction."

Other neutral settings may include a park or other secluded setting—particularly if you are trying to iron out grievances in a relationship. If you are holding a group meeting, meeting rooms are often available in public buildings such as libraries or museums, commercial structures such as banks, and shopping malls.

One of the best places to negotiate can be in a car—yours or your partner's. People searching for a site often forget this possibility. You can drive to a quiet spot, taking whatever materials you will need with you. Some business people even use recreational vehicles for this purpose, converting them into convenient mobile offices.

If You Go to Their Place

It is widely believed that power usually resides with the side whose place has been selected for the negotiation. At the meeting this side will demonstrate that they are in charge—they are in control of their environment.

If they are the boss, they'll have subordinates serving them, answering phones, relaying important messages, bringing in coffee and doughnuts. They can take phone calls when they are supposed to be talking with you, demonstrating that whoever you are and whatever you have to say is not as important as somebody and something else. They expect you to be impressed with their power, and the negotiation between you may reflect this supposed advantage.

Tradition says that you should always try to get the other side to come to your place. I don't always agree with that point of view, which is given as advice in many books and talks about negotiation tactics. If you're clever, you can often turn a meeting at the other side's office to your own advantage.

Sometimes, in fact, I *choose* to go to their place. Here's why:

I get a lot of environmental clues about who and what they are. We women are usually better than men at picking up on the details around us. There's the physical structure itself: the building, the foyer, elevators or stairway, hallways, the entrance to the office I go to, signs on doors. Is there a receptionist, a secretary, an assistant? How does my negotiating partner treat these assistants?

Then I watch the process of receiving me there—how I'm handled. Does the person I am to meet come out to get me and walk me into the inner sanctum or meeting room? Does he or she stay behind the desk, as if defending it? Or come around to greet me and try to put me at ease?

I note the decor in the office, the size and composition of the desk (solid wood or veneer? metal?): I study the books on the shelf, see the view from the window, look around for clutter, dust, spots on the carpet. I learn things about them from the pictures on the walls, from photos and placards on their desk. I become a personality detective. How could I possibly get the same information if I see them elsewhere?

Most of all, I like the freedom to exercise a particular strategy that women don't use often enough. Walking out. I do this when I feel the need of some cooling-off time—time to gain perspective, to regain control, to think before making any decisions. This is hard to do when you're negotiating in your own office. You can't easily get up and leave. You have to persuade or ask your negotiating partner to go. In someone else's office, I can say, "Well, it looks like we're bogged down here. Let's both do some more homework, and maybe get back together again sometime." Then I walk. I take control by walking. And as I start walking out, they may say, "Wait! Maybe we can discuss this some more. . . ."

If I handle it right, I can control the situation when I'm in someone else's environment. That extends to exercising some say in how they want to seat me. For instance, sometimes I've been put initially in a seat where the sun was in my eyes; I couldn't look at the partners but they could look at me. Some people I've seen in that position don't move; they act as if they have no right to object to discomfort. But I put up my hand—I call it my police gesture—and say, "Stop! Before we start talking, can we pull down that shade?" Or I'll move my chair and say, "I'm doing this because I can't see your face."

You've got to take your position when something like this happens to you. Often, the other side has deliberately set it up in a particular way as a test for you. For instance, they may give you a huge chair— so big you almost disappear in it. I just say, "I prefer sitting in that chair," and choose a better territory. If I look around and find no chair that I want to sit in, I may then go out to the secretary and say, "Excuse me, may I take this chair? I prefer sitting in it."

I have a friend who takes a special folding chair with her when she goes to meetings. It's lightweight, beautiful, and expensive. If she doesn't like the chair offered to her, she sets hers up right next to the person she's come to talk with. In that succinct, nonverbal way she's let them know that she's just as much in charge of things as they are.

If you're negotiating for a job, you'll want to pay close attention to the ambience of the place where you'd be working. If you're a

Butterfly and you enter a cool, high-tech climate filled with Data-crats, it should alert you to adjustments you'd have to make to work there.

If It's at Your Place

It's true that, by being on your own turf for a negotiation, you can exercise control over various factors. But be aware of disadvantages: if your place is not first-class—even close—and theirs is, you may lose by sheer contrast. You won't be able to match their apparent success.

Increasingly, people with small, independent businesses of their own use their homes or apartments as offices. If you do, and you have suggested that an initial negotiation meeting for professional purposes take place there, make sure you use space that is dedicated to your business and away from visual and auditory distractions.

Refrain from "over-hostessing." Your focus should be on the business at hand, not on providing a nice tea service. Women tend, of course, to give in to the expectation that they must be food and drink providers. Carefully consider whether or not this is the image you wish to present in a negotiation.

And what about smoking? If you smoke and they smoke, or if neither side smokes, no problem. If one side smokes and the other does not, there is a problem in the negotiations. One person's habit or objection may be a source of annoyance and irritation to the other. It's best, then, to acknowledge the issue—in advance—as a mutual one, and arrange appropriate smoking breaks in an area removed from the nonsmoker.

Ever Heard of Carbo-Sabotage?

People hosting a meeting, at their place or in some neutral ground where they're footing the bill, can control what you put in your body—and brain—if you let them. Let me tell you a tale about this.

My Citicorp team was negotiating in Japan. The situation caught me off guard—an example of not having enough advance information. Four of us Americans met with six Japanese men. They put out a beautiful spread: pastries, espresso, all kinds of rich foods. We were thrilled. During the nine-hour negotiation, food kept coming, and we gorged ourselves while drinking soda pop and coffee. Around 4 o'clock I began realizing that our team was both hyper and tired, experiencing a lot of highs and lows. On the other hand, the Japanese were calm and collected. And then I realized it: all day long they had drunk tea and eaten bland sugar-free food. They very nearly got us.

From then on, whenever I am supposed to negotiate, I watch carefully what I eat beforehand. Your chemical balance is important. Every morsel of your mental and physical energy has to be focused on your job.

When negotiating, you can also be seduced by ambience.

They called in the morning and asked me to meet them that very night at a restaurant renowned for its French cuisine—where I'd never been. We'd have a few drinks and then dinner, and all the while we could talk about the deal they wanted to make with me. The background? For twenty years I'd been holding onto a business property in a seedy downtown area, netting in rent monies only enough to pay taxes. The lot value hadn't noticeably escalated. I was getting restless, but hadn't put the place up for sale yet.

Somehow these two fellows found out about me. They had formed their own architectural partnership, one said over the phone. They'd like to buy my building and upgrade it, converting the four stories into lofts for artists and craftsmen. I looked forward to meeting these young, gung-ho idealists.

Well, they wined and dined me. Completely charmed me. They detailed their plans: downstairs there'd be a cafe where creative types could hang out—drink espresso, eat borscht and pasta, show off etchings and watercolors, read their poems, play zithers and recorders. The kind of place I would have loved forty years ago, when I was a young textile sculptor. I was amazed when I finally looked at my watch and saw that it was eleven—an hour past my normal bedtime. We still hadn't really negotiated.

"Well, guys . . ." I started to say, yawning. Right then the one in the gray sweater pulled out a typed agreement. "This preliminary contract contains our bid," he said. "You'll see we're offering you a very fair price." Indeed they were; it was five thousand more than what a similar place had sold for a half-year earlier. I liked them, trusted them, wanted them to be successful. I knew they'd have to invest effort as well as capital in their dream. They'd made me feel like I'd even be a part of it all.

So I signed the papers, took my copy, and drove home. I must have been brain-dead. Next morning when I read the front page of our local paper I saw that the city council had just approved a development center in my section for upscale housing for urbanites weary of commuting. Lot values were expected to double in value immediately. I got on the phone right away with a realtor friend and then my lawyer. No use: that agreement hastily and trustingly signed the previous night was a valid legal document. I'd been zapped by Bordeaux wine and my own foolish romanticism, which still lurks around in the nighttime.

Ever since then, I've done all those *what ifs*: If I had only asked to think it over for a day or two. If I'd kept informed of the latest urban planning proposals. If I'd just gone to bed as usual, instead of out to dinner, where I'd been swept away by the lovely ambience of that meeting. But I let them select the time and place, and they came in with their own hidden agenda. They renovated the old building, made fancy offices for themselves, and installed a pricey boutique on the ground floor.

On Negotiating with Drink in Hand

Often I look like I'm playing when I am really negotiating. That's true of a lot of people. But when we are socializing while going about our business, it's smart to keep our wits about us.

People often negotiate by drinking together. Certainly that went on in my corporate days in New York. I noticed as I began my job as a Citicorp vice-president that important information was disseminated and decisions made elsewhere—during after-hours get-togethers at the club across the street, where the "inner circle" regularly met. I saw I had to go out boozing with the boys, even though I wasn't a drinker. That put me further on the "outside." (In those years, choosing not to drink was seen as strange for an executive.)

I decided to drink with the boys without really "drinking." Since they went to the same bar all the time, I visited the place on my own first, and introduced myself to the manager as the new member of the Citicorp "team," whom he knew well. "I don't drink alcohol," I explained to him, "but I don't want to make a big deal out of it. When I come in with the guys, I will always say to the waiter, 'I want the same.' Now, I don't want any remarks from him, ever. What I'll always expect to get is club soda on ice with a lemon twist."

That was how I negotiated my future at Citicorp. I set up exactly what I needed so I could be part of a group that exchanged information and made decisions.

Ironically, I got a reputation as a masterful drinker. This all came back to me a few years ago, when on an airplane I met a man who'd been on that same Citicorp team. "What have you been up to?" he asked. "The guys still talk about you, Nicole! How you drank everyone under the table! And, the next day, you could tell us exactly what we decided and what the insider scoop was. Remember?" I just smiled. Today, of course, I simply say, "I don't drink," and leave it at that. Always be wary of the effect alcohol has on you and on your negotiating partners. It's a potent "third party" that will be present during the negotiation.

The Agenda

The issue of agenda setting is an important facet of preparing to negotiate. There are always several agendas: yours, your negotiating partner's, and perhaps one or two hidden ones. An agenda is a structured plan to consider or act upon. The official agenda for the meeting is the one held in common. It will be in writing, particularly if the meeting is a formal negotiation. You'll have one of your own, with possibly several different items that you may keep in your head but will present, and promote and push, in the discussion. Your negotiating partner will probably have an agenda, too. Hidden agendas aren't talked about, but usually emerge sometime during the discussion, to be spotted now by astute negotiating partners who may already have anticipated their presence.

Let's think of an example here. An agenda for a small business meeting might be to decide how the public relations will be handled in the next six months. Participating negotiators would be a contracted publicity person and the entrepreneur. A formal written agenda would be provided, as I'll describe in detail shortly. The common agenda would be to support the company's recent targeted marketing plan with publicity in the appropriate local papers. The entrepreneur's *direct* agenda is to get a specific plan in action by the end of the month. The publicist's *direct* agenda is to present ideas that are do-able in a short period of time. The entrepreneur's *hidden* agenda is to ask for more work and a rush job without increasing the monthly retainer fee. The publicist's *hidden* agenda is to extend the short-term projects into long-term ones to ensure a renewal of the yearly contract.

A business meeting—particularly with more than two participants—is usually more productive when a formal agenda is set and followed. When negotiating, it's important to stay on track if some resolution is to be reached. An agenda also provides a rational structure that will remind the two sides in a conflict that they are there to resolve their differences. Discussions between two people, whether for business or personal reasons, would rarely necessitate a written agenda given to the partner at the meeting—unless you both find it helpful in covering all points. In situations where emotional issues have created a conflict, an explicit plan outlining the discussion might appear pretentious or offensive. Yet if you wish to exercise some control (if only self-control) in a potentially volatile negotiation, you might well want to design a progression of the talk between you, in hopes of keeping it on track and beneficial.

A formal agenda is set down on paper and duplicated so that everyone attending the meeting will get one, preferably in advance. The sequence of dialogues at the meeting is outlined in this general way:

  I. Introduction
 II. Agreement on agenda
III. Purpose of meeting (summarized)
 IV. Presentation of side 1
  V. Presentation of side 2

VI. Discussion of two sides' points of view
VII. Stage of decision, agreement, or resolution
VIII. Scheduling of next meeting
IX. Adjournment

Meetings often go better if one person assumes the role of discussion leader, conductor, or moderator. This does not mean that he or she cannot participate in presentations or debate. But it does mean that there is responsibility for maintaining the agenda, enforcing courtesy (controlling interruptions and outbursts, for example), timing the stages, and furthering the action by pushing it along.

How an Agenda Should Work (Ideally)

The introduction phase allows people to introduce themselves: name and position. It is not just a nicety and ice-breaker; it provides crucial information. Some important meetings are allowed to take place without everyone really knowing who all the others present are. People who come early (or are on time) can introduce themselves to each other, of course. But people who arrive late, or if the meeting starts promptly, won't benefit from that social exchange.

Timing can be imbedded in the agenda schedule by allotting a specific number of minutes to each stage. Or, if the meeting is to start promptly at ten o'clock, say, the times for each stage to begin would be noted: 10:10, 10:25, and so on. This form becomes confusing if a meeting begins late or a particular segment runs overlong—though that should be avoided, allowing limitations of only several minutes more. If an ending time is set (which is a good idea, for it puts pressure on people to get something accomplished within a definite time frame), the agenda setter would work backwards from that time, designating appropriate time periods for each phase of the meeting.

It is customary to assign responsibility for certain agenda stages to particular people. For instance, the meeting moderator would handle stage II by asking whether the people present agree to the written agenda as provided, or if they have suggestions for additional topics to be discussed. Then the moderator moves on to stage III by summarizing briefly the purpose of the meeting.

In stages IV and V, if teams rather than individuals represent the two sides, each will have a leader: side 1 presents the position that is primarily applying for a decision or a resolution that it is hoped will be achieved through discussion with and consideration by side 2. That side may begin with a proposal (positive) or a grievance (negative) aimed at side 2. The negotiating partner (side 2) should refrain from interrupting the presentation with outbursts, rebuttals, or debate. (This issue could be part of the ground rules set up by the moderator when the meeting begins, with all attendees having responsibility for policing it.)

Side 2 gets its turn later to present its point of view. It should initially concentrate on listening attentively to what side 1 is saying, and take notes on points to be brought up later. When side 2 responds in its time, side 1 is likewise expected to listen and take notes, preparing for the discussion or debate period to follow. If a business matter is involved and side 2 is interested, it is then that this side will establish an initial bottom line—the extent to which it is willing to become involved.

If both sides have managed to allow the other to present its case without interruption (difficult indeed to do when a volatile disagreement is being negotiated), and have made real efforts to hear the other position, the discussion period is apt to be fairly rational. It is important to deal with specifics and to avoid generalities that go nowhere.

Stage VI usually constitutes the bulk of the meeting. It can seem to rush past, whether a lot gets said and accomplished or if things bog down. The moderator as time watcher can push the sides first to focus on points of agreement and concessions made. The tougher work follows, dealing with disagreements and rigidly set and held bottom lines. Some issues that seem irreconcilable may have to be tabled for later, so that others perhaps more solvable can be considered.

When the meeting time is limited, time is running short, and the discussion is making little or no progress, stage VII obviously does not occur. At this time the moderator should summarize what has been provisionally agreed upon and what remains to be decided. Then he or she should ask the two sides to consider whether they wish to meet again and carry on the discussion further. If so, in stage VIII a time and place are set between the two sides, and the outline of a new agenda can be agreed upon. Tabled issues may be specifically noted on the agenda. Any additional information, materials, or participants needed in the future meeting will be brought up at this time.

Even though the initial negotiation meeting may have failed to produce a decision or an accord, if it did not end disastrously in a walkout by one or both sides, and if a second meeting has been arranged, there has been some progress. There's still hope for the negotiation process.

Who's Producing the Meeting Agenda?

In many people's minds, producing an agenda, getting approval of it from all persons concerned, and distributing it is a thankless chore. You may not regard it that way. Just as the side that hosts a meeting may have some obvious power, the person or side that puts the agenda together has a certain unstated power. This person may or may not be the moderator. An agenda maker may be an introvert—comfortable with words and paper. A moderator, on the other hand, should be an extrovert—someone who won't be fearful of keeping unruly debaters in line. (It might, as a matter of fact, be fair and appropriate to divide the two responsibilities.)

If you have volunteered for or been asked to produce the agenda, use this job to your advantage. You can strategize within it to construct sequences, such as by introducing subsets A, B, or C within some units. If two groups are involved, you will communicate with people on both teams, and become conversant with personalities, issues, feelings—ending up knowing more, probably, than other people there.

Use the phone to get overall approval of the divisions and timing. If there is time, send copies of the agenda well in advance of the meeting. The top of the page should contain the overall purpose, time, and place of the meeting, with names of attendees. A note can provide directions for getting there, information about parking, and so on. Give your phone number, and ask for any feedback, questions, suggestions, or concerns—anything that might be communicated to the moderator or other side, or might be incorporated into the final agenda to be prepared for the meeting itself, with a copy for each participant.

Organizational considerations may have to be taken up prior to discussion. Remember always the type you're negotiating with. Datacrats want and need the details; Steamrollers will hate them. Send brief memos only, but say you can send more details if requested.

Negotiating an Agenda Without an Appointment

Much of the negotiating we do with other people—and almost all we do within ourselves—is in an impromptu form. We simply go about our business of living, working, and relating and negotiate as things occur that require examining and settling. Our heads are always working on agendas of many kinds, vague or definite; when an urge or necessity comes up to trigger our negotiating interests, we proceed, without announcing it or making a special appointment. And we don't really think of this ongoing, inner and outer decision-making process as negotiation.

Some people—Steamrollers particularly—regularly negotiate in an on-the-run, spur-of-the-moment way. Clearly, it's their way of life. They often expect other people to have the same ability and willingness, so they can't understand it when they face resistance or are asked to make an appointment to discuss the matter they brought up.

Confrontation is a variant form of negotiation. Time, place, and agenda are all set by the initiator, sometimes in an elaborate way and involving other people; but rarely is the other side alerted to the impending event. Confrontation puts the other side immediately in a defensive position because it stands accused of offending the confrontor or someone else. So the ensuing negotiation may become almost a trial, which is scarcely the best atmosphere for partnership negotiation.

You may have to plan some of your own negotiations as confrontations. The other party won't be warned or advised of your intentions. Some examples of this are collecting a long overdue debt, evicting a tenant, or firing an employee.

▪ EXERCISE ▪

Think of some situation confronting you now—in your business or personal life—that needs to be negotiated and resolved. Write it down.

Now, consider the logistic questions for discussing this issue with your negotiating partners.

1. When should you meet?

2. Where should you meet?

3. What time of day is best for your purposes?

4. Who should attend the meeting?

5. Will there be refreshments?

6. How will people be seated?

7. Should you have a formal or an informal agenda?

8. What is your direct agenda?

9. What is your hidden agenda?

10
READYING YOURSELF

"Nothing works unless you do."
—Terry Cole Whittaker

What's my most winning negotiation? Getting the job I have now, as sales manager in a software firm launched a year earlier and growing fast. After getting the interview call, I started to prepare; I studied up about the firm and its products, as well as its main competitors. Fortunately, I already knew quite a bit about computer software—and had opinions about what sells well, and why. I knew I'd be on firm ground there. I also made sure I'd be neatly groomed—the first impression is the right impression—which I'll admit hasn't always been a priority with me. I got a haircut the day before, had my favorite wool dress cleaned—it's a conservative yet warm gray. I even polished my shoes and matching handbag.

My newly done résumé was current and well organized, and featured the background experience relevant to the position while showing a balance of interests, and I had printed it up in magazine type so it would appear ultraprofessional. The morning of the interview, I showered early to have plenty of time, ate a sensible breakfast, then dressed. I put on my makeup deftly, to enhance my features but not bedazzle anyone, and finally sprayed on some subdued cologne. I knew I looked good on the outside—important in selling. Equally important, I felt good about myself on the inside!

At the interview with several people, including the company

president, I spoke clearly, quickly, and to the point without appearing anxious or nervous, covering all aspects of my work career with confidence and ease. If I hadn't taken time to prepare myself, I might not have gotten the job.

I was asked to speak at a convention given by a renowned national charitable organization. The man who had hired me was the husband of a magazine publisher. I often wrote articles for her and knew she wore hats wherever she went—luncheons, business meetings, even on stage when giving speeches. Deciding that I'd please the meeting planner by following his wife's style, I wore a hat—something I do occasionally, but not when I'm doing training. I thought I'd done a great job (and heard so from attendees), and was surprised when I was not invited back for another such occasion. I decided to find out why, and asked the magazine publisher. "Oh, my husband told me that the feedback on you was this: good content, but she seemed just too sophisticated. Her outfit clashed with her down-to-earth message." What a difference a hat made! In planning what to wear, I had chosen to play to the wrong audience.

During the preparation period, you've been readying yourself to negotiate effectively your appointment or meeting. As the time draws near for a major presentation or discussion, you'll want to focus the "package" you are putting together. This package will consist of you, the person, and of the proposal or plan you bring with you that's aimed to sell—not necessarily in a monetary way, but to persuade your negotiating partner to buy into, to agree to. We consider in this chapter the external facets and internal contents of that package. Both are vital elements in achieving your goals in the negotiation.

Creating the right elements and effects for the last stage of your homework have a great deal to do with self-negotiating—with convincing yourself beforehand to put time and effort into doing a super job.

So if you've taken the preparation road this far, why not go a bit further?

Looking Like a Winner

Recently I went to Orlando, Florida, as the keynote speaker at a realtors' convention. As I rode down in the hotel elevator, a woman got on dressed in a perfect golfing outfit. She pulled along a large leather cart, with beautifully crafted golf clubs peeking from the top. In my customary expressive manner—I will talk to anyone, anytime, about almost anything—I said, "Those look like serious golf clubs." She looked at me and smiled. "They are," she said. "I'm not sure that I am a serious player, but looking like one is half the game." I agreed with her; I know it well enough.

Obviously, this golfer has been doing more to win the game than just working on her strokes. Whether it's participating in a game of golf, playing the piano at a recital, designing a marketing plan, or preparing to negotiate for a higher budget, we should look good and dress the part, which means paying attention to our physical appearance.

Remember: strategies, skills, and commitment come together in image creating.

First Impressions Count Most

How many times have you walked into an office, into some meeting, or into a party and made up your mind about the entire place just on the basis of your first, almost instantaneous impression? Either you want to sit down and talk intensively, comfortably, with people about whatever it is you've come for, or else you just want to turn around and go home because you're sure you won't like whatever is going to go on there. Most likely things will go as you felt they would from the start.

We make quick appraisals. In just sixty seconds we make fifteen to twenty-five quick decisions, sizing up both people and environments. And while we're doing that, of course, others may be doing the same with us! Plan your first appearance well. Heed the expression, "You are your most important audiovisual aid." The information you give out must be balanced by the way you do it: how you look, sound, move. Projecting a positive image—in whatever terms are appropriate for the work you do—will give you that special competitive edge you might need in your profession.

What Image Do You Want to Project?

In strategizing our physical self-presentation, we should consider first the goal we want to achieve in the negotiation. The way we appear should be appropriate to that goal. The immediate goal in your self-packaging—much smaller than your overall goal but nonetheless crucial—is to instantly persuade your negotiating partners to reduce their resistance and listen carefully to you.

When I went to Detroit to assist an auto workers' union in preparing to negotiate with management, I knew my favorite corporate-style suit—which surely had won me lots of clients—would instantly create a great gulf between them and me. If I dressed as I would when meeting with their bosses in corporate headquarters, I'd be immediately spotted as an outsider, and meet with suspicion, even hostility. I chose a pantsuit, and rolled up the sleeves of the jacket so I'd look ready to sit right down and work with them. I wore a cotton shirt, not a silk shirt, and shoes with low heels that looked comfortable and safe.

Ask yourself these questions as you think of assembling an outfit, and sift through your wardrobe closet, searching for just the right item for D-Day:

- With whom will I be negotiating?
- What values and norms does that person (or organization) hold near and dear? (For example, conservative or liberal, somber or playful, casual or formal.)
- How do those values get translated nonverbally? In other words, what sensory elements—visual ones especially—would convey pleasing messages to them? Displeasing messages?
- What words describe the company image: current, quality, conservative, innovative, relaxed? Will both my image and my own comfort zone match them?

Images are extremely important to corporations, which spend millions of dollars just to redo their image when they feel it should be updated or changed because its current one seems off the mark.

If you are planning some pitch to a company or association that is obviously image attentive, make sure that you and your presentation are designed to merge agreeably with theirs. You don't want your image to fade into it, but to match it in a way that generates exciting compatibility, a bit like the courtship dance of made-for-each-other mates.

What Role Will You Be Playing?

I have many "looks," and am sure you do too. It's more than having a closetful of clothing we can select from, choosing some item to wear to achieve particular effects. Image combines the visual part of our statement with subliminal signals. In the alchemy of our psyches we put together elements that will convey particular non-verbal messages. By dressing, speaking, moving about in certain ways, we can virtually tell those people we want to impress such divergent character themes as: "I am a serious, very reliable person. Trust me." "You'll find me generous—and awfully fun to be with." "I can be creative yet practical at the same time."

It's good strategy to know what values are important to the other side, and match them in your personal "statement"—your appearance and demeanor when you meet with them to negotiate. If you are not aware that you can bring about such subtle transformations, you might give it a try at your next negotiating session.

It isn't all such hocus-pocus, either. There's a science to it, based on observations, measurable data, behavioral experiments, elaborate surveys. Innumerable articles and books have been written on the psychology of color, shape, and texture. Women's magazines for decades have offered useful tips on improving or altering your self-image. A number of highly reputable and successful people have based entire careers on teaching others to understand how one's appearance—or the appearance of an advertisement or cereal box, a shoe or a bottle, an automobile or book jacket—affects people. All those people are buying, reporting, voting, falling in love, hiring, and signing contracts.

And you can read these articles and books, take classes from local experts, attend seminars conducted by traveling gurus, or go to fashion and makeup services who will customize their hands-on advice to your needs, personality, and physical being.

Do We Still Have Dress Codes?

Today in most places we women have earned enough credibility through our abilities and accomplishments to drop some rigid "packaging" rules and requirements. Whether they were set for us or by us, these regulations restricted our choices, cramped our individual expression, often made us uncomfortable. No longer need we try to resemble men in order to pass muster as professional people. We never really did that disguise well, anyway, so why even try?

What we must pay attention to, however, is wearing clothing that is environment appropriate. Before I leave my home to negotiate somewhere, I always look at myself in the mirror one more time. I ask myself, "What do I see?" I want certain words to come to mind as I see my reflected image—words like *organized, competent, friendly, neat, well groomed, serious, dedicated, energetic, professional.*

Try this yourself. Look for items that pull your eyes' attention away from your face. A fancy belt buckle, fabulous two-tone shoes, a bangle bracelet over your watch, designer buttons, printed skirt—all will distract from your goal and message. As one of my associates says, *"Your clothes should never have more to say than you do."*

When getting dressed to negotiate, make sure that your negotiating partner's eyes will be directed to the "information system" you are bringing to the meeting. This is your face, particularly your eyes. Wear eye color connectors—a scarf, blouse, or jewelry that enhances, not wars with, your eyes. Wear colors, too, that blend with your hair color, not fight it.

If you negotiate for a better budget, you want to look like a winner—responsible, organized, profitable. Ask yourself what a person in that particular industry looks like. How do the female executives dress? What colors do they wear, and seem to prefer? But if any colors make you look unattractive, don't wear them. For instance, when I wear gray I appear to be twenty years older. In this country, old is not often considered wise. So if anything does this to you, discard it; it won't help you get your negotiating partner to say yes. Make a conscious decision whether or not to "go gray" with your hair. What are the ages of your negotiating partners? How old should you appear to be taken seriously? (Too young can be a handicap, too!)

Very high heels make you appear off balance, as if you might tip over any second, or make it seem that you're selling something other than advertising space. Wear shoes that look good, yet enable you to walk easily and gracefully, and won't start pinching your toes if you must stand for a long time.

Apply any makeup that you wear carefully and conservatively. If your eye shadow stands out, change it; it should be used to make your eyes the center of attention; you want them to tell others that you are alert, lively, honest, intelligent, responsive. Lipstick should be subtle; your mouth is second in importance to your eyes.

Confidence and credibility also come from how you move and how your body parts are aligned. Pay attention to how you habitually hold your head when you walk and sit, and work on changing this stance if your head tends to drop forward, as if you're about to lose it. (Who'll want to negotiate with a woman without a head?) On the other hand, don't keep your chin too high; you'll look snobbish or snooty, though, ironically, we usually do this instinctually when overcompensating for anxiety and fear. Retain a neutral yet empowered look by keeping your chin parallel to the floor and your shoulders in line with your hips.

Consciously create a "doing business" image with everything that you put on or do with your face and body. (Remember? *Negotiare* means doing business.) But also make sure that you will feel comfortable in what you're wearing, and that it is in accord with a genuine facet of who *you* are.

Ask of trusted friends, men and women both, "When I come into the office in the morning, what three words could best describe the person you see?" If you can, ask a similar question about the person you're going to be negotiating with. If you hear one-word descriptions like *conservative, flashy, nondescript,* or *casual,* you have definite clues as to how you might "pace" that person in your own attire. You will be liked better, of course, if you appear to resemble his or her own style.

Don't Go Out Encumbered

As you leave your home or office, see just how much you are carrying along with you. Do you look like an overburdened mule?

Don't give the impression that you'll be willing to carry *any* load. People may start regarding you, and treating you, like a workhorse.

Watch closely how successful businessmen go about the world. They are usually unencumbered, look flexible, available, free. One of the best preparations for negotiating I ever saw was made by a woman at an ad agency. She bought a jacket with an inside pocket just big enough for her credit cards, driver's license, her car key, a pen, a lipstick tube, and a $20 bill. She did away with her over-stuffed handbag.

We women almost literally immobilize ourselves with all the junk we carry around with us. Much of it we don't really need or use but keep with us "for emergencies"—ours or someone else's—as if we're obliged to schlepp doctors' medical bags. Women who are, or once were, mothers of young children may particularly think this way. Then, when someone wants to borrow a pen, they open up their satchels and paw around for five minutes, revealing the contents of their lives but possibly not producing the pen.

A leather briefcase containing requisite paperwork for a meeting is highly serviceable, of course. And looks highly professional. But you ruin the effect if you make it an addition to your purse. You'll spoil your businesslike impression when you open it up to get the handouts for others, and your makeup kit spills out.

The future belongs to the women who can move fast, think large, and bring solutions, not to women who are weighted down, anchored to the ground. Reduce what you take with you to a bare minimum. Leave that extra stuff at home or in the car. Or if you're away from home base, keep it at the hotel, or rent a locker at the airport or train station.

For strategy purposes, at some point in your negotiating career you might deliberately try to look your worst to achieve a particular goal. Think of the TV series "Columbo," whose hero-detective with a bumbling demeanor is portrayed unerringly by Peter Falk. He perennially throws off big-shot mobsters and cunning murderers with his slovenly appearance.

Deliberately designing a less than wonderful appearance is one thing. Conducting a negotiation by putting on a seemingly "weak" demeanor is another. Sometimes they can be used together to get the results you are after.

A real deadbeat had owed me a substantial amount of money for months and months, and nothing I could write or say or do seemed to impact him at all. No check was forthcoming, though sometimes one had been promised. Letters went ignored, phone messages were not returned. A few times I'd dropped by to hound him, but he always stiffed me.

I knew this guy was out there making lots of money, so a lack of wherewithal was not the issue. He just couldn't be bothered by going through the routine of paying me off. Obviously I had run out of negotiating possibilities.

So I devised a special strategy for the occasion. I didn't wash my hair, put on a dirty old raincoat, and I went off to camp out in his office until he came back from some power lunch. There he found me in his waiting room, looking almost like a bag lady. I acted nervous and fearful, and my voice quavered when I talked. And I kept coughing. I intended to look and sound very ill.

It worked. He wrote out a check on the spot, to pay me off quickly before anyone else might come in and witness the misery he'd apparently reduced me to. Maybe he himself even felt a touch of remorse.

Not a very elegant way of getting to my goal, but I got there.

The very thought of such a cop-out may well appall you, particularly if you're forthright and strong-minded, but there's a survival tactic in using it as a desperate measure.

What About Using
Your Sexuality When Negotiating?

Some women say it's tragic if you're born beautiful and then have to deal with the inevitable focus on sexuality. But I say that being feminine can be an important negotiating difference between women and men. Any attractive woman who dismisses this in negotiation is a fool. Use it; it's an absolute gift!

I consciously make a physical imprint with my presence. After all, people listen to about 80 to 90 percent of what you say, but retain maybe only 10 percent. The emotional impact you make is what's left—so it's almost everything.

When I'm going to negotiate, that's why in the morning I dress up with a flair, with colors, and prep myself up psychically. It would be hard then for me to look invisible!

I know how to walk into a room and get all eyes on me. How to put intonation and rhythm in my voice. When to be sassy or disruptive. I watch what gets people going—and use it.

Yet all the while I am very careful about being truthful. Do I really mean what I'm saying—and believe it? So I work on the quality of what I'm saying. For I always want to be remembered as genuine, honest, full of integrity.

Is using feminine attractiveness and sexual lures as manipulation bait in a negotiating situation a sell-out? My advice is that if you feel comfortable with your own physical being—sexual and otherwise—regard it as one of the tools of negotiating. If your attractiveness to someone else assists you in getting and keeping their attention, so much the better. They can be attracted to you as a total package—your personality, warmth, honesty, humor. Don't forget, too, that most women respond positively to another woman's attractiveness.

Using one's sexuality as bait and then as a concession point in getting what you want can be exceedingly dangerous, however. It often backfires. If you do it, you may well conclude afterwards that it was scarcely worth the risk or bother. Have confidence in your eventual success with men with genuine power; if they like you, that will help you toward your goal without needing to extract sexual favors.

Make Sure You Know
What to Say About You—and No More

It's often said—by ourselves, too—that we tend to talk too much about personal things in inappropriate settings. In negotiating, you want to design and carry out your strategy so that only gradually do you give out the data relating to your position and goal that you want your negotiating partner to receive. You want to take it step by step, holding some things back quite deliberately until you are sure that he or she will understand and value whatever you choose to tell now. This is a wise, time-proven tactic. You are not lying or deceiving; you're simply withholding information until the proper time for its appearance. You don't spill out the contents of the entire bean bag.

Second, sometimes the other side, knowing the female tendency to be open, honest, and overly revealing, will pump you for information that will ultimately be used against your negotiating position. Say, for instance, that it looks as if a company is preparing to offer you a job, and you go in for what appears to be the final stage of negotiation—for salary, benefits, title, and the name on the door and rug on the floor. And now the human resources manager starts asking some very personal questions.

What do you say? Always anticipate such a possibility when the appointment is made. And in your strategic preparations, rehearse *exactly* what you want to say about your private life. Know how you can deftly deflect questions that you consider prying and inappropriate, where you may reveal something that could disqualify you—from somebody's viewpoint—for a position for which you are eminently qualified. Often even outside consultants can be interrogated in a similar way.

The interview may start out very informally (calculated), which could get you chattering in a friendly way. You like this person, and this person likes you. Then the offhand questions begin. You start to get uncomfortable, but think you must respond to them. You do not have to lie, but you can evade or provide ambiguous answers. You can turn the question around: "Why do you feel you need to know that?" and so on. Above all, know your rights. You can report situations in which you have been asked improper personal questions when negotiating about a job.

Increasingly, of course, human resource departments are thinking up more and more ways to probe into our psyches and intimate selves. From their point of view, there are highly practical reasons—economic ones, and often security ones as well—for their concerns. You may be subjected to a battery of management-skills tests, for example, that can actually be utilized to scout out matters about which others may make moral judgments.

If you refuse to provide sufficient information about yourself—such as your financial status, whom (if anyone) you're sleeping with, your political beliefs, your life-style, the health problems of your children—and you don't get the job, figure you're better off in the long run. That kind of snooping and spying, or forms of sexual harassment, surely goes on in that company from the top level all the way down.

What If You Want to Delay or Even Call the Whole Thing Off?

Whenever I'm playing it close to the edge—say, when I desperately need some new account—I don't negotiate well. By now I know I've got to go in with the up attitude that works well for me; it lets me walk out the door without caring what happens. I need to come across as strong and powerful; it'll show in the way I walk and talk with utter confidence. Whereas if I'm weak, scared, and fragile, these feelings just seep through, even when I try to deny them. So I always want to negotiate only when I've got real control over my life and feel positive about the future. Not when I'm traumatized by all that stuff: kids, lovers, hormones, the depleted bank account. It's then, too, that I just can't seem to find the right outfit to wear. I simply call the negotiation off for a bit and don't go out that day. By tomorrow or the day after, I'm usually strong and powerful again, with the stars lined up in my favor.

At times you just won't feel like negotiating. Find out first of all whether your intuition is telling you that you really don't want to negotiate something; that the people or situation involved, say, aren't really to your liking; that the effort of making that connection isn't worth it and, in fact, might take you in the wrong direction entirely so that you are picking up on "bad vibes."

Or maybe some Steamroller has been pushing you into negotiating before you're fully prepared. They often like to catch people off guard that way. They also know that many women have trouble simply saying no and are banking on it. So learn to say no nicely but firmly whenever you're not confident of holding up your side of the negotiating, whether it's unanticipated or prescheduled.

You can always just walk away from an impromptu negotiation. Or if you're on the phone and somebody's badgering you, just put the receiver down, right in the middle of your own sentence. (Who would think that you actually hung up on them?) But if you're truly interested in discussing the matter further, set up a date, time, and place to do so. And give yourself enough time to be prepared.

Sometimes—allow for the remote possibility—you may simply not be up to negotiating. You may be sick, you may be dealing with extreme stress or loss, or you may not be fully prepared. If you're on a team or you have an associate as competent as you to do one-on-one negotiating, bowing out may not be a big problem. But if everything depends on you, and you're just not up to your usual acumen—in fact, far below it—what will you do?

In past years, I went through with it at the appointed time, come hell or high water. Now, though, I approach things differently. I do not always feel at my best—who does?—and don't expect that of myself. Ordinarily, I can pump up enough energy and adrenaline to get me through a negotiating session, training workshop, or speaking engagement. But I can only push myself so far and so often. Sometimes, now, I have to postpone, cancel, or bow out. I am only human.

You may find yourself having to make similar decisions. As far as meetings set up for negotiating purposes, it may not be difficult simply to reschedule them. After all, you wouldn't expect your opposite to appear if he or she were really incapacitated. People cannot negotiate effectively when they are physically or mentally down. When negotiating was widely done in a victor-victim manner, this suited the adversary's purpose. Nowadays, in the partnering mode, this is scarcely a desirable way to conduct negotiations.

Dealing with a Lack of Self-confidence and Experience

"Oh, but I'm just not *ready* to negotiate yet!"

Did you say that?

Realize—again—that you've been negotiating all your life. You may just not have been doing it very effectively. I often playfully remind women, in negotiating none of us is really a virgin.

Whether you were born in the United States or came here later, you've had to protect your own interests. Your family possibly talked a lot about the need for money, work, food, or keeping a roof over your head. Getting a job, almost any job, and keeping it might then be the highest priority—certainly not higher education, a white- (or pink-) collar management position, a big new house on the hill.

The tactics that enabled your family and others to cope with difficulties may not necessarily work for you in your quest to thrive. Non-Anglo cultures, for instance, tend to raise female children to be helpmeets rather than autonomous, ambitious, professional women. Black Americans, on the other hand, have a culture of strong women who model female strength for their daughters whether or not they are household heads.

If you are caught between two cultural patterns, it will not be easy for you to steer your own course as you work to resolve the differences. It may be that, in your family's culture, men are usually the principal authority figures even though women may possess a great deal of unacknowledged, positive power. If this is the case, regard this intrinsic female power as a strong resource whenever you prepare for negotiation. Let it infuse you with confidence in dealing with whatever personality types and negotiating styles confront you.

Whatever your cultural and family roots, as you prepare to negotiate recall and review the strengths and resiliencies rather than defects, weaknesses, and failures. Search for positive images of people, incidents, and accomplishments that will reinforce your self-esteem, not negative memories, hurt, or angry feelings that might undermine your position of intended control.

Don't Forget to Take Along Your Mental Billboards!

Attitude management is crucial in the final phase of preparing to negotiate. Keep your big goal well in mind. (Remember? It should be phrased in such a compact form that you can write it on the back of a business card.) Repeat it often—like a mantra—to yourself. If you get distracted during the negotiation, your billboard will keep you from getting off course.

Manage your part of the negotiation by creating an appropriate "attitude environment." Part of your role as a negotiator is to control the temperature during the process: your attitude can function like a thermostat in the proceedings, heating up the discussions, cooling down the disagreements. Staying consciously competent, you can regulate the negotiations and see that they stay on a course that is consistent with your strategies and your goals.

Here are a few of the billboards I use:

DEPERSONALIZE: IT'S NOT ABOUT YOU, IT'S ABOUT THEM.
IT'S NOT WHAT HAPPENS, BUT HOW I RESPOND TO IT.
YOU CAN'T SHAKE HANDS WITH A CLENCHED FIST.
SHIFT HAPPENS.
COMING TOGETHER IS THE BEGINNING. KEEPING TOGETHER
    IS THE END.

Find—or make—your own billboards, perhaps special ones for each negotiation. Put them on three-by-five cards, stick them on the refrigerator door, take them to bed, memorize them.

Get Ready, Get Set . . . Go!

Tomorrow can be a new beginning, particularly if you are going forth to negotiate something important to you. Don't start out by shoving things into your computer brain like: "Oh gosh, I'm going to have to deal with that jerk again." "She's going to give me all these details I can't stand to hear." "They're going to try to bully me and wear me down one more time."

Think positively. "It's going to be great!" See the positive outcome of your vision. You made the commitment, then you did your homework and came up with the plan. Now go out and *do* it!

You can try out your new negotiating knowledge and skills at work, at home, while buying something or selling something. Start with the simpler situations and move on to more complex and difficult negotiations as you acquire confidence and experience.

And before you know it, you will be a fully conscious competent negotiator, winning or scoring big in most of the negotiation games that life sends your way.

▬ EXERCISE 1 ▬

MANAGING YOUR "INFLUENCE IMAGE"

The old line is "You never get a second chance to make a first impression." In negotiating, it is critical that that first impression be exactly the one you have strategized as part of your preparations for reaching your negotiating goal. As a refresher, go over the following questions:

1. People's—customers, suppliers, team players, strangers—first impression of me is usually:

2. For this negotiating session, I want (names, titles) to think:

3. The results I expect to achieve from this impression are:

4. To achieve these results it will be necessary for me to: (Join a gym, enroll in a health program, hire a professional image consultant, purchase new equipment—computer, calculator, recording devices, etc.—purchase new clothing, have voice lessons, practice with a professional speaking coach, design new business cards, and so on.)

▬ EXERCISE 2 ▬

THE POWER OF YOUR VOICE

You will notice that in the last exercise, I suggested that voice lessons or practicing with a speaking coach may be something that would contribute positively to making an influential first impression. How important in making a powerful impression is your speaking voice?

I was consulting with a group of health-care women at a hospital in Oklahoma. We taped a negotiating session with the doctors and administrators who were overwhelming men. The women were well prepared in terms of what they were requesting and in negotiating strategies, and they did all right but could have done better. My role was to observe, to give feedback for improvement, and to train them in better negotiating skills.

I asked them to listen to just voices, no content, then to listen to content. I asked them to write down feelings and observations as they listened.

Some of the results were:

1. They found their voices were far less audible than the men's (others had to strain to listen when they didn't want to be heard).

2. They used many more qualifiers: "It might not be that important." "I am sorry, but. . . ." "You might be surprised, but. . . ." Along with content they lost tone power.

3. Their voices went up at the end of each statement (and sounded as if they questioned their own proposal). "We need to have this completed. Is that OK?"

Using the form below, analyze your voice:

1. Record your telephone speaking voice during a business conversation (most answering machines have this function). How do you sound? Is your voice strong and confident? Does it waver between shrill and steady? Does the tone of your voice "give away" your position or your feelings (remember, over the telephone, without the use of body language or eye contact, your voice carries far more information than when you are negotiating in person)?

2. In face-to-face conversations, ask your friends and colleagues to give you honest feedback in how you sound. Do you use a different voice for one-on-one talks than you do in a meeting? What is the quality of each voice?

3. In analyzing your voice, pay particular attention to tempo, volume, pitch, quality, and articulation. Also, what general impression are you "voicing"—friendliness, dullness, alertness, indifference, vitality, laziness?

PART III

NEGOTIATION IN ACTION

"It isn't until you begin to fight your own cause that you really become committed to winning."
—Robin Morgan

11
GETTING INTO
THE GAME

*When negotiating, listen naïvely. Stay curious: you don't know what they're going
to say.* —Nicole Schapiro

Whenever I go in to negotiate some business deal—I run a
building-cleaning service with a dozen employees, and also
buy and fix up houses to rent out—I want to come across as
strong and powerful. But sometimes—when I need an account
badly—I'm playing it close to the edge. I can't afford just to
walk away if things don't go the way I want them to.

I don't negotiate well when I'm feeling needy or scared; my
fragility somehow seeps through. That's why I try to negotiate
only when I have a positive feeling about my future, when I
exude a sense of control over my life. And I won't go out if I'm
traumatized by stuff about kids, lovers, checkbook . . . or even
if I can't find the right outfit to wear, because that's a sure sign
that I'm down.

My aim in negotiating any deal is to be a good communicator.
The key is always being absolutely myself, and not being uptight about the deal making. I keep in mind I can always walk
away.

I pump myself up beforehand. I do these affirmations: looking in the mirror at myself—all fixed up to go—and saying
"Yes, yes, yes!" to get my energy flying. I wear whatever is de
rigueur, so I'll feel comfortable. In Hollywood it's something
casual and bright, in New York, the equivalent of three-piece

suits. When I was doing some heavy-duty, long-term negotiating in Europe, in some places I wore jeans and sweatshirts—very chic and very American; in others, a conservative suit—very American, too.

Because I'm usually successful at what I do—I'm a lawyer, a financier, a producer—I don't have to kowtow to anybody. They know I am a woman to be reckoned with. So I may walk into the room where the meeting will take place and do something funny or say something outrageous . . . just to break the tension. Either they'll hate it or love it, I don't care. They'll at least know who I am.

When you can be yourself, you'll be okay. You may even manage to have fun.

You've prepared everything you need to negotiate effectively. Now you're going to go out and see what happens in real life, whether in business, in some practical need, or in a personal relationship. Apply the information in this chapter selectively, to the specifics of each unique situation.

Tending to Logistics

Design your day's schedule, if you can, to leave ample time for getting to the meeting. Never arrive late; being flustered and apologetic puts you at an immediate disadvantage. Arrive at the station early to catch the train, or be on the freeway before the worst congestion hits. Allow for possible delays en route. If you've given yourself leeway of at least a half-hour and you're held up somewhere—stuck in gridlocked traffic, say—you have a cushion of time as a safeguard.

When you do arrive at the meeting place early, use that extra time to good purpose.

- "Freshen up" in the restroom.
- Sit quietly somewhere and review your notes.
- Rehearse your opening.
- Replay your choices of strategy; don't ever freeze the picture!
- Sense the ambience of an office you may be visiting for the first time.

- Call up a few billboards on your mental computer and let their energy-boosting messages enliven your attitude.
- Ask someone on the premises if you may go into the meeting room, and choose where you want to sit for watching people enter the room.
- Busy yourself with your own material.
- Reflect on your negotiation strategies.
- See yourself in the many conflicting roles you might have to play during the negotiation: analytical, flexible, firm, practical, tough, sensitive.

When your negotiating team or opposing partners come through the door, become an attentive observer. Identify personality types by how they walk, dress, talk—and what they bring with them. Datacrats will be loaded down with papers, female Butterflies carry large purses, Nice Guys have food to share, Streamrollers come unencumbered. You'll soon gather up plenty of information to clue you in on negotiating styles.

Observe how everyone greets each other or handles introductions, how they shake hands with you, where they choose to sit, and what papers they arrange before them. Study their body language. (See the particulars of this later in this chapter.) You'll especially want to note who seems to have the *real* power; that's the person you want to influence. Watch carefully; it may not be titular power, and perhaps won't be obvious at first. But you'll see other people's eyes veering in that person's direction, and there will be a special respect accorded when they talk to that person—small nods, fewer interruptions, more agreements. Your intuition should also pick up indicators. Listen in.

Before the Real Business Begins

Socializing before a formal meeting is often considered a requisite nicety, particularly at the beginning or end of a working day. An early-morning meeting may feature coffee, fruit, and rolls; the afternoon, cold drinks and snacks. This prelude period accommodates latecomers while getting people to unwind and mix.

Don't ever forget, though, that this is negotiating time, not party time. Plan your strategy as if you were at a conference table.

Use these informal occasions for two purposes: to spot the different personality types; and to personally connect to help build trust with persons on the other side. Establishing a bond greatly assists in bringing about partnership negotiation, especially with people inclined to be hardliners. Socializing, as many cultures know, lays the groundwork for the business ahead; it's scarcely frivolous. People who come just for the meeting, or who arrive late, miss out on this important pre-negotiating opportunity.

If you are hosting the event, you'll need to circulate, introducing people to each other, always with a plan: who needs to know whom, and who needs to be kept apart. Draw out persons standing to the side, alone, and unnoticed. Not only is this humane and courteous, but it could be smart. Datacrats, for instance—who might act aloof because they are shy and feel awkward socially, may be dismissed by Butterflies, who gravitate toward all the fun and chatter. (Or, conversely, you might have to protect them from voracious Butterflies by leading them away to a quieter, more comfortable conversation. But those Datacrats could well be running corporations or at least controlling the budgets.

If the meeting is taking place at your office, make sure you adhere to the schedule. Terminate the pre-meeting socializing promptly. If you are elsewhere and nobody else is paying attention to the clock, remind them that it's time to get on with the business of the day. Give them windup time of seven to eight minutes. Make sure you negotiate the end of the pre-meeting appropriately, or delegate it to someone else.

Where Do You Sit?

At some negotiation meetings, you're given assigned seats at a table, perhaps even with place cards. In team negotiating, often each group neatly occupies one side of the table. At most meetings, though, you can pick your own spots. There can be leverage in choosing the type of table. For instance, round equals power, and an action-grabber can increase the power game when nobody's at the "head." With a long rectangular table, as with a dining table, whoever sits at the ends may be seen as king and queen. If a relatively informal meeting is conducted in a living-room setting, first arrivals get their pick of possible places on "insider" sofas and armchairs, and latecomers make do with what's left at the periphery. If you have a choice of seating, choose a chair where you won't feel rigid and confined, or which is too big for you to get out of easily when you might choose to pace. Avoid soft sofas into which you may sink into obscurity, or become so comfortable you may get sleepy.

Geographic placement is important. *Where* you sit is part of your strategy. Usually, people try to avoid sitting close to someone with whom they're in an adversarial relationship. You think, "I can't stand that man," and sit as far away as possible. Or, when this other person enters the room and you're already seated, you may quickly move your stuff over so it looks as if the place next to you is already occupied. The same holds true for someone who is very abusive verbally—characteristic of some Steamrollers.

Good tactic: If you really want someone you don't like to agree to a solution you'll propose, *sit right next to him or her.* You'll show both bravery and confidence in your ability to handle pressure. That way, when your space is invaded it will be hard for the person to call you names or disagree with you. Proximity somehow breeds rapport (except, notably, with certain Datacrats who may become nearly catatonic if you get too close).

If you sit next to someone, however, it's hard to make eye contact or pick up on body language. Despite the confrontational aspect, sitting across from a person forces eye contact between you; you'll also observe much more in terms of body language. This information-gathering opportunity is important if you don't know the person well and need to carefully "read" his or her personality profile and intentions.

If you know who will be most influential at the meeting, try to sit at the right of that person. (And not always will he or she sit at the head of the table.) Sometimes you can arrange that ahead of time by a phone call from your secretary. Or you can simply take the chair, saying, "I'd like to sit next to you, as it will be easier then to share some of my material."

If your organization has sent two people and the other side has four or five, consider several seating strategies:

1. Sit opposite each other so as to use prearranged signals as you negotiate.

2. Sit together so you look like a more powerful block of negotiators.
3. If your strategy is a Good Guy/Bad Guy one, sit at opposite
ends of the table.

Temper Your Expectations

Before the negotiation begins, rerun your expectations and all the
scenarios you practiced in the preparation days. Move them out
and along. Settle on various possibilities and then narrow them
down to one or two likely scripts.

Don't get misled, though, by your own notions of what will
happen during negotiation, based on what you think *should* happen
. . . or perhaps what you fear *might* happen. Even though you did
your homework, do not assume that people will do as you have
predicted. Be prepared to listen attentively—and naively, too, as if
whatever your negotiating partner says is fresh and unanticipated.

I always go into a negotiation with a certain goal or outcome
in mind. But I never go in expecting people to play fair, according
to certain rules. I suppose the one rule I do hold to is that there
are no rigid rules.

All negotiation begins with yourself, and nothing works unless
you do. Find in each situation the best way for you to do your
work.

Ready?

How to Focus Your Attention

In each moment of negotiation, *you should be present when you are there.*
Ahead of time, clear your mind of any extraneous matters that will
distract you from giving it 100 percent of your attention.

Here's a technique I use; try it if you're preoccupied with other
matters before a negotiation. Ask yourself, "Can I make any difference about things I'm worried about today while I am here?" On a
piece of paper write down three things you're concerned about. If
you can't do anything about them while you're in the negotiation
process, cross them out. Fold the paper and put it away. Clear your
mind before you negotiate.

Sometimes you may need to push yourself. If it's negotiating you haven't done before, as on a new job, you'll need to be either a conscious competent or a consciously incompetent negotiator. Know what you *don't know*. Review previous negotiations. What worked; what didn't? Know your skills bank. "I am good at understanding the meaning, not just the content." "I am good at opening positions."

Still, as you assume the responsibility of sitting or standing in front of other people to present your position, believe in *you*: know that you will be excellent. You must put your prime energy into what you are saying and doing in this place, and not permit your thoughts to wander. You know who you are, inside and out; and you know how you want to appear to others. And you are confident because you have prepared well for this meeting, and practiced a sense of detachment.

You also know what you want—what your goal is in the negotiation. Remember? It's so concise and well formulated that you can summarize it on the back of your business card.

If you have come to a meeting to present a proposal for doing some form of business, you'll first have to sell the opposite side on the idea: the benefit of a cooperative environment.

Stage one is persuading. ("There are more efficient computer systems.") If they are interested in hearing more, you go on to the next stage.

Stage two is detailing, which includes answering specific questions about your expectations and demonstrating benefits that will serve their needs. ("You'll save money and get the work done faster.") If they remain interested, you will begin the process of examining the bottom line.

Stage three is bargaining over cost, deadlines, service contracts, gain, commitment, and so on. ("This is the kind of deal we're prepared to make for you.")

On the other hand, if you're meeting to iron out a conflict, address the matter. You need to choose: talk with the person directly, or talk with a representative. The partnership attitude is that you assist the other side to reach satisfaction in negotiating. Focus on the system, not the person. Use first-person plural words: *we, our, us.*

Discussion will be more productive if the meeting begins with a review of the conflict's history, giving each side a chance to present its perspective and experience. Often, when the negotiating partner listens attentively to the other side's view, maybe for the first time seeing the opposite perspective, the chance for conciliation starts.

Handling Surprises

Nobody likes surprises during a negotiation. Sometimes you'll discover that the opposite side has inserted a surprise attendee. This can be either a thoughtless action or a tactic to throw you off. How you handle this will, of course, depend on whether or not you object to the presence of someone you weren't expecting. Your permission may not even be asked for this change; if it's "you against them," and you are already numerically outnumbered, you may wish to state your objection.

The inserted person might turn out to be innocuous, even helpful to your side, or he or she may pose some threat. How will you know? You may have some option in the matter. You can say something that will indicate your dissatisfaction over a violation of your prior understanding, but doing so may bring unfavorable consequences.

I was prepared to negotiate for a special, three-part management seminar program that would sensitize executives to the concerns and needs of female and multicultural employees. My understanding was that I would meet with two vice-presidents and the CFO. Lo and behold, when I arrived, another person was present. He was introduced as the human resources manager. As he shook my hand in a stiff way, almost reluctantly, he glared at me.

"Ms. Flanders, you won't mind if Mr. Jenkins sits in with us, will you?" one of the VPs now asked me. "Yes, I do mind," I said. "Why was that decision made, and who made it? The program I want to give has no connection, I am sure, with Mr. Jenkins's own expertise in the company. If he remains here, we'll have to restructure the purpose of this meeting."

I knew, of course, that Mr. Jenkins was threatened by the program. I'd heard from several people who worked at the company that Mr. Jenkins was hostile toward both women and minorities. I knew he'd try to veto the whole plan. Because I voiced an objection, Mr. Jenkins was uninvited. Afterward, I used my reason for not wanting him present as a way to alert the three men present to the firm's reputation among employees and the outside world. It was probable they'd face future lawsuits if they continued discriminatory policies and practices. Was I correct in assuming that they emanated from the human resources department, or was upper management responsible? The men made a quick decision to let me give a brief demonstration program, after which they'd make a decision about a contract.

When I gave the program, Mr. Jenkins attended it along with a dozen other managers—only two of whom were women, I noticed. Win turned into long-term loss. The next contract was given to another consultant, thanks to Mr. Jenkins's efforts to torpedo me within the organization.

This woman's experience shows how not to handle surprises. Her goal was a long-term contract worked through forming supportive relationships within the corporation, not a one-shot program. She made two basic mistakes upfront. One was to say, "Yes, I do mind." Don't be argumentative or put down anyone else's expertise. Then, "the program I want to give" failed to use the mutual-ownership statement, "The program we want to offer." She got torpedoed because she focused on the fearful possibility of being torpedoed. She also assumed negative energy and acted as if it were a fact.

If presented with this circumstance, how could you do it better? First, say whatever you like in your "private talk." "Oh no! Of all the people to spring on me!" But you *negotiate* with public talk by replying differently, such as, "Oh good—that will give all of us the chance to agree about where the women's and cultural diversity programs should be headed. Mr. Jenkins, what do *you* think?" Involve him upfront; make him your partner; model your intent to cooperate, listen, and get commitment.

Or say, "I always like working with human resources people. After all, they are the ones who will continue all our training efforts after I'm gone. So Mr. Jenkins's input is vital to our needs here in initiating these programs." Another variant would be, "Should we go over the agenda again since we have a new participant? We'll all need to know where we're heading." If you do not wish for any more new people to be added, that at least alerts the opposite side that you won't happily accommodate any more surprises.

Exercise caution about becoming too indignant or cynical. Be as diplomatic as you can in getting more information about what the reasoning is. The new person brought in might be the one who makes the final decision, or at least has a large say in it. If you've prepared yourself effectively for the meeting, you could save yourself time and more preparatory efforts by wrapping up the deal right now.

Handling surprises that come up now and then when you negotiate might sometimes be an important part of a particular position or responsibility. It could be your chance to prove your flexibility. Your response to a surprise ingredient or an impromptu negotiation might well determine whether or not you'll continue to be considered a candidate for some position. If the goal you're after is crucial to you, don't allow yourself to get rattled by unanticipated scenarios. All surprises can offer a gift. Stop . . . breathe . . . summarize. Say, "Oh, Mr. Jenkins, won't you join us?" Gain time to deal with your private talk: "What the heck am I going to do now?"

Here's a memorable surprise I got long ago. Just given a big promotion and the title of vice-president, I was new on a banking executive team that met weekly. As my first meeting was about to begin, I felt all eyes were upon me. Someone said, "Nicole, you won't mind getting some coffee for us, right?"

Not having anticipated this request as part of my perceived function there, I was stunned. I took a deep breath; that's a good way to gain time and get oxygen into your brain, to think more clearly (you've got to do it, though, without gulping). Then I looked back at them, keeping steady eye contact going from one to another. "Sure, I'd love to get the coffee today. But before I do, let's make a plan. Now, next week, John, you can get the coffee, and the week after, you, Frank. . . ." I wrote all the names down, with dates attached. Then when I left the room to get the coffee, I handed the list to the secretary and asked her to make copies for us all.

I'd turned the surprise into an opportunity. They surely resented me for breaking into the "boys' club," and had expected me to snap angrily at them. Instead, I was polite and cooperative. I used this calculated affront as a chance to show that I could delegate responsibility, solve problems, and stay clear and cooperative. And handle unwelcome surprises, too.

You may run into unanticipated scripts. Surprises can come from different directions, such as:

HISTORY

- "Do you know that your ex-husband is a new partner in this firm?"
- "Didn't you work for General Dynamics? What made you leave that position?"

GEOGRAPHY

- "Let's meet in the cafeteria instead" (or the corporate office, the golf course, the conference room, etc.).
- "Can you drive me to the airport? We can talk then."

DELAYING TACTICS

- "Oh, did I forget to tell you to bring the Canadian sales figures? I'm sorry, but I won't be able to discuss this without them."
- "My son has soccer practice, and I've promised to pick him up at four today, so we'll have only fifteen minutes to talk."

You'll need to handle each separate surprise as it comes along, but certainly if too many of them accumulate (such as repeated delays), you're amply warned that something is wrong here. It might be just the style of the company. Start anticipating it. Call ahead and ask, "Are we still meeting at your office?" You can also educate them by letting them know how these surprise moves and decisions affect you. Help manage more consistency.

Just as you'll dislike it if your negotiating partners introduce some new element you didn't expect, so they should equally dislike it from you. Even though pulling some trick like this can be effective strategy in unsettling the other side, it ends up backfiring because it gets people angry or makes them feel foolish or inadequate. This mitigates against having any long-term relationship. If you have reason to bring new persons or elements into the negotiation, it is good policy to alert your partners in advance, explain your reasons, and get their agreement.

Your Opening Gambit

Always have several possible openings ready, so you'll be able to shift them as necessary.

Remember one of my favorite definitions of negotiating? It's "mutual education." It's also a process or journey of determining and meeting both partners' perceived needs. It is also important to review what negotiation is *not*: it's not a confessional, not a boxing match, not coercion.

Even if you're the one who has requested this meeting, it does not mean you have to start. But if you are handling the opening, regard yourself as an educator. Explain the underpinnings of the task for the hours of work and study ahead. It takes most people four times to hear something and really "get it," which is why repetition, with variations, is a major technique in teaching. And you may have four personality types to educate about what you propose.

Are you on first? Don't fuss over your first sentence. It's a throwaway; nobody listens to it. Make it casual, affable, humorous, welcoming. Be sure to address the person with power with your *second* sentence. Look right at him or her as you start talking; afterward, you can "play the room." You've determined that this person is one of the four personality types, so you assume the remark should contain one of those key words: *what* (for a Steamroller); *how* (for a Datacrat); *who* (for a Butterfly); or *why* (for a Nice Guy). This translates to: what we need to look at, how you want to handle it, who is involved, and why we need to talk.

Watch what happens. If you say "This is *what* I propose to do for you" and the Number 1 person leans forward attentively to hear you better or bolts upright, you've hit the target. If not, you move on. "And this is *how* I am going to do it." No sign yet of a response? Play now to the Butterfly. "And the people who will benefit from it are. . . ." Sooner or later, everybody will want to know that *why* anyway: *why* you want to buy or sell, do something, get them to do something, or resolve some conflict or disagreement. None of your points needs be lost.

What you now do is focus your first, best energy on expounding upon and expanding one of those four categories while touching on the others, too. Later on, when you take questions, you can detail aspects of your proposal.

If you're negotiating with a group of people, the other side will probably represent several different personality types (or degrees and variations of a few types). If the group (as with a corporate identity) has no set style, or if no one is in absolute charge, you may find yourself dealing with some radically different individuals. Until you can sort out who is the real decision maker, you'll have to speak to several different styles quickly and sequentially. Then you wait to see what the reactions are, and design your future strategy by basically addressing the dominant personality.

It's possible, though, that decisions are made by consensus or majority vote, in which case you might have to carry through the entire negotiation session taking into account the differing styles and personality needs and concerns. This requires a skillful balancing or juggling act during the negotiating—sort of being all things to all people—while watching the level of response in your partners.

If a Steamroller is present, usually he or she will run the negotiation process, or at least attempt to seize control. A Datacrat or Butterfly with more actual decision-making power may just sit back and allow this to happen; that may in fact be part of the other side's strategy. So make sure that you don't get led astray by thinking that the tough-talking bottom-liner is the real chief. The person in positional power may simply be sitting there, quietly watching—which may be his or her strategy.

Moving Along

When you go into any negotiation situation, you know what you want out of the process: your goal. So you present your position, which is your plan to achieve that goal, in your terms. But that's only the beginning. Another way to look at this is the me-thee-we progression. Taking care of the me first comes in your preparation. Because you have clearly defined your own issues, at the opening you can get into the *thee* issues—those of your negotiating partner. At the outset, you put your own stuff "on the shelf." You now sit back and listen to the other side. Finally, you come back in and get into the *we*—both of your issues together. Now the task has become mutual: define and solve something together that incorporates both of your positions as much as possible so you both will gain.

Establishing initial bottom lines becomes necessary early on in the negotiation in a business deal. If the other side responds in an interested way to what you offer, they've got to know what you need from them in explicit terms—price, quantity, timing, and so on. If what you propose is completely out of line in their view, they must now educate you about why this is so. (And vice versa, if you've been approached with a deal.)

Information exchange and mutual education should be provided by each side in a manner that is straightforward and calm—nonaccusatory, nonreactive, nonblaming. You listen attentively to the other side's needs, concerns, and interests; after all, they must protect their own position at all times. And you expect them to listen just as carefully to your circumstances.

Whether you're going to do business together or resolve some problem between you, the mutual respect that comes from educating each other puts you in good stead. When a reasonable deal between you seems possible, you work together to find a bridge between your two sides. Keep the dialogue open until mutual satisfaction is achieved.

In the process, the initial bottom lines become soft, and one or two are modified up or down, each moving in a direction toward the other. It's a serious miscalculation, then, to establish a *hard*, intractable initial bottom line on either part. Always have at least two bottom lines you can descend (or ascend) to.

Opening a Negotiation
for Conflict Resolution

Negotiating between two warring groups can be fraught with tension and emotional displays. We're not just talking here about Arabs and Israelis, or street gangs, or couples in arms. This happens to all of us. One group of neighbors wants more streetlights and is willing to pay higher taxes; another adamantly opposes the plan. Parents of a child who got AIDS from a transfusion have enrolled him in the local school; other parents are vocalizing their outrage and fear. A group of female employees feels slighted and angry because the company passed out free tickets to a soccer game only to the men. Trouble is brewing between one side and the other, and it should be resolved through negotiating. A meeting has been called to air the positions taken.

Perhaps you have volunteered or been asked to provide the summary overview of the meeting's purpose. If so, be brief. Let the others know you won't welcome interruptive questions or comments. Set guidelines for acceptable behavior before openings. Don't go into details; those come later. Avoid making statements that might trigger inflammatory reactions, especially likely if the negotiation is a dispute between two warring sides.

If someone else is handling this initial phase of the negotiation process, give respectful attention to what is being said and refrain from saying anything unless a question is put directly to you. If the opposite side presents its case first, concentrate on listening well. The person who listens is the person in control. Listen with a goal in mind: "I need to hear what is the real concern." Take notes to remind you of specific agreements or disagreements with statements in their presentation. Written information often serves as a leverage.

Maintaining an interested, calm, and rational demeanor will work in your favor, particularly when it's known that you strongly oppose the other side's position. Not showing your feelings is a strategy. If this initial opening is phrased in a manner unfavorable to your side, don't let it rile you and throw you off. It might be a test strategy. You may register a complaint to this effect in an even voice afterward, or explain how the comment affected you. Always consider the purpose of your comments: do they support the negotiation? You will soon get your turn to talk. And if you don't seem to be on the agenda to talk, you must then assert your right to have it.

If you're not a disinterested moderator, when you present your position, expect courtesy from your negotiating partners. If you're meeting over a conflict between you and they start to interrupt your opening remarks, ask them to stop, and assure them that they'll have their chance to question or challenge you later. Say, "I need three more minutes." If they persist in interrupting you and nobody else at the meeting backs you up, you may then just stop in the middle of what you are saying, pointedly gather up your papers, and make an exit. You must serve effective notice that you will not participate in a negotiation where the ground rules of common courtesy are being broken at the very start. It can only get worse unless attention is given to proper procedure.

You will have your own agenda in your head, and put yourself "on the shelf" while you hear other people's experiences and ideas; that way, you'll know how different they may be in their views and solutions. You co-partner by summarizing what you have heard but others may have missed. Now you are ready to put your own proposals out, and start building up the *we* toward *our* common purpose and goal.

Watching Body Language

As the meeting begins, closely observe what partners *do* with their physical selves. It will be easier for you to read other people's "body language" when you aren't talking—at least until reading it becomes second nature to you. (You can practice some "tactical silence" here.) Trust is built or broken by what you say and how you look when you say it. Your jawbone, set firm as you say, low and slow, "I'm fine," may read differently.

When you're negotiating in person, face-to-face with people, you have a marvelous opportunity to learn about the other side with your eyes and ears. You may have special advantage here. Experiments done through the years have shown that women generally are better observers than men of details in the appearance and outward behavior of others. Here's a case where women's intuition and presence in a relationship pick up sight and sound clues. Men's tendency to move quickly and stay with the big picture can be a disadvantage.

About 65 percent of the strategy used in face-to-face negotiation comes from reading what is going on in the opposite side. Body language, as it is widely called, is a large subset of applied psychology. Many books and articles are available for learning the particulars of "BL." Conscious competent negotiators depend considerably on scientific findings based on practical research among people. (Practicing every day by closely observing one object or person in your environment will help prepare you for studying body language when you're negotiating.)

Skill at reading body language can be a distinct advantage when negotiating. Moment by moment, you can skillfully track what is really going on inside the negotiating partners—as they talk, as they listen, as they respond to you or others—and this will enable you to revise your strategy as the negotiation process unfolds. You will look and listen for signs of tension, distrust, guilt, irritation, distortion, smugness, withholding, nervousness, anger, empathy, relaxation, fear, trust, deception, and so on. But you must closely watch and hear while you participate. Take time for silence, for if you are talking much of the time, or are not so much listening as planning what you're going to say next, you will have little time to attend to your negotiating partner or your larger goals.

Watch particularly (with warning caveats to follow):

• Eyes. Not just if they maintain eye contact with you, but where they look: up, down, sideways to left or right (each direction has meaning—to the right for right-handed people means they're considering). Darting glances, or fixating, staring. Rapid blinking, or tears. The "look" in the eyes: fearful, angry, sympathetic, friendly, remote, etc.

• Nervous Mannerisms. In general, running hands through hair, pulling on fingers, cuticle chewing, nose scratching, chin rubbing, ear pulling ("I'm not sure I hear this right").

• How They Sit. Bolt upright, slouching, constantly shifting; at the edge of the chair (low trust = ready to go).

• Face. Rigid with wooden expression, scowling, frowning, overanimated, trembling.

• Mouth. Downcast, pursed lips, constant smile, open with teeth bared, grimly grinning.

• Head. Held with chin elevated or drooping; cocked to one side or straight; motionless or flexible; stiff neck.

• Using Hands. Frequent gestures (and what gestures); using both hands or only one; thumb; which fingers (such as frequent pointing, as accusation or indicating away from self?). Many cultural meanings.

• Legs and Feet. Legs rigid, feet flat on the floor; legs crossed at knee or ankle; foot swinging or banging, erratic or rhythmical. Which way legs are crossed—e.g., when they are crossed away from you means a shift, so recheck agreements or reintroduce benefits.

Remember, since our first negotiation is self-negotiation, body language in the first thirty seconds is the true unabridged version of others' thoughts and feelings. They might adjust in the next half-minute to poker face or some other disguise of their strategy.

Warning: These body-language indicators are all situational in interpretation and variation. People's cultural roots, health, and age create variables. You shouldn't isolate one action or factor and then decide on the reaction or feeling behind it as a "fact." Someone with a limp handshake may have bad arthritis. A person with chronic back pain may seem stiff and cold. People whose head position is up or down may be wearing new bifocal glasses.

Certain BL aspects inevitably vary from culture to culture. For instance, the direct eye contact that Americans normally expect from each other, proclaiming honesty and self-worth, can be offensive in some places, especially in women. Asians are more likely than Americans to mask their faces with bland expressions, intended to disguise what they really feel. And like cultures, individuals may vary widely and not totally abide by the BL "rules."

Remember that while you're studying your negotiating partners, they too are watching—and listening—to you. So periodically "check in" with anything you may be doing inadvertently with your face, body, or voice—mannerisms and nervous habits—that are revealing thoughts or feelings you want to keep under cover or that might irritate others.

How They Say What They Say

Just as faces and bodies become graphic displays of emotions, voices provide auditory clues. If 65 percent of what informs us in negotiation is attributable to our interpretations of others' body language, that leaves 35 percent for feedback from what we hear.

Interestingly enough, people respond much more (30 percent) to one's *tone* of voice and talking *style* than to their *content* (5 percent). (DON'T CONFUSE COMMUNICATION WITH UNDERSTANDING is one of my billboard messages.) Word choice, tone, and pauses all have meanings. Pace as well as accent indicate the speaker's geographical origin—Southern, New Yorker, Midwestern. Clever negotiators can use their voice for particular effect, such as to soothe your anger before you have really worked through its justifiable causes, or to "get your goat" by using a condescending tone. Such tactics will throw you off.

Again, listen naively when you negotiate. Don't believe you know what they're going to say. Know in advance, however, what words to listen for in both positive and negative ways; how to listen for them; and how best to respond when you hear them. That's part of anticipating scenarios, and now you should be tuned to the real dialogue.

The pace of speaking can indicate various things. Rapid speaking may show quick information-processing capability. But glibness also may indicate a memorized script, frequent spiel, or nervous tension, or a strategy. Slow speaking may indicate slow-paced processing, cautious thinking, painstaking search for the proper word (not everyone is fluent in English), or lack of interest or enthusiasm. Normally you want to pace your negotiating partner's speech.

Listen for the speaker's customary language, such as favorite words or expressions. Also, listen for the sounds used in pausing while thinking or collecting oneself—insertions like *well, you know,* and *uh,* as well as blank spaces and unfinished sentences. Some people show their nervousness by filling up any silent moments with words that approach babbling. Others—notably Datacrats—remain so guarded in their speech that they utter only monosyllables.

How your negotiating partners use their voice is a key indicator of how they feel inside. But with loudness, say, distinguish excitement from anger or style and energy. As discussed earlier, when pre-negotiating or even negotiating over the phone, we depend greatly on voice clues. In a direct meeting, we also can see whether the people are a good "match" for their voice. Don't make fatal assumptions. Sometimes, for instance, a man with a deep, forceful voice can look like a pip-squeak, or a man with a light, high-pitched voice may resemble a football player. Listen and observe.

Do not confuse silence with a different pause habit. Women

tend to jump in faster to "plus" you than men. Silence can be a powerful tactic. When people become aware that you are not contributing anything to your side of the discussion, though you are actively listening (and taking notes), they may ask you to talk and then give you their full attention.

A Note on Keeping Notes

Some people have fantastic memories, but most of us do not. It's highly useful to jot down notations about what people say as proposals or responses, arguments or counterarguments, concessions proposed or offered.

Also, what provisions have been made for taking notes or minutes that will conveniently and officially summarize the main points considered and positions expressed at the meeting? If this is a major discussion to solidify business arrangements or resolve differences, note-taking should be arranged for in advance. Remember that secretaries have informal power, and part of negotiation is knowing when and how to use power.

Has someone been designated to provide the written report? Who must approve the notes? How soon can copies be made and distributed? (Today, a quiet notebook computer for taking notes streamlines this work.) This point is particularly important when negotiation is done in stages. People need to review what went on before making additional decisions. Also, people who missed the meeting or may be key decision makers should know what went on.

If you're part of a team and have volunteered to handle the recorder's job, you may not talk as much. But in that position you can deftly influence the people who read the document you produce—people on both sides of the negotiation—by language (word choice and placement, style, even rhythm) and overall tone, as well as select and highlight particular points while downplaying or editing out some others. Though you may appear to be only a secretary to the other side, you are one of the most important attendees there.)

Another person who wields quiet power is someone who writes on a flipchart or board, visibly summarizing what has been said. This may or may not be the discussion leader or moderator.

He or she can exercise considerable control by detailing specifics as the meeting proceeds, and also by summarizing the separate agendas.

You will find taking your own notes handy as the meeting rolls along. Mark the turning points in the discussion; you will want to refer to them when you summarize—periodically, and aloud for the others' benefit—what is happening in terms of concessions and compromises.

As the Agenda Unfolds

Is this meeting basically formal or informal? (Formal meetings have written agendas, prearranged minute-taking.) If the meeting has an agreed-upon agenda (as discussed in Chapter 9), you and your negotiating partners will want to adhere to it as closely as possible. This structure assists you in moving the discussion forward at all times. Frequently the reason for the meeting is multifaceted; there's not just one problem or possibility, but several. At such times an agenda reminds you not to stay just on one point, but at least cover them all in a preliminary way, for it might be possible to agree on one thing if not some others.

As a conscious competent negotiator, you know your goal well. Sometimes, however, you may need to assist your negotiating partner in determining what his or her goal is (or should be). Here again, there's the educational element at work.

How might you help your partners identify their goals? First, by asking questions, listening, and writing down what they say. Then repeat back to them what they've told you. Record it on a flipchart or chalkboard, where they can see it. Yes, now they can see that this is what they must know, or get, or become—or what must be changed, or what must happen—in order for their own needs to be satisfied. From there, they can talk about their agenda in the matter to be negotiated at the meeting.

Now you are ready to tell them, clearly, about your agenda, and answer whatever questions or concerns they may express. As the result of the opening gambit, both sides now know what the separate issues are, and are positioned to move into the we issues, working toward a mutual goal that will contain, as much as possible, each side's goal.

Building Trust

Negotiation is all about building mutual trust; no one will change a position if there isn't some level of trust and that means that you should not lie. Being caught in a downright deception is deadly. If you lie, it's also hard to remember what you said before—to this partner or to somebody else they may check with. Inconsistency can also be perceived as a lie. It's impossible to negotiate successfully when everyone mistrusts everyone else.

Not trusting at all can get you into as much trouble as being gullible. Many of us operate with an unconscious negative mindset. We believe everyone is out to do us in. Our inveterate suspicion hardens into cynicism, paranoia, and hostility. After a while, most people stop trying to deal with us. What's there even to negotiate?

To demonstrate that you are open to negotiation, show an open spirit initially. If you expect the best of people, often they will oblige and give you their best. On the other hand, let's be realistic. Con artists do exist. Watch for signs of their presence. Frequently, they are expert deceivers (they have no consciences to report to), so you may not easily spot them at first.

Ask these questions when you suspect that someone may be putting something over on you:

1. Do you find yourself uncomfortable, doubting what the other person is saying "for no reason"? Trust your intuition.

2. Is the deal too good to be true? In a business setup, everyone should profit in a clear, open way. Something that is too one-sided—you "get" everything because they're such nice guys—is probably not for real. There's some hook here somewhere (which may be intangible, such as power over you).

3. Does the other person's behavior reflect what you expect from someone in that position?

4. Is he or she telling the truth? How do you know if someone is lying? Does it "compute" with the homework you've done? Calibrate the lie. (Ask several questions about the company or the people, to which you already know the answers.)

Watch Your Timing

Good timing means knowing exactly what to say, when, and how. Run a litmus test on your timing by seeing what your negotiation partners are doing while you talk. If they interrupt you often, if they drum their fingers on the table or kick the floor, if they start packing up their papers or study the wallpaper designs, they are frustrated or bored.

In negotiating, pay attention to subtle, nonverbal, quick signals that show when your partners are wearying: darting eye movement, "plinked" eyeballs, a quarter-turn of the shoulders. You should know that you have just lost these persons. If you don't want to lose them forever, you've got to come up with another hook to grab them. I suggest these hooks:

- Summarize what you have already agreed upon.
- Reiterate what concessions they've already won.
- Ask them to be more specific about their goal—what they'd like to get out of the negotiation.
- Come up with new enticements that you've stowed away in your mental grabbag.
- Call time out for a brief recess or to meet another day (because you don't know what to do next).

Some persons—men probably more than women—become so intent on their negotiating that they are insensitive to the need to pace the negotiation to the personal and situational needs of their partners. They rush through or apply ever-mounting high pressure. If rebuffed or frustrated in getting a yes, they may become indignant, even mean. All the while, they don't seem to realize how they are putting the other side off so much that they lose any chance for making a deal.

Then there's the flip side of the time coin. You can take too much time presenting your proposal or detailing things people don't really need to know about now. You can waste time allowing somebody else to do the same to you. With most negotiating, patience can only be a virtue for a while. The difference between negotiating and arguing often is time management. Setting a time limit or pretending you have all the time in the world is a strategy and can be a negotiation leverage. The purpose of negotiation, after all, is to come to some agreement, even if that agreement is to end the negotiating before a solution is found. If nobody is pushing the agenda along, you may get caught in the backwaters somewhere.

Always be aware of the passage of time as you negotiate. Don't waste time—yours or, just as important, your negotiating partner's. But if you sense that his or her pacing needs are naturally slow and relaxed, and you love to rush along, if this deal is crucial to you, for heaven's sake follow your partner's style to succeed. But set limits on how long you're going to dally, and stick to them. Some people never agree to anything until you start walking out the door. And if they let you go, so be it. You can now move on.

The Patience Factor

There's a difference between a negotiation set up to arrange a business association of some kind and one that is intended to resolve a dispute. Sometimes a solution can be found in five minutes. At other times, it may take five hours, five days, or five months of concentrated negotiating. Expect that an agreement involving, for example, large sums of money or the employment of many people will require many meetings, reports, and reviews. But if it's only one person, say, for a short period at a reasonable fee plus material costs—when there is no huge commitment—the deal might be made very quickly.

Grievances between people or groups may take more time, patience, and human effort to settle, particularly if the disputes are longstanding. Cultivate the ability to be patient in working toward a decision or solution, along with a good sense of timing. Make sure that you also preserve the ability to be persistent and assertive all the while. Some people will keep you dangling for months if you do not seek closure. It is better to get a no now instead of a no ten months from now, if that no is truly inevitable.

Things to Remind Yourself to Do

There are a few simple but critical commandments to keep in mind as you negotiate, especially if tension is building. Make them into habitual billboards so you can consciously call them up.

- Separate issues from positions.
- Keep in mind: Intent before message!
- Observe and check out clues to any hidden agenda your negotiating partner may have.
- Negotiation is trust, attitude, information, need, and time management.
- Stay in contact with your negotiation partner's hopes.
- Be patient with the other side.
- Depersonalize any remarks that seem calculated to upset or offend you. "It's not about me, it's about them."
- Leave room in your position and bottom line for maneuvering.
- Pay heed to your pacing in order to create trust.
- Use silence as a tool.
- Go for satisfaction; success can kill you!

Above all, start with people "where they are at." Realize that you cannot change people's minds, but you might influence them to change their own minds about the negotiation taking place.

Watching Your Blind Spots

Blind spots happen when we are afraid, when we do not listen, when we are frozen in a decision or don't understand the culture of the setting in which we are negotiating. Here are some words of special warning. Some of us "go Catholic" when we negotiate: we somehow think this is the place for a confessional. It can occur particularly when we are nervous or unguardedly overconfident— we spill. When we do this, we give away information—and leverage—to the other side. We unintentionally provide the data that may prove detrimental to our position.

A few common blind spots are:

- Failing to read your own or the other side's body language
- Not recognizing nuances of timing (such as when to take a break)
- Losing track of the rhythm (discussion has moved to another issue and you didn't realize you had lost the point)

- Uncontrolled fear (You need the raise so desperately, you missed the opportunity to pick up on counteroffers: "We can give child care, stock options.")
- Unable to determine the true source of power or not noticing shifts in power

When Negotiating Gets Stalled

When negotiating is going well—in a direction and at a pace everyone's satisfied with—people relax into the style basic to them. But when it's going badly—when they feel pressured or fear they're losing ground—they either switch negotiating styles or go to the extreme of their normal style, adding to the confusion and heading backwards from any progress that's been made.

These are warning signs. You're probably showing some of them yourself. You've got to come up with some new options and proposals for consideration, or call the negotiation off before the scene gets worse. Schedule another meeting, or even end the effort.

Or maybe the other side introduces an issue that you haven't given prior thought to. You will probably then need to re-prepare. In that case, call time out. Schedule your next meeting, and try to end up on a still-hopeful note.

When you're in somebody else's office or on neutral ground, you can always get up and leave, giving whatever reasons that seem cogent at the time. But when you are on your own terrain, you will want to bring the meeting to a swift end in a firm but tactful manner. You can study your watch and find that it's time for an appointment elsewhere.

In the next chapter, we explore techniques of getting a stalled negotiation process back on track if you really want to hang in there and get to your goal.

12
WORKING TOWARD AGREEMENT

"There is more to life than increasing its speed."
— Mahatma Gandhi

One day in our conference room, while co-chairing a negotiation between our bank and a big corporation, I looked down that long, solid oak table. A dozen financial wizards, lined up in neat rows on each side, were scowling at each other. After an hour and a half of haggling, we were getting nowhere, and not fast.

Well, I leaned over and took off my right pump. It was high-heeled, of black calfskin. I fetched it up and banged it on the table, just like Khrushchev at the U.N. In the first second or two, they were all shocked silly. But this outrageous act somehow expressed our collective frustration. It broke the tension. They howled their approval.

Relaxing a bit now, we saw how we'd been unduly stressing ourselves. After a half-hour break, we came back and settled our business, to the satisfaction of everyone.

When you're negotiating, avoid taking yourself or the situation too seriously, as if everything in your life hangs on the outcome. A sense of humor often helps to filter what the world throws at us, and we gain some perspective on what's going on. Laughter can give some quick relief and new energy during pressured negotiations.

However, humor has to be done with respect for you and others. In serious negotiating, humor can offend, which means you lose in the long run. Avoid put-downs of anyone, including yourself, just to be "funny." If you need a fresh viewpoint and some respite, call time and take a break.

Are You Getting Somewhere?

When the negotiation process is going well, there's a continuous sense of progress. Not that the action is always easy; there may be arguing back and forth, tough bottom-lining, and feelings of anger, resentment, or suspicion. Still, when you're participating in partnership negotiation—to resolve a conflict fairly, say, or to set up a mutually profitable business deal—you won't have the same battle for dominance that characterizes victor-victim negotiating. In that negotiating style, the struggle for power compels you to protect your ego at all cost while competing aggressively.

In partnership negotiation, both sides try to see each other as equals, even if the playing field isn't level. And if you've looked after both of your needs and there is mutual trust, you should be able to hammer an agreement.

If you don't have a feeling of progress—if it seems stuck—analyze where the problems are. Call time. Even a five- or ten-minute break may help you gain some perspective on what's happening.

During this break, ask yourself: Am I so fixed on my goal that I'm not conveying some crucial verbal and nonverbal messages? Replay the verbal-nonverbal exchange. Quickly sequence the events.

If we bear down too hard on most substances, they will resist us, condense, or break apart. That can happen when we keep pushing ourselves in negotiation. We must be sensitive at all times to the climate of the meeting. People get bored or tired, frustrated or angry, fearful or tense. At such times your strategy must shift gears. Identify where a blockage may be and try to deal with the problems outright. If a momentary pause for refreshment seems desirable, lift the pressure.

Lighten Up! Do you know why angels can fly? Because they take themselves lightly.

Creating Alternatives to
Influence Momentum

When you seem to have hit a roadblock or brick wall, yet both sides are intent on working through to a resolution, what can you do?

I move into the solution-thinking mode. There are problems. To deal with them effectively, we must know exactly what they are. Sometimes the apparent problem isn't the one that's blocking the negotiation. It's a problem we haven't acknowledged. Or maybe it's a side problem not taken up yet but demanding attention. Or even something that happened earlier—a concession maybe, or some statement made—that is now resented or regretted.

Articulate and write down whatever problems are perceived right now by both sides. Is there a "deal breaker"? Are any of the problems unsolvable—that is, potentially fatal to reaching an agreement? Why do you or your negotiating partner think so? Deal with that issue. If you're confident that the problem can eventually be solved if you move on to other issues, table it for now. Give it prominence in a future agenda.

Now work on what you're confident you *can* solve. If issues are interconnected, list them in the sequence in which they should be decided. When the negotiation is jammed, it often helps to focus on matters that can be readily dealt with and agreed upon, to give both sides a feeling of accomplishment.

If you have devised an approach to resolving some matter, you'll want to persuade the other side to see it your way. Use persuasion to reach an agreement.

- Start with easy-to-settle issues.
- Send the most desirable message first.
- Always stress the need for agreement.
- Present both sides of an issue—yours *and* theirs.
- Remain open and flexible.
- Reaffirm the benefits from an agreement.

In your preparation, you decided on the various directions you might take if you encountered resistance. One is the Three Yes

Questions approach. You ask three questions that inevitably elicit positive responses from your negotiating partner, thus shifting the process in a positive direction.

Another is coming up with four alternative solutions to a dilemma. This tactic works especially well with Steamrollers. You explicitly state your various proposals, one after the other. You've placed the one you prefer third. Your partner will probably say, "No . . . no . . . yes . . . no." He or she wants to show his power by saying no emphatically, so the individual is pleased to have that chance. At the same time, if he or she wants to make a deal with you, the person knows there will have to be a yes sometime. And—clever you!—the one you prefer is really the only one he or she is apt to buy.

Still another tactic is to make a concession or two at this point. In your preparations, you strategized the order, type, and magnitude of concessions you might make. The first ones—for showing goodwill, perhaps—are really throwaways—those you can best afford to grant. (Any leftovers you might reserve for closing time throw in as little gifts.) Save the heavier concessions for times when the negotiation appears to be totally bogged down, but always try to keep one or two big ones as spares. Dramatize your concession making, too, so it's clear that you're not giving this up without some pain.

You can also brainstorm.

When things get stuck in a negotiation, I send up trial balloons. You know, the "what-if-we-were-to-do-this?" kind of solution. They're a bunch of ideas I come up with—on the spot, or things I've thought up earlier—that might help unjam the proceedings. And I never float just one; I always do at least three or four.

The responses I get from the other side can tell me a lot about their thinking and feeling. From that, I'm better able to search further for solutions and ask them for their own suggestions, which often inspires them to think creatively along with me. We're partnering.

But suppose you're still not close to reaching accord. What then?

- Check the level of trust.
- Are you really listening?
- Make sure you are being heard.
- Reassess the needs of both sides
- Is one side "winning"?
- Does the other side feel it is "losing"?
- Create new alternatives that satisfy both sides.

Other Ways to Get Your Way

What's that maxim? "All's fair in love and war." Some people would apply that to negotiation, as well. How much do you need what you want? How much is the goal worth to you? Whether you're negotiating on your own, for someone else, for your employer, or for the good of the world, at times you will aim to win, whether you feel you must or the cause is absolutely worthy.

I won't say these tactics are dirty tricks exactly, but I don't encourage women to use them regularly. They can become habitual. You will be resented and will lose trust when people see through what you've been doing to get your way.

You'll need to know these tactics, however, not only for contingency use when you're in a tight corner, but also because you should be able to recognize them when they are being used *against you.*

- The "broken record" technique—repeating the same things over and over so as to "brainwash" the other side.
- The old good guy–bad guy routine—when one person can switch back and forth; best done in team negotiating.
- Verbal assaults that unnerve the other side.
- Righteous indignation—the morally superior position.
- Acting nervous or fearful—to catch the other side off guard because you seem so weak.
- Looking sad, even crying—giving your opponents guilt, so they'll make concessions and even let you "win."
- Playing "dumb little me"—a cute, vulnerable bimbo.
- Flattering the big daddy on the other side, who is going to take care of you.

- Playing "big mama's going to do it for you, honey"—which works particularly well for older women.
- Flirting and other sexual wiles.

Men who believe that most women don't know how to win are apt not to be as much on the defensive or take the offensive when negotiating with women. Actually, partnership negotiation can often work well with them—far better than coming in as a hardliner. They may not even realize that you are negotiating, it is such a different style from theirs. Pulling the "gender card" on men who play by these rules can be a way women can cleverly manipulate their partner's sexism. Either the men are so obtuse that they don't notice it, or they feel so invulnerable they don't care.

When you know or suspect that any of these underhanded tactics are being used against you, refuse to role play, and tell your negotiating partner of your disapproval.

Be a Bit Outrageous

Only worry about something you can do something about. If you're stuck in a situation that you cannot change, at least you can work on changing your attitude about it. Humor may work better than outrage or anger.

I was driving on the freeway one morning when my car stalled in heavy traffic, in the outside lane. The man in the car behind me, trapped along with me, began leaning on his horn. I got out of my car and slowly walked up to him. As he rolled down his window, he looked ready to holler insults at me.

"Sir, you know what?" I said. "If you'll fix my engine, I could blow your horn." He looked at me then, like, Huh? "Okay," he finally replied, "I'll see what's going on." "I put the hood up already, so you can look at it while I sit in here and blow the horn." "Oh, you don't have to do *that!*" he said.

He couldn't fix it, but he ended up using his car telephone to call AAA for me. Frustrated to be trapped like that on his way to the office, an appointment, or maybe the airport, he had been ready to kill or explode. Fortunately for both of us, I managed to shift his attitude. You can't change anybody's mind, but you can help them change it.

That was a good example of my epigram, "Two people can't go crazy at the same time." Sometimes using humor will relieve a bad situation and move it to your advantage.

In the tactics just mentioned, there's one I didn't list. It may be a form of manipulation, but it's a category all its own, involving what we might consider reverse psychology. To do it well, you've got to be willing to distort the situation that's frustrating you and take it almost to an extreme. You can do it tongue-in-cheek, even with zany humor. At first the serious person on the other side may not realize what you're up to, but usually he or she finally gets it. By then, it is hoped, you've not only made your point, you've also persuaded your resistant or singleminded negotiating partner to budge.

Like everyone else, I don't win all the time. When I was negotiating to land a consulting position with John, who was the CEO at a garment-manufacturing firm, he clearly wanted me for the job, but balked at my fee. "I know a consultant in your field who works for half that price," he said. Which meant, since he felt he could readily obtain my equivalent, I should drop my fee 50 percent.

Right then, I decided to "crazy the crazy." This technique's always worked well with my three kids. "John," I said, "I know you can get a consultant for $30 an hour or less. Even for $5 an hour. I might even be able to find a person like that for you." And on and on I went in my crazy-making way. But this time my partner didn't say, "Okay, Nicole, I got the point! Let's make a deal." So I lost out with John, who did hire someone at half the price I'd have charged him.

But John came back to me a half-year later, looking sheepish. "The consultant I got really messed us up," he admitted. "I was a real jerk not to hire you, and pay the fee you asked for. It would have cost me a lot less in the long run. Because I want to hire you now."

A conscious, competent negotiator tries to educate her negotiating partner and, at times, help that person save face. So now I said in a measured, kindly voice, "John, you weren't a jerk. You just did not have all the information you needed when you made that first decision. Obviously you have it now, and you've made a good decision."

When you're negotiating, there's public talk and silent talk. Whenever you feel really frustrated, upset, or angry, talk any way you want to—*inside*. You can say the nastiest things about people, and in your mind's eye you can hang them with a noose, run them over backwards and forwards, do anything you want. You've created your own brief fantasy world as an outlet. Then you can take a deep breath and go back to negotiating with new calmness and purpose. In winning some negotiations, you've got to reach that new level, the "Shift Happens" plateau.

Have You Really Reached the Bottom Line?

You previously set limits on just how far down or up you'd be willing or able to go without losing. So has your negotiating partner. You also established how many concessions and what concessions you can make, or expect of the other side. If you have both reached the bottom line and you've still not attained an agreement, consider what else you might do.

For example, a company that has extra warehouse space can offer no-cost storage space to a supplier whose own facility is cramped, in exchange for a lower per-unit price. A corporation may provide free monthly parking at its city headquarters to a legal consultant whose retainer fee was over the budget. Similar non-money exchanges like this can be proposed to help sweeten the deal for both sides. Last-resort brainstorming and option seeking may turn up such possibilities.

Let Some Unresolved Issues Hang

For the sake of reaching some accord after hours, days, or even weeks of negotiation, you may want to come to a basic or interim agreement that encompasses all the points in dispute that you *do* agree on now. You can write that up and sign it, as evidence of the progress you have made, which may now be acted upon, if even in a limited manner.

At the same time the two sides can acknowledge in writing those that you have not as yet been able to work through. And you can also affirm in writing your intention to conduct further negotiations to resolve these remaining named issues, including any others that the process has stirred up. A schedule for resuming negotiations may even be set up for the future.

In most cases, it is better to have a limited understanding or resolution than none at all. It shows some positive outcome of time and effort expended, and displays the goodwill of both sides to continue the discussion that each side hopes will lead to further problem solving or conflict resolution.

Calling Off a Negotiation

Somewhere along the negotiation route you may realize that either agreement is possible now, or it's nowhere in sight. You are stalled. Everyone is frustrated. You must decide whether or not to end it. If you decide to end it, try to move off from it with as little rancor as possible. Be philosophical. If there's something worthwhile between you, maybe you'll want to do business or renew a relationship another day.

Making that connective spark between you usually means searching for some common ground. But you can move only so far from your side. Therefore, if your partner appears intractable in spite of all your efforts to get him or her to warm up or budge, before you give up totally see if you can get, straight out, an explanation—however brief—for the virtual refusal to negotiate. You may then have things to say yourself. Through this dialogue, each of you may then learn something important. Remember that mutual education is part of negotiating.

Some Negotiations Are Clearly Hopeless

Whether it's an unresolvable issue of price, principle, personality, or some other discordant element, many times you'll get to the point in a negotiation when you see it's fruitless to try further. Just throw in the towel as gracefully as possible. Move on and out, if you can; if not, just do your best with something you're stuck with, despite your arguments against it. And later, reflect upon what you've learned from the process. That's what you'll gain from it. It won't be the goal you'd set, but greater wisdom is something.

■   ■

Some of my most frustrating negotiations involve dealing with higher-level management, whenever they just can't or won't "get it." Where I work, they shoot from the hip. The worst instance was when my firm's executives decided to introduce the concept of performance quality to our division, probably because it was the latest "in" thing among those MBA types. First they sent three of us off on a mission to get information about training programs and write up reports. Then it turned out two other people had done the same thing—showing the higher level wasn't well organized about this plan.

Now they arbitrarily decided we could turn what's normally a two-week experiential course into a two-day lecture class. They just said, "Team together and do it, a month from now." "But this is premature," I protested at a meeting. "None of us is properly prepared to do this yet." "But we're going to do it, and you're going to teach it," I was told. So we did—and it was a total disaster, from Day One. At least I got them to call off Day Two.

Management in its infinite wisdom then decided a person on a higher level should take over. The man they put in charge took a stab at conducting another quality program with a different approach. Well, he bombed out worse than we did. He even got fired.

Gauged from outset, obviously there was less than a 50-50 chance of succeeding even minimally. But I couldn't stop the program; they simply wouldn't listen to me. Though I knew it was wrong to do the course that way, I didn't have all my ducks in the row so I could explain all the whys to them. Also, I should have proposed alternative recommendations, since I knew management was set on doing something about the quality thing. From the experience I've learned this: Don't take a problem in and not offer a solution.

Just bringing some matter into discussion raises the consciousness of all parties involved. But since the basic purpose of a negotiation is to come away with some agreement, without that agreement you cannot claim any real success. That comes with closure.

Getting to the Close

Have you taken the negotiation to the point where both sides are coming to an understanding? Maybe you've recognized what you both need to do business together. Or you're starting to formalize an agreement that will settle some conflict between you. Thus you are closing in on your aim in the negotiating process: reaching a resolution of some kind. You may not attain exactly the goal you'd set; still, if you've gotten anywhere near it, you can feel satisfied—or relieved, anyway.

But your work isn't over yet. Getting closure is the first of the final steps in the negotiation process. If it's a business or some other kind of deal, there will be paperwork going back and forth, money transactions, and more phone calls. Depending on your position, you may be involved in handling the subsequent follow through details.

If you've kept good notes and nobody else has, you may find an excellent use for them when finalizing the terms of the agreement, which will take into account the concessions, compromises, and other points negotiated.

In various situations, it is sensible for you and your negotiating partner to discuss now, openly and candidly, the possibility that someday things might go wrong between you. This may seem remote at the time, especially if the whole negotiation has gone smoothly and amicably. Naturally, you'll be hesitant to bring this subject up; it's a bit like discussing divorce during a honeymoon. However, in agreements you make with others you may wish to have provisions for handling future disagreements, as a sensible contingency measure.

Contracts and Agreements

If the negotiation is a business arrangement and has taken place over something you have proposed, in your preparation for it you'll be advised to draft an agreement, preferably using a word processor. Take copies with you when you negotiate so that, at the appropriate time when you're getting into the closing, you can pass them out for study. If you have left blank spaces for issues to be arranged in the negotiation—such as delivery time, price or fee, and place—they are filled in now. Whole new clauses can be added, or contents may be altered with deletions and insertions, done either on a typewriter or in handwriting and then okayed by two sets of initials.

This preliminary document may thus be officially signed once there is complete agreement on terms, so there is already a surety of agreement. When time, effort, money, or risk-taking—in business, it's often all four—are involved, you will want this legal document as insurance against the other side's possible failure to meet its obligations. Until you have a signed commitment or a written purchase order, it is unwise to proceed further. If the changes to the preliminary agreement are major, the document can be reprocessed.

To some people, a contract may seem coldblooded and overly rational. However, whenever you put yourself in a vulnerable position—financially, legally, physically, emotionally, socially—you may wish to obtain a written agreement. It serves as a reminder of the terms on which the relationship exists, and may even spell out consequences if those terms are ignored or are violated.

But it wasn't always like this.

At a business conference where I'd given a keynote speech, an elderly man with a white mustache and full head of hair came up to me afterwards and gave me his card. Gustav said he was a first-generation American, from Eastern Europe like me. Right on the spot, he asked me to come to his manufacturing firm in the Midwest and give a three-day training program for middle-level managers. We agreed on the various terms and shook hands.

When I got home I mailed off a contract to Gus. But it wasn't returned to me, nor did the man respond to several letters and then two fax messages. The time for the trip was fast approaching, and by now I assumed our deal was off. But just to make sure, I decided I'd better call Gus. He came on the phone. "Yah, sure I want you here!" he boomed. "But why do I have to read all those papers you are sending me?" I began laughing. "Well, I really blew it with you!" I admitted. "I should have remembered my grandfather. In his time and place, nobody signed contracts. For them, a handshake always finalized any deal. You and I *did* shake hands, right?" "So you'll still come, and I don't have to read that junk you sent?" "I'll come," I assured him. But there aren't many people, companies, or organizations I'll work for without a signed contract. With Gus, I knew his handshake had a moral force behind it, even better than a signature.

People and companies may readily "forget" about a deal you thought you made with them, which was all-important to you but of little consequence to them, or something they conveniently choose to retract if cash-flow became a problem. Remind them about you, wait, and hope all's still okay. If you've got your prior understanding in writing with their signatures on it, so much the better.

You might be concerned that being businesslike and serious, not casual and informal, is inappropriate in certain negotiating situations, even if they involve crucial matters. If you feel, however, that a written agreement is essential, and come with document in hand or prepared to produce one, getting the other side to see this as important will be part of your negotiation—as, for example, in personal relationships where you may wish to set down new understandings. This is standard and customary when conflict resolution has involved professional assistance or mediation.

Investigate the availability in stationery stores and bookstores of paperback manuals and boilerplate forms. These generic contracts can be photocopied and altered for your situation. Some software programs also include alterable agreements.

Since handwritten documents, signed and dated, are also legal instruments, don't hesitate to produce one if you really want to bring off a deal but you're negotiating far from a typewriter, computer, fax, or copier machine—in a restaurant, say, or on a vacation to Bali!

And don't forget that fax machines instantly relay contracts for review and signing, a real boon with phone- or letter-negotiated agreements. Consider employing other high-tech assistance, not just when finalizing your agreement but at points in between. Use the photocopy machine to produce agendas, proposals, contract drafts, and other documents for all who need them; audiotape the discussion leading to agreement; use portable computers for notetaking and office computers for electronic mail and other communications; access information through modems; obtain documents (and technical backups, designs, plans) through fax transmission.

Don't Forget Those Followthroughs

The results of a good negotiation should stay with you, so don't forget these points:

- Come through with all you've promised. (Check your and their expectation vs. reality.)
- If you're running into any problems with followthrough, alert your negotiating partners as soon as possible and try to renegotiate so that both sides are satisfied with the deal and you don't lose credibility and trust. (I did provide that delivery date and I can't . . . new solution.)
- Keep close track of your negotiating partner's side of the deal. (Let's be sure you won it without its costing you too much overtime.)
- Keep in touch even when you don't need your agreement partner. (For example, send articles, or call and say "How about a cup of coffee?")
- Be available when they need you.
- Prepare them and yourself for the next negotiation by reminding them of the positive results of the past negotiation. ("We made some good decisions.")

Why Some Negotiations Fail

Let's look finally at the main reasons why things can go awry. These conditions can occur on either or both sides, and the existence of only one of them—let alone several—may be enough to doom a negotiation and future goodwill.

ORGANIZATION FACTORS

Wrong opening move
No game plan
Poor preparation
Not being clear on the bottom line (when to walk)
Insufficient information or wrong information
Mixed up facts, assumptions, hopes

Lack of experience in organizing
Inability to measure up to superior competitors
Incompatible schedules, time frames
Unsuitable goods (quality, quantity, type)
Bad planning
Evidence of poor followthrough ability
Lack of implementation plan
Absence of specific date, verifications
Unrealistic goal setting, unclear, unrealistic expectations
Inadequate resources

INFLUENCES AND PERSONALITY FACTORS

Fear as the motivator
Not clarifying or managing the kind of negotiating climate you want
Bad (unethical) intentions
Personalizing issues when you lose your energy and time
Distrust and suspicion of other side
Constant one-sided compromise
Clearing up historical negative perceptions
Cultural misunderstanding or insensitivity
Other side doesn't know how to negotiate and you don't recognize it early enough
Not celebrating small movements or not declaring others' wins
Hidden agenda
Too many bluffs
Mutual dislike, hostility, psychological warfare
Wrong person negotiating the deal
Vengeance toward or sabotage of other
Too few or too small concessions against demand
Habitual mistreatment of other person
Lack of goodwill and respect
Not observing nonverbal clues until it's too late

MISTAKES AT MEETING

Accepted first offer
Wrong place, wrong time

Irrationality, emotionalism
Not knowing how to get back what you've given away wrongly
Changed issues, not declared
Unfocused or lethargic interest
Wrong presentation of information—too much or too little data
Loss of the sight of the goal
Defective communication
No review of options or evidence why your offer is valuable
Defensive, offensive, without counting concessions and release
Poor timing (too slow, fast, inappropriate)
No agenda or no involvement of partner in agenda
Unmatched style and pace between partners—nobody stretches to
    adopt
Too serious—forgot it's a game
Unresolved, unrecognized, and unmanaged power and control is-
    sues between partners
Inflexibility when maintaining position—aggressive vs. negotiative
Misread shifts of style
No attention paid to others' comfort or discomfort zones
Bottom lines rigidly set on both sides
Adverse attitude, such as cocky or frivolous
Resistance to persuasion
Overpressuring the other—not knowing when to stop, back
    up, go
Indecisiveness at the wrong time
Backing away from any conflict vs. moving with the conflict to res-
    olution
Threats (outright or veiled)
Failure to push toward closure—visiting too long
No risk or too much risk—no clear rewards

If any of the above negatives characterize one or the other party's position, attitude, or action, the negotiation will be pointless
unless the problem is addressed, negotiated, and corrected to mutual satisfaction.

NEGOTIATING FOR YOUR LIFE

- EXERCISE -

Think of an unsuccessful negotiation experience

1. What went wrong in terms of organization factors?

2. What went wrong with the influences and personality factors?

3. What went wrong at the meeting management?

4. What can you commit to do differently in a similar situation?

5. What skill do you need to sharpen or acquire more of to implement commitment?

6. What payoff can you anticipate if you will change your approaches?

13
TACTICS FOR SPECIAL CIRCUMSTANCES

"Winners dwell on their desires, not on their limitations."
—Martina Navratilova

Robin was promoted to a new position as the Number 2 person in a large transportation company. I asked her what her title would be. She said, "Who cares?! As long as they pay me!"

Sometimes, as a teacher, I think that I do nothing but negotiate with the thirty kids in my care. I also find that I am a teacher of negotiation—helping the children achieve their goals, resolve their conflicts.

The spectrum of negotiating situations in our professional lives is infinite, from obtaining a job or a contract to functioning successfully within that job to exiting a position or terminating an agreement. There are many books, manuals, classes, and advisory services that focus on successful job hunting. Here, we concentrate on specific potential aspects of job negotiating. Let's start with money.

In the initial interview, unless it's with the key decision maker for hiring you, you probably won't negotiate the details of salary and benefits. You should always go in, however, with an explicit idea of what the position is worth. If a job ad did not state a salary or salary range, find out—if you don't already know—the usual range for positions in that classification, whether calculated on an hourly rate (typical of professional trades) or in monthly or annual earnings. Professional associations can be helpful here (National Association of Women Architects, National Association of Home-builders, etc.).

Do not be naive about what you should earn. Ask upfront, at the initial interview, what the salary or salary range is for the job. Even a ballpark figure will do. If it is too low, you may decide to remove yourself from the running. On the other hand, if the situation interests you and there's strong interest in hiring you, you might be able to talk them into a higher figure, plus other benefits. Salary is important, but it should not necessarily determine your decision. In your homework, determine what your specific goals are in negotiating a position. If you are offered two different positions in the same time period, you may be willing to take the one with a lower salary because it promises more challenge, empowerment, title, connections, and learning opportunity.

Look at benefits and perquisites (the "perks") in addition to salary. What is the health insurance package worth to you? (It may include dental and eye care, for example, and have monthly value of over $200.) Could you get a company car and also have gasoline paid for? What's a free garage parking space worth in a downtown area? Will you have a commission and bonuses? An expense account? Travel opportunities (if you want them)? Will you get credit for unused sick leave? Is child care available? What kind of vacation leave is there, including sabbaticals? Could you get additional education through company sponsorship, such as enrollment in an MBA or other master's program, and special professional training? Can you have some choice about projects you might work on and new equipment you might need to do the work in a more efficient way? Will the company pay for membership in a civic or professional group that would give you information and business contacts along with conveying prestige and social exposure? Is it possible to work out flex time, coming in at alternative hours and even working some of the time at home? Companies are increasingly less rigid in the setups for employees, especially those who are valued for their creativity and problem-solving abilities. These are other items that could be used as trade-offs when negotiating salary, with some of them bargaining chips when later seeking a raise, after you've been hired.

When a salary range is specified, say $25,500 to $32,000, fight hard to end up in the middle, or a little above if you can't make it quite to the top. If your experience is minimal, however, show your fast learning skills in previous jobs. Remember as you negotiate salary that women often earn less than men in equivalent positions because they tend to accept a lower salary to begin with, and then find it hard to "catch up" with male associates of the same seniority.

If you sense that the company wants you, realize that it may not want to quibble over a few thousand dollars. Leave some "win" for them. You start high so they can say, "We got her at a good price." They won't lose respect for you; after all, you didn't agree to take the position "at any price." You should then be earning the income you need and deserve, but also gaining others' respect along with your own.

Once at your job, some initial negotiating issues in setting up the position periodically recur in different forms, as when asking for a raise or a promotion; these are covered later in the chapter. Much of the time, however, your negotiating will be concerned with handling relationships or situations with associates, subordinates, internal management, and outside vendors and customers.

Negotiating the Situation You're in

Let's say that you decide to attempt changing bothersome circumstances about your job. First, make a list of the things that bother you, then group them, such as:

1. Management issues, derived from people in executive positions who may be overbearing, inattentive, insensitive, ignorant, wasteful, temperamental, and reluctant to share information.

2. Problems with associates and co-workers, or people in other divisions—all of whom function independently of you— who may be undependable, time-wasteful, ill-functioning, inexperienced, unwilling to cooperate, undermining, harassing.

3. Problems with persons in subordinate positions whose job performances are erratic, inferior, or inadequate but whom you cannot or do not want to fire.

4. Problems with clients, suppliers, or other outside people with whom you do business, whom you do not like or trust but must nonetheless deal with.

5. Annoyances about the physical workplace—lack of or inferiority of equipment, air or noise pollution, cramped quarters, dirty or rundown and depressing appearance.

6. Your own resentment, based on a sense of being taken advantage of as an employee; expectation of working long hours and on weekends (with possibly unpaid overtime), salary lower than merited, poor benefit package, too much traveling, unreasonable demands and expectations.

7. Dislike of other aspects of the job, such as commuting distance, time, expense, and traffic congestion; no parking space available; remote or inconvenient plant location; little or no rapport with other employees, lack of team spirit.

8. Inability to see a challenging and rewarding future for yourself in this job; you have possibly reached limits of further advancement.

Let's discuss negotiating tactics for some of these common situations.

Problems with Higher Authority

The situation's dynamics are different, of course, when you occupy a subordinate position. Your boss may be an individual incapable of partnering with anyone, including people on his or her level, and possibly a spouse at home. But do not assume this because it seems so and others say so. Unless you personally have already attempted a dialogue, perhaps several times, and found that the effort is futile, don't back away from trying to negotiate. Remember, because you will be seen as an "inferior," you cannot demonstrate an egalitarian or partnering approach unless the person relaxes and allows it.

The "boss" whom you must approach about particular issues that bother you and you wish to negotiate may in actuality be a management hierarchy or a system that is or has become nearly impenetrable. Within that seemingly rigid structure, however, there usually are some accessible human beings who have remained open to others, are willing to talk with you, and can pass on their own opinions to other people, ultimately reaching the decision-making level. Your assignment is first to find these people, then to negotiate with them and coach them how to help you. Within a large corporation, locating possible key advisors and coaches in higher places is not easy, however.

You must also decide whether you will be better served dealing directly with people or through writing a memorandum or report, solicited or unsolicited, that details your observations, facts, and suggestions for change. A combination of the two may work most effectively, since all personality types and negotiating styles (Steamrollers and Datacrats, particularly) will be accommodated. Summarize the issues you make at the start of a long memorandum, and also end with a summary statement.

Sometimes you encounter problems with supervisors and managers who are veritable workaholics and expect you to be the same. You may frequently be expected or required to work in the evenings and on weekends. On occasion, when handling a rush deadline or a crisis, extraordinary 105 percent participation is essential. But normally it should not be, and reflects poorly on someone's management skills. It means that work allocation is inappropriate and unrealistic, and there are insufficient resources in your sphere of work. If your manager goes along with this, and expects his or her subordinates to do the same, you're caught in a bad situation. Try to get your co-workers to make a concerted protest to management about an intolerable situation.

Some people live for their jobs. If such a person is doing his or her own thing capably and happily, why care? But if your life gets affected by a manager's work addiction, you've got to set limits on what you'll do when, how often, and why. Psychologically speaking, some managers—by overworking themselves and you—are evading problem situations at home. Others simply don't seem to understand that there's a life outside the workplace. You can talk to them about your need to live your life, but they may not quite understand this until they "get a life" of their own.

I first met Tom when I was giving a seminar on hiring issues at a high-tech firm. How could I ever forget him? He asserted that he'd never hire a person who was unwilling or unable to work a minimum of fourteen hours a day, as he did. "That's our work pace here," he said, obviously relishing it.

Three years later, I came back to do a training program. Tom attended it. During one session, he said that everybody working for him should be able to do their assigned jobs within an eight-hour day. "If they can't, and they're capable, there's something wrong."

"Tom, what happened to change your opinion?" I was amazed. "Oh," he told me, "when I got married, my wife said she'd like to see me once in a while. Then we had a baby. I don't want to come home every night too late to have dinner and play with our little boy. Having that kid shifted my priorities; until then I couldn't understand what most of the women project managers were talking about."

When we, as women, start negotiating for a balanced life, we're indirectly and directly modeling ways for men to have it as well, when they give themselves permission to negotiate for it—which begins with self-negotiation. Because he was a project manager, Tom could control assignment scheduling and fulfillment better than those who worked under his leadership. That doesn't mean, however, that team associates can't negotiate for improved working conditions.

Marina works for a traditionally all-male transportation company, where to succeed you are married to the job, especially if you're single. Though Marina is single, she wanted to have a life away from work.

When I told my project manager and team members that I had to leave each night by 6 P.M., the manager said, "So what's the big rush?"

I showed empathy. "I can understand your concern," I said, and I am willing to work five hours extra each week, if necessary. I will also work late—under unusual circumstances."

"But what do you have to go home to?" he asked, disbelievingly. I offered more solutions, such as taking work home at times. And I proposed better approaches to producing quality products more consistently and cost-effectively than we'd been doing it so far. But I said I needed time for myself.

"Buy why?" he persisted. My tactic was to keep going back to my original statement and repeat my offers of compensatory commitment and working to make the "system" more efficient.

He finally gave in, and agreed to anticipate emergency situations that would sometimes require occasional overtime from me.

In this example of professional partnership negotiating, Marina set her own limits and then took a risk in negotiating for them. She didn't lecture the manager. ("You should go home, too!") She wasn't carrying a chip on her shoulder, which would have caused her to attack. ("So because I am single, you think I don't need to have a life?") Instead, she stayed calm and didn't personalize the situation. She offered both options and solutions. She used the "rescue" method of repeating her original statement in a neutral tone and kept clearly focused on her goal: to leave time and energy for a separate life to be enjoyed away from her job.

When men and women become partners in negotiating for a more humane workplace, we'll all be better off. Job overload and stress now and then may be tolerable, and some people who like being challenged by deadlines actually thrive at such times. But keeping up such a pace continuously is hazardous to your health. Know your limits as a worker. And know your rights as an employee. Information is power when you need it. Health problems traceable to stress-related situations at work can be litigated, and negotiating with your employer may involve a brief reminder when there's no letup in sight.

Desensitizing Yourself
When Dealing with Difficult Clients

Most of us have frequent or constant contact with people outside our place of work with whom we negotiate to buy or sell goods or services, or make arrangements relevant to our company's interests and concerns. Inevitably, disagreements and problems arise. How we handle them, as representatives for our employer, reflects on our own qualifications for the job.

If we're naturally quick-tempered, for example, we have to learn to curb that tendency. Or if we're too easygoing in a fast-paced, tough-bargaining business game, we'll have to adapt our character to a different mode if we're going to succeed. You're now back to self-negotiating—to asking yourself what it costs you to adapt, and where and what the benefits are.

> For several years I've worked in customer services in a large department store, handling customer complaints. Each day, dozens of phone calls come in from angry people, and sometimes irate customers come into our office and yell at us.
>
> When I got trained for the job, I was advised never to get emotionally involved in whatever was said, no matter what. To stay pleasant and detached. To listen very carefully and never argue back, especially getting mad. This was hard for me, because I fight back when I feel attacked.
>
> I always try to agree with the complainer in a mild way that helps defuse their disturbance. "Yes, sir, I can imagine how upset you feel." "Sure, ma'am, I can understand how disappointed you are." If they exaggerate the circumstance and obviously distort the truth to get some reaction from me, I'll go along with it, and repeat back what they've said. When it comes back to them like that—and I sometimes do this in a humorous way—they'll usually grasp how ridiculous they sound. I don't feel that the customer has a right to abuse me. However, I make a game out of redirecting their angry energy by listening, and not judging their feelings.
>
> Once they've vented, they start calming down; I've made them feel "heard." Then we can start negotiating the problem. They are able to listen to me and together we'll usually work out a solution that satisfies them, whereas if I'd shouted back at them at the start, the problem could never have gotten resolved.

Taking an approach like this may work out well for you in a variety of situations where you or the company you work for comes under a barrage of attacks from outsiders. Remember, "You can't fight fire with fire. All you'll end up with is ashes."

Asking for a Raise

Years ago, when asking for a raise, I brought in a journal that had entries for each workday showing on one side what I had accomplished and on the other side what I had learned. Another time, after I'd initiated a new program that saved the corporation many thousands of dollars through reducing costs, I asked my boss the Three Yes Questions, the last one being whether he thought my actions merited a raise worth 15 cents per minute. (That was way back in the 1970s, equivalent to about 50 cents today.) He immediately agreed to this minuscule incremental increase, not thinking at the time that in an eight-hour workday, this amounted to $9 an hour or $72 a day—or $360 a week, about $1,450 a month, to a grand total of more than $17,000 a year! Soon afterward, though, this banker did the figuring, and when he spotted me in the hallway admitted, "You sure got me!" However, he didn't renege on the deal. A Steamroller himself, he surely felt I deserved it for sheer cleverness.

Requesting a higher salary is a challenge for anyone, particularly for women. There's often this issue of feeling inherently that we don't merit more than what we're already getting; we may even suspect that we don't deserve that. We can be intellectually conscious of the absurdity of not getting equal pay for equal work. But emotionally we feel those old undercurrents that make us hesitant to demand more.

We're also schooled not to ask for things, and to believe that we'll be rewarded if we're good. If we do assert ourselves, people will think we're pushy; they're going to dislike us and not want us around, as punishment for our presumptuousness and for drawing undue attention to ourselves.

These two tendencies—feeling undeserving and reluctant to request something for ourselves—cause us to refrain from asking for something better, which we may know we deserve on the basis of our value, accomplishments, dependability, and commitment. A better salary, a better position, better benefits and perks, better acknowledgment and visibility, and so on.

In some workplaces, unless a freeze is on, raises are automatic. You're there for six months or a year, and if your work is good you get a specific increase in your paycheck. There are also merit raises, given at the discretion of the employer. In many jobs, though, you have to ask for an increase in wages. When you take a job, you'll want to know who decides the issue of raises, when, and how. You may set, then, a specific period of time after you start work when you can be expected to bring up the matter. (If during the interval you're promoted, that's of course an earlier time to renegotiate your salary and benefits significantly upwards.) If in your initial negotiation you held out for a higher salary then they intended to give you and you won, you may feel sufficiently rewarded to hold off a request for a while.

If a raise is dependent upon a job performance review at the end of a year, you should keep that in mind as you build your case. Employers and the managers who represent them may use minor strikes against you as reasons for not giving you a raise, or for giving you only a small one, not what they might have originally implied would be due you.

If defects have been noted in your job evaluation, you'll need to be prepared to counter damaging assertions, in a calm and rational way, with your demonstrable value. Handle criticism that is given to you at such reviews or at other times by your superiors as calmly as you can. Do not leap up in anger, and get defensive or accusative. This behavior won't help you; will only aggravate your situation.

If you tend to cry when criticized, whether or not you believe there's any merit in the criticism, don't stiffen up to fight back the feelings so that you'll become rigid or inaccessible. If you cry, you cry; just try to keep from a noisy or wet display, particularly with Datacrats and Steamrollers, neither of whom are comfortable with emotions.

Here's a helpful tactic to use whenever you feel attacked by someone in the workplace who's judging you. Visualize your whole self swathed with a layer of soft white gauze as light as air. The layer between you and this outside skin now becomes flooded with warm golden sunshine. You are protected from direct contact with whatever information is given to you. You hear it, but it doesn't quite touch your body, your mind.

If told about a person's negative perception of or specific experience with you, you might say something like, "That's not how I see it," and perhaps briefly say why. Remember that the informant actually may not be a favorite of the reviewer, who is only reporting that point of view. You may have gathered up, for instance, appreciative notes from department heads in other divisions, and from customers and clients for work you did in their behalf. You may have assembled before-and-after statistics that measurably demonstrate your achievements in bringing in or saving money, or in saving time, which has value too. You may even have prepared lists of accomplishments, and graphs that visually show the positive side of your work, which the reviewer or review committee may have failed to notice.

If you feel shaky in approaching your boss for a raise, worry over being seen as a malcontent for protesting aspects of your job, or are concerned that criticism about your job performance may lead to getting fired, always keep in mind this reality: it will cost the company a large sum, probably at least several thousand dollars, to fire you and then replace you with someone else, who'll take time being trained and brought up to speed. If a confrontation with higher authority threatens you with dismissal, you may want to remind this person calmly of that cost. (Try to find out from someone in human resources a fairly exact figure.) Unless you're a serious nuisance, they may not want the expenditure of both time and money.

Negotiating for Opportunities Instead of Raises

A higher salary is usually welcomed by us all. It sets a new figure compensating us for the work we do, and that has transfer value elsewhere. A raise also means that we'll pay higher taxes, and in some income brackets and households that isn't necessarily desirable, especially if it means you'll net about what you had before.

It often happens, too, that your employer can't afford to give you a raise—at least a significant one. He or she can show you the annual and monthly budgets, and you'll see that the cash just isn't there right now.

Be concerned if other people are receiving raises—the word does get around—and you aren't. Find out why. Notice whether males have been favored over females. (There's still that lingering opinion that men "need" the money more than women, and are also more valuable as workers!)

If your work has been good and they know it, try to negotiate for things that may actually be worth more to you than additional money. You might want to cut back on your work week by job

sharing (go back to school, take a second job, start a business of your own on the side, spend more time with your children). You might ask to do some of your job at home, especially if you're involved in creative endeavors or computer work, saving yourself commuting time and other hassles.

Another thing you can ask for is the opportunity to represent the company with one or more civic and professional organizations that meet locally, regionally, even nationally. Often managers are burned out on meetings and avoid them unless absolutely essential. Having your own membership in the chamber of commerce or the Lions Club might be worth several hundred dollars to you. You could write off lunches and dinners, and meet a number of people who would be useful contacts for the future if you need to look for another job.

You can also volunteer to be a liaison between the company and visitors, including prospective employees and people from other organizations who are touring the facility. Doing extra work like this gives you special credit. It also puts you in a position to acquire more and updated information that others on your level do not have, and allows you to become known to influential people positioned in other departments.

Negotiating for a New Position

Sometimes managers recognize our abilities early on the job and begin promoting us into higher positions. Nowadays younger employees coming into entry-level or management-grooming positions, probably out of technical and professional training schools, expect to move rapidly up the ladder. In the past, significant moves might come every decade. Now we expect them to take place every year or so. If they don't, we're apt to question why not. Is it something in us that is preventing the forward and upward motion? Or could there be something in the system at the company that is retarding our progress?

Women, it's often been noted, tend to make themselves comfortable in the job they've been given, especially if it has some room for them to expand while they settle in. For instance, you may take a new job with a company, work hard to prove yourself loyal, worthy, likable. You become a good cooperator and supporter of others' efforts. You are efficient, organized, good at training others to learn new tasks. And managers might say to themselves, especially if your predecessors bombed out, "Why not keep her right where she is?"

If you're ambitious and are becoming resentful of this help-meet role, do several things. Let your superiors know that you want to move ahead yourself, and don't want to spend the rest of your work years enabling others to do so. And if your position allows it, hire an assistant whom you can deliberately groom to replace you. Some of us are apt to feel uneasy about doing so, out of fear that this person will then look so good that he or she will show us up and take over our job. Let both the managers and this assistant know what you're up to. At the same time, start investigating jobs with other companies, just in case your message of warning didn't get through.

We are told often of the glass ceiling that keeps women from being admitted to top management. There is evidence, on the other hand, that women who are determined, bright, diplomatic, resourceful, self-confident, assertive, and in control of their lives have an excellent chance at succeeding in some high places—including a company of their own making, should they be prevented from rising to the heights elsewhere.

If you ever feel you're getting stalled on your route to your job goal, start questioning the system if you believe that you're doing everything right. Watch out for a growing number of lateral moves, in which you're shunted sideways rather than upward. (A certain amount of experience in various divisions, however, in house and in the field is traditionally expected of people moving up through management. Make sure if this happens with you, that is the firm's express intention.)

When you're feeling stalled and discounted, do a private assessment of your strengths and weaknesses on the job. You may get useful feedback from associates whom you trust, who also see you objectively. Let the information you assemble sit on the paper for a few days and ponder it. There's a possibility, once you decide to move off a defensive and subjective position, that you'll see areas where you should improve your job performance if you intend to advance.

If you still think you're encountering unreasonable resistance

to further advancement, instead of growing resentful or bitter, try discussing your impression with management. "What must I do to get where I want to go?" Tactically speaking, do not overtly accuse them of a male conspiracy, even though you suspect it.

Actually, most corporations nowadays have been sufficiently sensitized about, and warned against, preventing women from occupying high-level executive positions. If they find just the right person whom they'll feel comfortable with while they respect her abilities, they are likely to pick her, for sheer public relations value if nothing else. You might in fact persuade them through the way you conduct your campaign that you are the one to move into the highest position as yet given to a person of your gender. So just because you don't see any women in the upper echelons does not mean that you cannot be the first one in the boardroom.

■ RENEGOTIATING YOUR PAST

My boss obviously remembers how a month ago I cried after getting some negative feedback in my job performance evaluation. I know he's hesitant to approach me now with any corrective criticism at all. He's not the kid gloves type, and he doesn't like holding back. I'll bet he's going to fire me one of these days; it would be easier for him than to walk on eggs around me.

Last week I really blew up at a staff meeting. To make matters worse, it was the first time I was chairing it, in my new position. I got out of sorts during a heated argument over some problem-solving matter, and gave a few people hell. "That heavy-duty job's too much for her," is probably what my associates and subordinates are saying behind my back. By now my boss has probably heard about it, and worries that I'm not hacking it. What on earth can I do to change the prevailing impression?

People tend to peg others as always being or doing something in a particular way, partly so they can accurately predict behavior. If we don't like being stuck in a tight box with a label on it, whether it's a box someone else has put us in or we've inadvertently climbed into it ourselves, we should always keep this in mind: We *can* renegotiate our reputations with others. How? By doing things differently than people expect us to, based on their previous experience and observation of us.

If this is your situation, you must visibly and consistently change your pattern of responding and behaving to get people to see you in a new light and trust any transformation you make. You want to break out of that old image. Just as in negotiating with others, you must prepare for this—plan how you'll do it.

In the examples just given, for instance, the first woman could tell her boss calmly and candidly that, in reviewing their discussion, she realized that she overreacted when advised of areas in which she should improve on the job. And then let him know that she hopes he won't hesitate to alert her to any shortcomings in the future, though she hopes to have fewer of them. In the second case, the woman could make sure that she won't lose her self-control in future meetings she presides over. Also, she can level with her boss about what happened, admit the error, and solicit his advice on how to handle similar predicaments. It is far better to acknowledge mistakes that are evident to and involve others and try to amend them than to ignore them and hope they'll disappear.

It may take more than one scenario to establish a new, improved you. If you're really determined, go at it consciously, consistently. Suppose you come in late for almost every meeting, and maybe even to work in the morning. People make running jokes about it in front of you. But if they need you to be there, they are sure to become increasingly annoyed. Nobody likes to wait for someone else, or be otherwise inconvenienced; we all have schedules to follow. A person who cannot respect other people's time will not be tolerated for long. If you are needed at your desk or at a meeting at a particular time, it won't matter to others that you stay in the office and work late. Your excuses and apologizing will not mollify them. The only way you can correct the impression of near-perpetual tardiness is to change your own behavior: rearrange your life habits so that rarely if ever will you be late, anywhere. At first you may elicit surprise and more jokes, which at least draws people's attention to the fact that you *are* now on time. Let others know, too, that you are deliberately making an effort to reform.

Renegotiating your reputation naturally requires negotiating with yourself first.

What to Do in a Downturn

The big boss came into my office yesterday and said he had to lay off 50 percent of the employees. "We've got to downsize," Larry said. "Hardly anybody's buying, and nobody's paying their bills." Bankruptcy might be avoided by cutting all expenses to the bone. "We want to keep you here at Foodpak, June. Your expertise in handling sales and marketing needs will be real assets. But . . ." he paused, "if you stay, you'll have to take a 50 percent cut in your salary and commissions until we come out of this tailspin."

"Hmmm," I said, knowing he wasn't done yet.

"Another thing," he went on, "is that you'll have to take over other people's duties. You can use all those practical skills you came here with how many years ago?"

"Twelve," I murmured.

"Started as a secretary, right?"

"Yes," I said, "while I was working on my MBA."

"Anyway, June, we'll all pitch in to save the ship. Work overtime and on weekends." Larry gazed out the window, stalling on giving more bad news. "The cutback also involves expenses the company's covered till now. We're dropping the leased company cars. I'll have to preapprove any expense-account expenditures. Most out-of-town conferences are out." So all those perks I love were going down the tube, too. "Well, how about it, June?"

"I must give it careful consideration, Larry," I said. "I can't live on just half of what I've been earning."

"But your husband's salary. . . ."

"Jim got laid off three months ago, and nothing has turned up for him yet."

As he headed for the door, Larry turned and gave a sweeping look around my office. "And June, the whole accounts receivable department is moving upstairs. Two or three people can use this space. So you've got to move out, maybe share with Ron. . . ." After saying he needed my decision by Friday, Larry was gone. Well, at least I wasn't laid off, as so many others have been.

Caught between a rock and a hard place, June was almost in tears. "Which do you prefer to do?" I asked. "Stay on at Foodpak, under conditions you obviously don't like compared with the past, or take your chances out in the open sea along with your husband?"

"Foodpak may be a sinking ship anyway," she observed.

"Maybe not, though," I said. "You and the others remaining there could work hard to save it. And even if you don't, for a while at least you'll have a salary coming in that's considerably more than unemployment compensation pays out. With that, you can buy time while casting your net out to catch another job.

"Another thing," I went on. "Could you learn new skills if you stay there? Use this as an opportunity to do retraining. Acquire some experience and expertise in other areas, which could look good on your résumé. This is a survival issue right now. If you can adapt to the company's desperate situation by responding to its needs, it will find a place for you. Otherwise, why keep you around?"

June seemed lost in thought. "Yes," she said finally. Then a bright look suddenly lit her face. "Also, I can tell Larry that if he really wants me to stay, working under the bare-bones conditions he's outlined, he'll have to make me a vice-president. Finally." June went out the door actually smiling at the prospect of that upcoming negotiation.

Like June, many of us nowadays must sort through similar possible solutions, choosing the option most practicable or attractive within a troubled work climate where employment is unstable and unemployment remains high for unskilled and skilled workers alike. The options often are:

- Search for another regular job, which can be full time but uncompensated work by itself.
- Start freelancing or register with a temp agency.
- Work as a consultant if you have special expertise.

- Become an entrepreneur, perhaps in a totally different field (such as acquiring a franchise).
- Undertake upgraded education or retraining for a new career or trade that may guarantee employment in future years for those with special skills and knowledge.
- To avoid layoff, accommodate an employer's production needs as much as possible without demeaning yourself or being exploited.

Perhaps prosperity is just around the corner. But the likelihood is that we may never return to the big-spending, lavish expense-account economy most people riding the crest of profit making took for granted.

You don't always know when a company that seems secure might begin right-sizing, get taken over, merge, sell out, change its whole management structure, close down some facilities or branches, or go into bankruptcy. Or that you or your team may inadvertently commit some fatal error that gets you into trouble with higher-ups, whose only thought is to dismiss you. Be prepared at all times to pack up your things and go. So once a year at least, make sure you apply for another position somewhere else, just to keep in touch with the job market.

If you are given an offer that is in some or many ways better than your current position, you may well want to take it. On the other hand, be careful about burning bridges behind you. Unless you have substantial, cumulative grievances against your present employer, let your employers know of the offer, tell them you'd really like to stay with them (if that is true), and give them the chance to keep you by matching the offer. Do not be surprised if they can't and don't. Companies are accustomed to having salary games played against them. They also realize that employees have their own needs and destinies, and know that you're going to acquire valuable experience elsewhere. If they want you back when you're better seasoned, they'll be willing to pay you more—maybe a lot more.

Unless you're absolutely secure and content where you are, always plan your next move, whether within your company or out in the world. While you're negotiating in your daily job, always be planning and negotiating for your future as well.

EPILOGUE

"It's not about gender. It's about an agenda of change."

—Dianne Feinstein

Whenever I take a trip—and most of the time it's either to negotiate something or to train people in negotiating—I wear a rubberband. That's an odd sort of bracelet. But it has an important purpose—it reminds me always to *stretch*. The ability to be flexible is crucial in successful negotiating.

I credit my psychotherapist friend, Lou Ann, for this metaphor. "I'm not a shrink, I'm a stretch," she commented. I was greatly impressed with the application of this symbol to my own profession.

Yet don't we *all* have to stretch in our careers, in our personal lives if we're going to accomplish anything? To make some positive difference in the world? As women, we know that. We've always known that as individuals we must stretch beyond the limitations imposed upon us if we're going to achieve personal and professional goals of our own, not just assist others in winning theirs. The past quarter century has shown us that we can accomplish much more when we work together in negotiating for our lives.

Partnership negotiation comes rather naturally to most of us. We don't really have to stretch much to see the benefits of solving problems and resolving conflicts through using cooperative decision making and action taking. We need to partner with the various selves within us as well as with others. When partnering with people who initially see things differently than we do or feel threatened by something we need or want, we both stretch to understand each other. Within a negotiating partnership, we can come to terms without selling out, internally and externally.

And that's how peace comes about.

Wear your own figurative rubberband. Stretch your vision and possibilities. Choose to become a conscious, competent negotiator in everything you do. As women in control at last of our own destinies, we can make a big difference—for ourselves and in the world we live in. Beginning now.

What is the meaning of life? . . . It is life.

INDEX

Aesop, 85
Age, 18–19
    appearance and, 167
    generational issues and, 71–72
Agendas, 155–60
    formal, 155, 156–59, 201
    hidden, 147, 155, 156
    taking charge of, 146–47, 159–60
Aggressive personality, 52, 53. *See also*
    Steamrollers
Agreements, written, 217–19
Alternatives, presenting of, 109, 210
Amiable personality, 52, 53. *See also*
    Mr./Ms. Nice Guys
Analytical personality, 52, 53. *See also*
    Datacrats
Appearance, 162–71
    clothing and, 162, 163, 164, 165,
        167–68, 181–82
    deliberately looking your worst
        and, 169–70
    first impressions and, 164, 177
    handbags or briefcases and, 168–69
    image and, 165–66
    makeup and, 162, 168
    negotiating style and, 69
    sexuality and, 170–71
Argumentativeness, 189
Aspiration level, 28, 29
Athletic activities, male-oriented, 43–
    44
Attitude adjustment, 18–19, 175–76

Authority
    higher, deferring to, 139–40
    over our lives, 20, 24–25
Automobiles
    negotiating in, 149–50
    negotiating price of, 87–88
"Avenger," 73

Bargaining, 27–28
    negotiating vs., 8–9
Baum, L. Frank, 126
Beck, Barbara, 6
Bill paying, in restaurants, 149
Birth-order placement, 35–37
Blind spots, 205–6
Body language, 141, 168, 183, 185,
    196–98, 203
Bosses
    problems with, 227–30
    workaholics as, 228–30
Bottom lines, 214
    establishing, 194
    of negotiating partners, estimating
        of, 99
Brainstorming, 79, 210
Briefcases, 169
Brozovich, Joan, 6, 38–39
Butterflies, 53, 71, 152, 183, 184
    anticipating scenarios for, 130–31,
        132
    do's and don'ts for dealing with,
        120–21

Butterflies (cont'd)
  general description of, 59–62
  negotiating with, 117–21, 145–46,
    149, 192, 193

Carbo-sabotage, 152–54
Chalkboards, 200–201
Chauvinism. See Sexism
Childhood
  gender differences in, 39–40
  negotiating style based in, 30–38,
    39, 48–49
Citicorp, 97–98, 122, 152–53, 154–55
Civic organizations, 235
Class identification, 75
Clients, difficult, 230–31
Closed-ended questions, 28, 29
Closure, 217
Clothing, 162, 163, 164, 165, 167–68,
    181–82
Coffee, going for, 70–71, 190–91
Cold buttons, 135–37
Communication
  body language and, 141, 168, 183,
    185, 196–98, 203
  foreign languages and, 77–78
  gender and, 44–46
Compensation packages, 241
  cutbacks and, 239
  negotiating, 87, 224–26
  non-money elements of, 225
  raises and, 140–41, 231–35
  research on, 224–25
Competitiveness, gender and, 41–42,
    45, 46, 69
Competitors, comparing yourself to,
    95–97
Concessions
  allowing for, 98–99
  non-money exchanges as, 214
  stalled negotiations and, 210
Conflict
  common sources of, 12
  within ourselves, 10, 12–13
Conflict resolution, 10–11, 187–88
  defining purpose in, 89
  openings in, 194–96

  patience in, 204
  written agreements in, 219
Confrontation, 160
Conscious competents, 23
Conscious incompetents, 23
Consensus, 41, 42
Contracts, 217–19
Control, 20
  authority vs., 25
  and proposing of time, place, and
    agenda, 146–47, 150
  self-, losing of, 237, 238
"Control Freak," 73
"Cookie Grabber," 73
Corporations
  images important to, 165
  personalities or cultures of, 132–33
Countermeasures, 28, 29
Counteroffers, 28
Criticism, handling of, 233–34, 237,
    238
Crying, 233, 237
Cultural differences, 75–77, 78–81,
    175
  body language and, 198
  mutual education and, 78–79
  women of color and, 80–81

Datacrats, 53, 61, 109, 118, 120, 152,
    160, 183, 184, 185, 199, 228
  anticipating scenarios for, 128–30,
    132
  do's and don'ts for dealing with,
    116–17
  fears and concerns of, 58–59
  general description of, 56–59
  negotiating with, 113–17, 148–49,
    192, 193
Deal breakers, 28, 209
Deception, 202
Decision making
  authority over our lives and, 20,
    24–25
  in daily life, 20, 21–22, 23–24
  deference to higher authority in,
    139–40
  examining results of, 23–24

identifying person with power over, 107–8, 139, 183, 193
patterns in, 22, 24
Delaying negotiations, 173–74
Demeanor, 166
gender and, 43
Deserving, feelings of, 92–93
Difficult people, negotiating with, 138
Discrimination, gender, 70–71. See also Sexism
Discussion leaders, 157–59, 200–201
Dowler, Susan, 7
Drinking, during negotiating, 154–55

"Ego exchange," 9
Eisenhower, Dwight D., 16–17
Emotionalism, 42, 46, 47
Exercises
on first impressions, 177
on goals, 101–3
on jargon of negotiating, 29
on negotiating style, 48–49, 83
on negotiating tools, 49
on personality types, 66–67
preparation worksheet, 125
on rating of skills, 14–15
on scenarios, 143–44
self-contract for negotiating change, 13
on tactics of time, place, and agenda, 161
on unsuccessful negotiations, 223
on voice, 177–78
Expectations, 93, 93, 186
Experience, dealing with lack of, 174–75
Expressive personality, 52, 53. See also Butterflies
Eye contact, 55, 57, 60, 64, 185, 198
Eyes, body language and, 197

Facial expressions, 197, 198
Fallback position, 28
Family, 19, 20
birth-order placement in, 35–37
negotiating style of, 30–35, 36–37, 48–49

Feet, body language and, 198
Feinstein, Dianne, 243
Financial arrangements. See also Compensation packages
negotiating, 17, 26–27
First impressions, 164, 177
Flipcharts, 200–201
Follow-throughs, 220
Food. See also Restaurants
carbo-sabotage and, 152–53
"Foot Shooter," 73
Foreign languages, negotiating in, 77–78
Future disagreements, provisions for handling of, 217

Gandhi, Mahatma, 207
Gender, 19, 78
athletic activities and, 43–44
chauvinism or sexism and, 70–71, 190–91, 212, 234
communication style and, 44–46
competitiveness and, 41–42, 45, 46, 69
demeanor and, 43
negotiating personalities and, 65, 69
negotiating style and, 38–46, 48, 68–69
and personalization of issues, 42–43
upbringing and, 39–40
Generational issues, 71–72
Gestures, 197
Glass ceiling, 236
Goals, 87–103, 187, 193
adopted from other people, 93–94
drafting your negotiation plan and, 94–95
exercises on, 101–3
"negative," 92–93
of negotiating partners, 90–91, 97–101, 201
"one question" technique for, 92
overall purpose for negotiating and, 89, 90
possible concessions and, 98–99

Goals (cont'd)
  research and, 87–89, 99
  setting, 90, 92
Grooming, 162

Handbags, 168–69
Hands, use of, 197
Handshakes, deals sealed with, 218–19
Harris, Gail, 7
Head, body language and, 197
Hesol, Howard, 3
Hidden agendas, 147, 155, 156
Higher authority, deferring to, 139–40
Hill, Jennifer, 7
Home offices, negotiating in, 152
Honesty, 68
Hot buttons, 135–37
Humor, 207–8, 212–13

Illness, 19
Image, 165–66
  first impressions and, 164, 177
Imaging, 80
Information
  exchanged in meetings, 193–94
  withholding of, 171–73
Interpersonal problems. See also Conflict resolution
  negotiating, 89
Interruptions, 203
  in conflict resolution, 195–96
Introductions, at meetings, 157, 183
Intuition, 46–48, 49, 196

Japan
  carbo-sabotage in, 152–53
  seeming Nice Guys in, 122
Jargon, 28–29
Job interviews, 162–63
  divulging personal information in, 172–73
  negotiating compensation in, 87, 224–26
  surveying ambience in, 151–52
Job performance reviews, 233–34, 237, 238

Jobs
  applying for, 241
  changing bothersome circumstances about, 226–27
  compensation packages and, 87, 224–26, 239, 241
  layoffs and, 18, 239–41
  negotiating for new position in, 235–37
  negotiating for special opportunities in, 234–35
  problems with higher authority in, 227–30
  raises at, 140–41, 231–35
Judgmental attitude, 138

Kennedy, John F., 1

Language considerations, 77–78
Lasker, Susan, 7
Layoffs, 18, 239–41
Legs, body language and, 198
Limitations, thinking beyond, 17–18
Listening, 50, 195, 199

Makeup, 162, 168
Manipulation
  in feminine negotiations, 40
  negotiating vs., 9–10
Maslow, Abraham, 11
Meetings, 182–206
  body language in, 183, 185, 196–98, 203
  breaks in, 207, 208
  delaying or calling off, 173–74
  discussion leaders or moderators in, 157–59, 200–201
  expectations and, 186. See also Scenarios
  focusing your attention in, 186–88
  formal agendas for, 155, 156–59, 201
  information exchange and mutual education in, 193–94
  introductions at, 157, 183
  losing self-control in, 237, 238

mistakes at, 221–22
note-taking in, 200–201, 217
openings of, 192–93, 194–96
seating strategies for, 184–86
socializing before, 183–84
surprise attendees at, 188–90
things to do upon arriving for, 182–83
timing in, 203–4
tone of voice and talking style in, 198–99
traveling to, 182
Mental billboards, 175–76
Me-thee-we progression, 193–94
Mistakes, negotiating your reputation after, 237–38
Mr./Ms. Nice Guys, 53, 69, 71, 183
anticipating scenarios for, 131–32
do's and don'ts for dealing with, 123–24
general description of, 62–65
negotiating with, 121–24, 148, 149, 192–93
women raised to be, 65
Moderators, in meetings, 157–59, 200–201
Morgan, Robin, 179
Morlen, E., 145
Mothers, as models for behavior, 32–35
Motivational issues, 72–73
Mouth, body language and, 197

Navratilova, Martina, 224
Need, 28
"Negative" goals, 92–93
Negotiating, negotiations
age and, 71–72
anticipating scenarios for, 88–89, 97, 126–44, 199. See also Scenarios
bargaining vs., 8–9
building trust in, 202
calling off, 215–16
closure in, 217
commandments for, 204–5
in conflict resolution, 10–11, 89, 187–88, 194–96, 204, 219
cultural differences and, 75–77, 78–81
defined, 6–8, 28
drafting of contracts and agreements in, 217–19
drafting plan for, 94–95
effective vs. ineffective, 22–23
evaluating tools for, 49
examining results of, 23–24
"feminine" tactics in, 211–12
follow-through after, 220
at formal meetings, 182–206. See also Meetings
gender and, 71
goals in, 87–103. See also Goals
handling surprises in, 188–92
jargon of, 28–29
language considerations in, 77–78
letting some unresolved issues hang in, 214–15
manipulation vs., 9–10
motivational issues in, 72–73
mutual education in, 78–79, 193–94
need for, 11–13
obstacles to, 19–20
patience in, 25–26, 204
over phone, 141–42
positional power and, 74–75, 111, 193
preparation needed for, 87–89
purpose of, 72, 89, 90
qualities needed for, 26
reasons for, 11
reasons for failure of, 220–23
risk-taking in, 20–21
and seemingly nonnegotiable facets of life, 18–19, 26
self-contract for, 13
self-packaging for, 162–71. See also Appearance
stalled, 206, 208–11, 215–16
surprises during, 132, 188–92
tactics of time, place, and agenda in, 145–61. See also Agendas; Place; Time
timing in, 203–4
Negotiating partners. See also Butter-

Negotiating partners (cont'd)
    flies; Datacrats; Mr./Ms. Nice
    Guys; Steamrollers
    Butterflies as, 117–21, 145–46, 149,
        192, 193
    Datacrats as, 113–17, 148–49, 192,
        193
    equals as, 147–48
    estimating bottom line of, 99
    goals of, 90–91, 97–101, 201
    hot or cold buttons and, 135–37
    identifying decision makers among,
        107–8, 139, 183, 193
    impatience with, 20, 25–26
    learning about, 104–8, 125, 139
    negotiating style of, 50–51, 104
    Nice Guys as, 121–24, 148, 149,
        192–93
    Steamrollers as, 108–13, 114, 115,
        148, 149, 173, 192, 193
    viewing negotiations from point of
        view of, 99–101
Negotiating personalities, 50–67
    anticipating scenarios for, 128–33
    of corporations and groups, 132–33
    exercises on, 66–67
    four basic personality types and,
        52–53
    gender and, 65, 69
    identifying before meetings, 183
    opening gambits and, 192–93
    sprites and, 81–83, 132
Negotiating style, 30–49, 103
    appearance and, 69
    childhood experiences and, 30–38,
        39, 48–49
    exercises on, 48–49
    gender and, 38–46, 48, 68–69
    layering of, 75
    mothers as models for, 32–35
    of negotiating partners, 50–51, 104
    women's intuition and, 46–48
Negotiation. See Negotiating, negotia-
    tions
Nervousness
    body language and, 197
    speaking style and, 199

Networks, 106–7, 125, 139
Nice Guys. See Mr./Ms. Nice Guys
Non-money exchanges, 214
    in compensation packages, 225
Note-taking, 200–201, 217

"One question" technique, 92
Open-ended questions, 29
Openings, 29
    in conflict resolution, 194–96
    in meetings, 192–93
Outrageousness, as tactic, 212–13
Owens, Juanita Lee, 7

Parentage, 19. See also Family
Partnership negotiation, 9
Past, renegotiating of, 237–38
Patience, 25–26, 204
Perez, Rosa, 7
Personal information, divulging of,
    171–73
Personal issues, primary types of, 51
Personality types, 138. See also Butter-
    flies; Datacrats; Mr./Ms. Nice
    Guys; Negotiating personalities;
    Steamrollers
    origin of, 51–53
Personalization of issues, 42–43
Personal relationships
    conflicts in. See Conflict resolution
    hot buttons in, 137
Peters, Thomas J., 16
Physical handicaps, 19
"Pie Slicer," 73
Place, 145–52
    ambience and, 153–54
    neutral, 149
    other side's office as, 150–52
    personal vulnerabilities and, 147–
        48
    selecting, 148–49
    taking charge of arrangements for,
        146–47
    your office as, 151, 152
Planned invulnerability, 71
Plussing, 96–97
Positional power, 74–75, 111, 193

Positive thinking, 176
Power
  identifying person with, 107–8, 139,
    183, 193
  kinds of, 27
  manipulation and, 9, 10
  men's struggles over, 41–42
  positional, 74–75, 111, 193
  Steamrollers' use of, 56
  table shape and, 184
"Power Monger," 73
Pre-negotiation phase
  arranging time, place, and agenda
    in, 146–47, 159–60
  telephone calls in, 141–42
Preparation. See also Research
  anticipating scenarios in, 88–89, 97,
    126–44, 199. See also Scenarios
  need for, 87–89
  stepping into your partners' shoes
    in, 99–101
Professional organizations, 235
Promotions, negotiating for, 235–37
Purpose, underlying, 72, 89, 90

Raises, 231–35
  job performance reviews and, 233–
    34
  negotiating for, 140–41, 231–34
  negotiating for opportunities in-
    stead of, 234–35
Recognition, men's need for, 42
Reputation, renegotiating of, 237–38
Research, 87–89, 99
  on competitors, 95–96
  on negotiating partners, 104–8, 125,
    139
  networks in, 106–7, 125, 139
  on salary ranges, 224–25
Restaurants
  negotiating in, 153–54
  paying bill in, 149
Reverse psychology, 213
Rich, Bobby, 6
Risk, 20–21, 68
Role playing, 126, 135
Roosevelt, Eleanor, 30

Salary. See Compensation packages
Sales personnel, 133
Satir, Virginia, 104
Scenarios, 186
  anticipating, 88–89, 97, 126–44, 199
  chain of command and, 139–40
  constructing, 127–31
  exercises for, 143–44
  hot and cold buttons and, 135–37
  judgmental attitude and, 138
  laying groundwork in, 143
  personality types and, 128–33
  personal or situational variables
    and, 133–34
  role playing and, 126, 135
  scripting, 134–35
  Three Yes Questions approach in,
    140–41
  worst-case, 127
Scripts, 134–35
Seating strategies, 184–86
Secretaries, 200
Self-confidence, dealing with lack of,
  174–75
Self-control, losing of, 237, 238
Self-negotiating, 12–13
Self-packaging. See Appearance
Sexism, 212. See also Gender
  coffee duties and, 70–71, 190–91
  raises and, 234
Sexuality, 39, 40, 170–71
Shakespeare, William, 68
Shoes, 168
Silence, 199–200
Sitting posture, 197
Skills, rating exercise for, 14–15
Smoking, 152
Socializing
  before meetings, 183–84
  negotiating while, 153–55
Speaking
  pace of, 199
  silences or pauses in, 199–200
  tone of voice and, 177–78, 198–99
Sprites, 81–83, 132
Steamrollers, 50, 61, 71, 72, 122, 160,
  183, 185, 228

Steamrollers (*cont'd*)
anticipating scenarios for, 129–30, 132
do's and don'ts for negotiating with, 111–13
fears and concerns of, 56
general description of, 53–56
men raised to be, 69
negotiating with, 108–13, 114, 115, 148, 149, 173, 192, 193
presenting alternatives to, 109, 210
Three Yes Question approach to, 110
Strategy, defined, 29
Stress, 93
Surprises, 132, 188–92
sexism and, 190–91
unexpected attendees at meetings, 188–90

Tables, shape of, 184
Tactics, defined, 29
Team negotiating, seating arrangements in, 184
Telephone calls
badgering, 173–74
in pre-negotiations, 141–42
Thoreau, Henry David, 87
Three Yes Questions approach, 110, 140–41, 209–10

Time
agenda schedule and, 157
frame of, for negotiations, 148
taking charge of arrangements for, 146–47
Timing, 203–4
Traveling, to meetings, 182
Trust, 196
building, 202

Unconscious competents, 22
Unconscious incompetents, 22

Voice
auditory clues provided by, 198–99
exercise for, 177–78
Vulnerability, 68

Walking out of negotiations, 151
Whittaker, Terry Cole, 162
Women. *See also* Gender; Sexism
intuition of, 46–48, 49, 196
of nonwhite ethnic groups, 80–81
raised to be Ms. Nice Guys, 65
Workaholics, dealing with, 228–30

"Yes" zone, 29

NICOLE SCHAPIRO is available for:

- Keynote presentations
- Customized development and delivery of training work-
  shops and seminars
- Individual and organizational consulting
- Retreat facilitation

Information on tapes, newsletters, and other educational products
is available by writing to or phoning:

Nicole Schapiro & Associates
110 Seminary Drive, Suite 1B
Mill Valley, CA 94941
(510) 939-5585

The NATIONAL ASSOCIATION FOR FEMALE EXECUTIVES,
founded in 1972, is the nation's largest business women's organization, with 250,000 members. NAFE helps women achieve career
and financial success through education, networking, and public
advocacy.

NAFE members are offered special insurance programs, low-
interest loans, credit cards, a career database, resume service, and
travel discounts. Venture Capital Fund invests in business plans
submitted by members that show high potential for return on investment. Perhaps the most popular feature of the organization is
its bimonthly magazine, *Executive Female*. NAFE offers national and
regional teleconferences in addition to local breakfasts and networking seminars.

The National Association for Female Executives is located at
127 West 24th Street, New York, New York 10011, (800) 927-NAFE.